D1572313

FROM
CARACAS
TO
STOCKHOLM

FROM CARACAS TO STOCKHOLM

*A Life in
Medical Science*

BARUJ BENACERRAF, M.D.

Nobel Laureate

Prometheus Books

59 John Glenn Drive
Amherst, New York 14228-2197

Published 1998 by Prometheus Books

02 01 00 99 98   5 4 3 2 1

Library of Congress Cataloging-in-Publication Data

Benacerraf, Baruj, 1920–
     From Caracas to Stockholm : a life in medical science / Baruj Benacerraf.
          p.   cm.
     Includes index.
     ISBN 1–57392–227–7 (alk. paper)
     1. Benacerraf, Baruj, 1920–   . 2. Immunologists—United States—Biography.
I. Title.
QR180.72.B4A3   1998
610'.92—dc21
[B]   98–23131
                                                                                  CIP

Printed in the United States of America on acid-free paper

Contents

5

This book was written for and is dedicated to Oliver and Brigitte Benacerraf Libby.

Introduction

Throughout my professional life, I had planned to retire at an early age, as idleness and the opportunity to be free of obligations and of starting on a new, more glamorous career has always had a powerful attraction for me. But the irony is that I am probably more afraid of being free of constraints, signifying the end of a life, than I am desirous of retiring or starting on a new creative path as the playwright or business tycoon I have often fantasized. Besides, there is always the possibility I might fail. In fact, my success as a scientist and administrator has always astonished me. I have regularly initiated new projects with the feeling of impending disaster.

Therefore, at seventy-six years of age I find myself, against all plans and expectations, still working in my office at the Dana-Farber Cancer Institute. But, at least I have officially retired, after serving as professor and chairman of the Department of Pathology at Harvard Medical School for twenty years and president of the Dana-Farber Cancer Institute for twelve years. Moreover, I finally closed my laboratory and wrote my last scientific paper in 1996, after more than six hundred publications over the past forty years.

At this stage in life it would be customary for me to make an assessment of my past experiences, and of the wisdom and beliefs that have withstood the test of a lifetime. I have been involved in this process, albeit unconsciously, for some time, and I feel an increasing urge to sit in front of my computer and confront my memories of past events and emotions. After a very active life as an investigator, I am at last infected with the introspective virus, which has affected some of my scientist friends and many others before me. It moves me to direct my thoughts to the mass of memories that has accumulated over the years. Occasionally, I am overcome with the fear of losing this precious data before successfully transcribing it, much as I would fear overloading my hard disk without the precaution of saving the valuable information.

I find the challenge compelling and fascinating but I am not sure of what I will remember or what I will find when I begin searching in earnest with the critical eye of a professional researcher. I pledge to adhere absolutely and without exception to the highest standards of accuracy and honesty, since this work is written first and foremost for me and may some day be read by my grandchildren. There is no valid purpose in fooling oneself or those who mean so much. Moreover, I pride myself on being professionally capable of objectivity and even hypercriticism, particularly when examining my own data, past errors, or mistaken ideas that I have entertained.

I have learned, indeed, that scientific progress is only built on the disproof and elimination of currently accepted paradigms, and that everything, and above all one's own contribution, is open to continuous and merciless scrutiny by others as well as oneself. I promise to be as accurate as my memory will permit and to be as critical of myself as I am of others.

Fortunately, I am a word-processor enthusiast. In fact, my life has changed dramatically as a result of the modern PC and its word processor. Although, I did not suspect it until I became an adult, I am a dyslexic. Now that this affliction is better recognized, my daughter, Beryl, who became a highly successful radiologist-ultrasonographer, and her son, Oliver, were recognized as dyslexic, at a time when special help could be provided to overcome this disability. As for myself, I had to work long and hard to learn to read at a respectable speed. Moreover, to this day I am a terrible speller in any of the languages that I have learned—Spanish, French, or English—and I have an atrocious handwriting which I alone can decipher. The word processor and particularly the spelling programs have made my life much easier and have provided the privacy I require.

1

—>—>—0—<—<—

The Benacerraf Family

I have a strong feeling of identity with my cultural heritage, which may have molded much of my personality. I am of Spanish, Jewish, and Sephardic* ancestry. My father, Abraham, was born in Tetuan, Morocco, when it was a Spanish colony, sometime in the last century. His date of birth was never ascertained. I could never settle whether he or his brother Fortunato was the oldest of the nine children—seven boys and two girls—who constituted the family. My father's family, as well as my maternal ancestors, were born and raised in Tetuan. The early members of my family probably moved across the channel from Spain during the Spanish Inquisition. My paternal grandfather, Salomon, whom I later got to know and fear, was the typical Spanish Jewish patriarch who inspired and demanded absolute obedience and respect from wife, children, and grandchildren.

---

*Sephardic Jews are the descendants of the Jews who were expelled from Spain by the Inquisition and settled in Morocco, Greece, the Levant, and Holland.

I was told that my grandfather managed to earn a meager living in Tetuan as a money lender when he felt he needed to work. It was a traditional family profession, which may explain the true meaning of our name. "Ben" means son in both Hebrew and Arabic and "seraph" is, indeed, the word for money changer in Arabic. I prefer the fantasy that the real root of my name is the Hebrew word "seraph," which means angel. Since my first name, Baruj, means blessed in Hebrew, I like to think my full name means "Be blessed, son of an angel"!

Salomon was not an effective money maker and his family was very poor; that explains the migration of his sons to Venezuela at an early age. His major concerns were the Jewish religion and the Jewish texts which he studied as a scholar. When I knew my grandfather, later in Oran, Algeria, where my father moved his family after acquiring wealth, my grandfather spent all his time either in the temple or, when my father gave him money, distributing alms to the poor Jews of the town. He lived a very austere life, occupying the smallest room in the apartment, furnished with only a steel bed, a chair, a table, and books. He was, however, fierce about enforcing the religious rules and teaching me to read Hebrew. As a dyslexic I did very poorly, of course, and was castigated regularly. It should be no surprise that I share no intimacy or real affection for my paternal grandfather. My paternal grandmother, his wife, Miriam, was already severely paralyzed and greatly diminished by a stroke when I first saw her in her house in Oran, but one could still detect that she, in contrast to Salomon, was a warm and caring person.

I had a stronger relationship with my maternal grandmother. My maternal grandfather, whose first name I bear, died when my mother was three years old.

When I was a teenager, my father took me to Tetuan to see the town of his ancestors and the house where he was born in the Jewish ghetto. It was a miserable house, without electricity, water, or sewage disposal. I readily understood why at the age of fourteen, alone and penniless, he left for Caracas, where a distant cousin, Nissim, assured him of employment in his little textile store.

My father, Abraham, was a fearless, determined, and highly intelligent young man who enjoyed both selling and buying. These qualities were gratefully appreciated by his older cousin who made him a partner in the business.

Abraham understood the advantages of wholesale over retail marketing or selling and the use of credit. Within a few years the little store became a substantial textile-importing firm with valuable lines of credit with the local banks. During this period, Abraham sent money regularly to his father to support the family in Tetuan, and arranged for his brothers Fortunato, Isaac, Moisses, and Leon to join him in Venezuela.

In time, his cousin Nissim retired, sold his share of the business to Abraham, and returned to Morocco. Abraham took on his least competent brothers, Isaac and Leon, as partners and established Hermanos Benacerraf and Company. The business thrived during the First World War, and Abraham and his two brothers began to experience wealth and comfort for the first time.

In the meantime, their brothers Fortunato and Moisses established an independent business in Carupano, dedicated to trading coffee and cocoa, and were equally successful. However, a tragedy occurred. Moisses, who had been despondent, decided to travel back to visit his family and was mysteriously lost at sea. He probably committed suicide in a fit of depression, but the matter was never discussed in the family. I only learned these details much later from business associates. Fortunato, who was particularly close to his brother, was very much affected by Moisses's tragic death. Either because of these events or due to the hazardous aspect of the coffee and cocoa business or because Fortunato was much more of a gambler and speculator than the more steady Abraham, he soon lost all his hard-earned assets and found himself destitute. Abraham, who appreciated Fortunato's business acumen and recognized that besides himself he was the only

brother with outstanding capacity, took him on as a full-time managing partner with an equal participation in the earnings of the
business. By then, immediately after World War I, Abraham was
ready to return to North Africa to find a suitable wife.

Abraham had realized a few years earlier that it was appropriate to move his parents and sisters from Tetuan to a more civi-
lized and enlightened city nearby where they would find themselves culturally comfortable. The city of Oran, in French Algeria,
where many Spanish Jews from Morocco had settled, appeared
highly suitable for this purpose. He arranged to move his parents
to Oran and bought a large apartment house, where they would
occupy the first floor. In 1919, Abraham went to Oran to visit his
parents and to seek a wife. Marriages, in those days and in that
milieu, were arranged, with proper attention to family background
and to religious, cultural, and financial considerations, without
any concern for the young lady's feelings or preferences, not to
mention her romantic dreams.

Abraham, who was about thirty-five, was told of a lovely
twenty-one-year-old lady, Henriette Lasry, who lived near Oran
with her mother, in the home of an older sister.

My mother, Henriette Lasry, was born January 12, 1897, in Sidi-
Bel-Abbes, Algeria, the youngest of eight children of Barouk and
Sete Lasry. My grandfather and his wife were both born in Tetuan,
but had lived, since childhood, in Algeria. He managed a successful wholesale business in Sidi-Bel-Abbes, selling colonial
agricultural products. I never knew much about him since he died
when my mother was three years old. Pictures of him indicate a
handsome, sensitive, serious man. After his death, his business
was taken over by his eldest son, Isaac, who was not successful at
it. As a result, my grandmother and Henriette lost their home and
went to live with my mother's oldest married sister, Simi, in her

beautiful country home at Eckmuhl, a suburb of Oran. Henriette was therefore raised very much by her sister, together with my aunt's own children, who were of comparable age.

Henriette was a beautiful young lady, very well behaved, serious, and proper. She had a very happy childhood with her mother, sister, and cousins. It was a united and warm family that I later got to know and love, when I visited them regularly on our yearly winter trip to Oran. Henriette had received a standard French education in the local French lycée, and had the equivalent of a high school degree, differing, in this respect, from my father who was largely self-taught and had barely enough schooling to learn to read and write Spanish. Henriette spoke only French and neither understood nor spoke Spanish when she met my father.

Although Henriette belonged to a highly respectable family, their modest financial resources caused her mother serious concern about her youngest daughter's marital prospects. She, therefore, gave very serious consideration to the inquiries made on behalf of my father. My grandmother was a very tough and realistic lady who had had a difficult life. The information she gathered about my father and his family and background was excellent. When she met Abraham, he impressed her as a serious, bright, rich, capable young man, and therefore suitable to marry her youngest daughter.

My grandmother, unlike her daughter, was fluent in Spanish and could converse with Abraham. Henriette, on the other hand, was totally unprepared for the traumatic experience of marrying a foreigner, fourteen years older than herself, who did not speak her language, and whose words she could not understand. The trauma was compounded by the expectation that soon after marriage, she would be leaving with this stranger—her husband whom she must swear to love, honor, and obey—for a distant and forbidding land, accessible only by a journey of many weeks. She was introduced to Abraham at an official reception, where they could hardly com-

municate. She proceeded, then, directly to her room and cried continuously for three days before finally agreeing to the marriage at
her mother's behest.

Henriette was not a sentimental or romantic girl. She was
clear-headed and determined. She was eventually swayed by her
own impression of Abraham at later meetings, and by her mother's
and sisters' insistence that he was a kind and decent man who
would make every effort to bring her happiness. Though worried
about being separated from the family she loved so much, Henriette was as keen and tough as her mother. I suspect she made up
her mind, at the time, that my father was a warm and sensitive man
and that she would be able, after the birth of a child, to convince
him to move from South America, closer to her family as, indeed,
she managed to do eventually.

This background will help the reader understand the characters of
my parents, the atmosphere of their home, and the nature of their
relationship. First and foremost for them, marriage was a lifetime
partnership, sacred and unbreakable, as well as the union of two
families of similar cultural background. It was designed to create
a new family.

Both of my parents came from large, united families who
depended solely upon familial relationships for protection against a
hostile world around them. They no doubt intended to have a large
family of their own since my mother loved children. She was deeply
disappointed, after my birth, that, due to a gynecological problem
which eventually required surgery, she had to wait ten years to
become pregnant again with my brother, Paul. I am convinced that
my parents were devoted and had enormous respect for each other.
But there was little tenderness that I could detect in their relationship, which was totally different from the very warm, loving, intimate relationship that I have experienced with my wife, Annette.

My mother was not a tender person and she was not prone to displays of affection to my father or to me or my brother. This is probably the reason my wife found me, to use her own words, "starved for affection" when I met her. But my mother was enormously courageous, loyal, and righteous. She had great expectations and ambitions for her sons, and no standards were high enough for the Benacerraf children to achieve. She was supportive of my father in every respect, and was totally submissive to his prerogative to make all important family decisions. She managed an immaculate home, without a speck of dust, but devoid of any personality. She was an excellent cook and enjoyed preparing meals in the Spanish, French, or North African tradition. She greatly enjoyed knitting, and I wore numerous sweaters that she made. But as she was color-blind, a rare affliction in females, the colors were disastrously dull. She hated to entertain except for her own large family to which she was passionately devoted.

There was, however, a distinctly out-of-character trait that amazed me. She loved gambling! She played for real stakes and was very good at it. She is the one who taught me both poker and baccarat, which she played flawlessly. She won at cards regularly, while my father lost, and she loved gambling in the French Casino at Vichy, where they would go to drink the waters, as was the fashion in the 1930s.

As for my father, he was a warm and generous man with great integrity and honesty. He took great pride in his name and in the reputation of his business. He was a man of his word. He had a terrible temper, though, and could easily get angry. Father on those occasions would shout in a manner that would readily frighten a small child.

There were few arguments at home, but when they did occur they were one-sided affairs. My mother never replied, but simply retaliated by withdrawing any comment and keeping silent and sullen until Father regretted his outburst and gave in. By this technique she managed nearly always to have her own way.

Toward their children my parents presented a united front. Efforts to play one against the other were futile. Moreover, Father was brought up in the Spanish tradition which demanded that, above everything, he was owed the kind of absolute respect, support, and obedience in his home that he had always shown his own father. As a consequence, he was very strict and unforgiving even of minor slights or disobedience. His had been a hard life, and he was totally self-reliant, trusting only himself or his brothers and sisters. He had a healthy respect for money and a total distrust of all governments, particularly concerning their capacity to display justice or fairness for the traditionally persecuted members of the Jewish race.

He tried very early to impress upon me that I had to prepare myself to earn a living, preferably by entering the family textile importing business. He wanted me to have the education that he never had, but he had very mixed feelings on this matter. He probably experienced some envy, resenting the fact that I was given free the education that he never could get—and considered to be an invaluable preparation for life's struggle.

Nevertheless, he wanted me to have the best education available in Paris, where we resided after I was five years old, and was proud that I did well at the lycée, even if the subjects I studied were foreign to him. But, the only higher education he truly thought appropriate for me was the law, which he felt would be useful to protect his business interests. Accordingly, throughout my childhood and adolescence, I expected that I would dutifully become a lawyer and a businessman to satisfy his wishes. This would have certainly happened if Adolf Hitler and the Second World War had not interfered with my father's plans.

Another important aspect of the home life my parents created for me was that, although very comfortable and luxurious by any standard, with numerous servants, a chauffeur-driven car, and vacations in the best resort hotels, it was culturally deprived. My parents never read books. Bookshelves did not exist in our home, except in my bedroom. After mastering my dyslexia, I loved reading above all else, and would wake up at four or five in the morning to read books or even sometimes the dictionary, occasionally with a flashlight under the cover of my blanket to avoid detection by my parents who were concerned that I woke up too early. As a consequence, my cultural education, beyond what I learned at school, was very uneven, and I had no notion of science until I reached the university.

The same is true of art and music. Art was totally neglected in my home. Mother felt that pictures on the wall gather dust so our walls were bare. I was never taken to the museums. As for music, Mother, who had learned the piano but had truly no taste for music, arranged for me to learn to play the piano. But, it was never very satisfactory, because my dyslexia made it impossible for me to read both clefs simultaneously. I had to learn both hands separately by heart to play a piece. After a few years of fruitless effort, I abandoned it. I returned to music and learned successfully to play the flute, a single-key instrument, much later, after I was married (to an excellent pianist, I might add).

The single cultural activity for which I am grateful to my parents is the theater. They loved all types of theatrical productions—plays, musicals, reviews—and had no hesitation in taking their children to the theater to see and hear everything that was shown in Paris. As a consequence I developed a love for the theater, and I toyed all my life with the temptation of being a playwright or a director (a fantasy that I indulged in at Columbia University, as I will describe later).

My parents, in contrast to my grandfather, were not deeply religious and only observed the Jewish holidays of Yom Kippur and Passover. They, nevertheless, insisted that I receive religious instruction from both my grandfather and a local Sephardic rabbi in Paris. These teachings, however, did not fall upon a fertile ground. I was not receptive, and never became interested in any aspect of the Jewish faith, or any other religion for that matter. I became rapidly convinced that all religions have caused considerably more pain and suffering than good to humanity. Because of their inherent dogmatic nature they have been historically opposed to the basic premise of science that everything is open to doubt and scrutiny by the minds of reasonable people. On the other hand, I have the greatest attachment to and respect for the preservation of historical and cultural heritages, be they Jewish, Spanish, French, or even Anglo-American, which, as I am deeply aware, have at various times molded my complex personality.

2

Childhood and Adolescence in Paris

Abraham and Henriette were married in Oran, Algeria, on September 11, 1919, and departed promptly for Caracas, Venezuela, where they settled in the large house in which Abraham resided with his brothers. It was a handsome Spanish colonial house, with numerous bedrooms, living rooms, and a dining room set around a beautiful patio. Henriette was not pleased by the lack of privacy or the need to supervise servants. The staff consisted of a cook, a dining-room maid, a bedroom maid, a laundress, and later a nanny for the baby. She, nevertheless, adapted rapidly, learned Spanish, and built a strong relationship with her husband based on mutual respect.

Henriette soon became pregnant, which had been her primary goal, and very much enjoyed the experience. I was born in my parents' bedroom on October 29, 1920. I have been told that she had a long and difficult delivery, as I was a breech presentation,* but

---

*Breech presentation is the birth of a baby buttocks first with legs extended.

otherwise both mother and child fared well. I was, of course, circumcised by a proper rabbi and named Baruj, which is the Spanish and phonetic transcription of Barouk, the name of my maternal grandfather. The tradition in my family was to name the first male child after the paternal grandfather and the next one after the maternal grandfather. In my case, to show respect for Henriette's dead father, Abraham generously offered to name his first son after him. I have a typically ceremonial photograph immortalizing this moment and depicting baby Baruj crying in his mother's arms, surrounded by the happy father, his family, and friends.

Though I lack personal memories of my early childhood in Caracas, there is photographic evidence of a pretty child with curly hair, in a little girl's dress, or playing with an automobile or with a wooden horse. Apparently Henriette, who very much wanted a girl, dressed and groomed me to fit her wishes. This behavior, however, had no effect on my sexual development, and I never had any doubt about my manhood. It is clear that the first language I learned was Spanish and that I was a happy child, brought up largely by a native nanny.

By the time I reached my fifth birthday in 1925, a major decision was made to move to Paris; this had been Henriette's intention all along. Abraham's successful business was the wholesale importation of textile goods, largely from England and continental Europe. The fabrics were sold to retailers throughout Venezuela on long-term credit. The business therefore required the expert purchase of goods suitable for the trade, at inexpensive prices, and the judicious financing of impoverished retailers who totally depended on the credit extended. This type of business, which could in part be likened to a form of banking, in the family tradition, required large profit margins, considerable capital, and close supervision of the customers. It also demanded a skillful selection of the goods, which were imported at bargain prices, and excellent credit relationships with the large foreign banks operating in Venezuela.

My father felt that, with brothers Fortunato and Isaac man-

aging the business in Caracas, he could profitably open a purchasing office in Europe to gain permanent access to the best
goods at the most attractive prices. He was, therefore, an easy
target for Henriette when she undertook to convince him to move
to Paris and open an office there. To help, he could take along his
youngest brother, Leon, who was always in poor health and who
hated the tropical climate of Venezuela. The move to Paris would,
in addition, bring him closer to his family in Oran, where he could
visit regularly, and provide better educational opportunities for his
son, who would soon be ready to enter school.

The decision was made. Fortunato with the help of Isaac was
put in charge of the Caracas end of the business and Abraham and
Leon left to establish the Paris branch of Hermanos Benacerraf
and Company. Henriette was overjoyed at the prospect of being
close to her family, which she had not seen for years. She and
Abraham rented a comfortable apartment on the third floor of an
old but respectable building in the sixteenth arrondissement,* one
of the most fashionable and pleasant sections of the city close to
the Bois de Boulogne, the prettiest park in Paris. My childhood
and most of my teenage years were spent in that apartment, which
I loved. It was the first home that I can distinctly remember.

My only memories of early childhood relate to this period of our
lives. I remember being an overly sensitive, impressionable child
with a vivid imagination, who would rather cry than laugh when, at
the circus, the clown would be slapped or fall. We lived in Paris most
of the year, except for the wonderful winter months spent in Oran,
Algeria, visiting my paternal grandparents. We stayed in the huge
apartment, which they shared with their daughter, my aunt Hassiba.

---

*Paris is administratively divided in separate sections called arrondisse-
ment.

Every afternoon, my mother and I visited my maternal grandmother at the country home of Henriette's sister Simi. This was by
far the most enjoyable time for me. The garden was beautiful and I
was treated like a little foreign prince by my cousins who were not
much younger than my mother. After a couple of idyllic months in
Oran, we would return to Paris and to the loneliness of our apartment. We had no family in Paris except for my uncle Leon, who was
single and lived with us at that time. My grandmother visited us
occasionally, but we had no real friends. I had no nanny since my
mother decided to care for me herself when we left Caracas.

For the first time in my life, when I was six years old, I was
sent to school. Unwittingly, my parents chose a private school that,
unbeknownst to them, was run by Jesuit priests, as were most private schools in France. When my mother asked what I learned on
my first morning, I said "I prayed sweet Jesus" and I asked "But,
who is Jesus?" After that episode, I never returned to the Catholic
school and was soon admitted to the Lycée Janson, a boy's school
and a major establishment of the Parisian educational system, free
from any religious influence. I spent twelve rewarding years at the
Lycée Janson and am immensely grateful for the French classical
education that I received from highly competent, dedicated, and
very demanding teachers.*

The French lycée of my childhood was severe and tough. A typical class consisted of thirty-five to forty students taught largely by
a single, well-trained teacher who had the equivalent of a Ph.D.
degree. Discipline was absolute and sternly enforced. Complete
silence was demanded in the classroom and the students were
never allowed to speak unless spoken to by a teacher. The curriculum, designed to be used nationwide by all French public

---

*It was therefore with considerable nostalgia that I returned to the Lycée,
several summers ago, to show my old classrooms to my grandson, Oliver. The
empty rooms (it was summer recess) were just as dirty, dusty, dark, and forbidding as I remembered them, or maybe worse. The walls had never been painted;
the tables and benches were the same old battered relics.

schools, was all-encompassing and very rigid. It was meant to provide the student a balanced classical education, with strong emphasis on French literature, Latin, math, history, and geography. The attitude of the school system was very competitive and elitist. Students were constantly urged to compete for the best grades in every topic taught. The test grades were ranked in numerical order, and announced publicly. The only weakness was the science program, which was poorly developed, organized, and taught.

Confronted with a foreign language in a rigid school system, and hampered by dyslexia for many years, school frightened me. I so dreaded going to class that I often hoped to be sick and allowed to stay home. In fact, I was often genuinely sick and experienced very poor health in those childhood years. I was distressed by a chronic asthmatic cough (to which I attribute my later professional interest in the mechanism of hypersensitivity and immunology, and my research in these fields). I also suffered from recurrent, severe attacks of gastrointestinal (GI) upsets, with diarrhea, pain, and fever, treated then, as in the Middle Ages, by starvation, liquid diet, and laxatives. I can personally attest, therefore, to the inability of medicine and of the physicians of that era to offer more than compassionate care.*

---

*The scientific medical revolution I witnessed in my lifetime has had an enormous impact on our attitude toward disease and on our ability to deal with it effectively, even if, sadly, the compassion has sometimes been lost along the way. In the fifth decade of my life, I became finally incapacitated by repeated attacks of a syndrome that closely resembles acute peritonitis and requires careful scrutiny and management. I was fortunate to avoid the surgeon's scalpel and, thanks to modern medicine, I learned that I was affected with "Familial Mediterranean Fever," or FMF for short, a recessive genetic disease of Sephardic Jews and other Mediterranean people, guilty of the type of inbreeding noted in my background. The gastrointestinal symptoms and recurrent fevers I experienced episodically, at various periods of my life since childhood, were explained as manifestations of this genetic disease. Fortunately for me, when the diagnosis was made, my close friend Sheldon Wolff had just established in a double-blind study at the National Institutes of Health that a drug, colchicine,

In primary school I was a student with only average grades, in spite of my efforts. I needed and was greatly helped by special tutoring, which was provided by older students desirous to earn some additional money.* Within a few years, however, I was able to surmount both language and learning disabilities. By the time I reached my teens, I began to enjoy the stimulation and prestige of being among the best students in my class, in mathematics and French literature particularly, and commanded the attention of my teachers in the lycée who only cared for the best students. I enjoyed the material very much, particularly history and French literature which I read avidly.

An important family event occurred when I was ten years old, the birth of my brother, Paul, on March 26, 1931, in our apartment in the rue Émile Augier. By this time my parents had realized the advantage of a Christian first name. Paul was, nevertheless, also named officially, Salomon, to honor my paternal grandfather. From the start, I have been very fond and somewhat protective of my younger brother, and have escaped the need for sibling rivalry, given the years that separate us. I realize that I must have felt some natural resentment at the obligation to share my parents' attention with an unknown newcomer. A proper French nanny was hired to care for Paul, and life continued as before. Later, during Paul's adolescent years, he would become very much my responsibility,† when my father became greatly diminished by illness.

---

used for many decades to treat gout, is able to prevent attacks of FMF, when taken prophylactically. As a consequence, I now take colchicine tablets regularly and I have been free of symptoms, ever since; one of the many illustrations of the miracle of modern scientific medicine.

*By a strange coincidence, I was reminded of this period of my schooling when, in 1980, among the hundreds of letters and messages of congratulations I received following the announcement of the Nobel Prize was a letter from Mr. Albert Glowe, one of my student tutors, who wrote from Rome recalling the days when he tutored me in Paris.

†I feel, therefore, proud of him and of his successes as a distinguished philosopher, Chairman of the Department of Philosophy at Princeton, and

✣ ✣ ✣

As a teenager, in the Paris of the tumultuous years preceding World War Two, I led an active, enjoyable, and interesting life. I was fascinated by Paris, and I would roam through its various "quartiers" by bus, subway, and on foot. I loved my studies and appreciated my friends. I accompanied my parents to every new theatrical production. But, most important for me, considering my passion for the theater, were my yearly season tickets to the Comédie Française where, with my school friends, every two weeks I watched the performances of the classical works of Molière, Corneille, Racine, Voltaire, Victor Hugo, and others, by the brilliant actors of that world-famous theater.

In spite of feeling very much at home in Paris and in the French cultural environment, after ten years as a student, I was still considered a foreigner in France, the Venezuelan son of Spanish citizens (my mother lost her French citizenship when she married a foreigner). The French, contrary to Americans, are very chauvinistic and not hospitable to foreigners, whom they suspect of attempting to establish themselves in their beautiful country. I was, nevertheless, fascinated by French and European political events of the time and was definitely attracted by the socialist philosophy. I read political newspapers avidly. Being very much interested in history, I was keenly aware that I was living in exciting, revolutionary, and probably dangerous times. I strongly felt the menace of anti-Semitism, not only from Hitler's Germany, but also in France, both at school and in the streets. I could see slogans every day in the streets and in the subway saying "Mort aux Juifs" (Death to the Jews). Every day, royalist and fascist newspapers were sold that openly advocated anti-Semitism. This was not sur-

---

Provost of the University for several years, as I would have been of a son. It is ironic that my father who so much wanted his sons to become big businessmen, in his own image, never had the opportunity to witness and enjoy their achievements in other fields.

prising in the country that had witnessed the Dreyfus affair.* I watched closely for the menace of a rearming Nazi Germany, bent upon destroying the remaining clauses of the Versailles treaty, and I was appalled at the inability of the French government to react to the remilitarization of their traditional enemy and to the occupation of the Saar. I also followed closely the traditional struggle between right and left that resulted in the victory of Leon Blum's popular front, which I cheered. I watched excitedly the riots of the fascist Croix de Feux against the French République which culminated in the events of February 6, 1934.† On that day, I ran through the city in the hope of seeing a real riot. But, alas, every time I arrived too late to witness anything more than broken pavements from attempted barricades.

Although I was politically very mature, I must shamefully confess that I had no inkling of the financial upheavals brought on by the major economic crisis of 1929. I was not interested in economic matters at that time. I perceived from my father that these were dangerous times for his business and that he was concerned enough to make long trips to Caracas, but nothing was explained to me, and our daily life did not change. Father had again clearly foreseen the danger ahead, trimmed his sails, and emerged from the crisis financially stronger than ever. He even managed, throughout this period, to make considerable real-estate investments in Casablanca and Oran, which he mistakenly felt would provide security for his family there.‡

---

*In the late 1900s, a Jewish officer, Captain Dreyfus, was wrongly accused and found guilty of spying for Germany. This created a major political conflict which fed strong anti-Semitism in France for decades. Eventually Captain Dreyfus was exonerated.

†On February 6, 1934, there were major riots in Paris on the Place de la Concorde and in front of the French Chamber of Deputies initiated by the Croix de Feux.

‡It is ironic that these assets were indeed totally lost, nationalized without compensation, when Algeria gained its independence in 1959, and those of my relatives who remained behind had to flee to France, leaving all their belongings. But this has been the fate of the Jews for centuries and, in the last analysis,

⚜ ⚜ ⚜

As a teenager, no one provided me with the type of information which is readily available to young people nowadays about sexual anatomy, physiology, reproduction, or sexuality. The attitude in my family was to consider these topics nonexistent. I was too bashful and timid to speak to friends about such matters. I had had little opportunity to meet girls except for my cousins in Oran in my early childhood and I experienced some very platonic romances during summer vacations. I was therefore very reserved and probably afraid of girls. Of course I never dated until at age nineteen I reached the United States. In my naiveté, I did not know that such relationships existed.

When I began to have wet dreams, I was very scared. I was convinced that I had a dreadful disease. It took considerable courage to approach my father, with whom I seldom had an intimate conversation, to tell him about my experiences, my fears, and what I described as my "symptoms" of this dreadful disease. My father simply said that he regretted he could not help me and that, under no circumstances should I mention my problem to my mother. He added that he would arrange for me to speak with my cousin Fernand, who had come up from Oran to study medicine in Paris and who visited us regularly.

Fernand was in a very mocking mood when he came the next weekend. He laughed and said: "Your father asked me to have you initiated into sex. It is healthier than wet dreams." He reassured me about the normalcy of my sexual urge and despite my fears and protests, took me to a whorehouse in the rue Monsieur Leprince. Prostitution was legal in prewar France, but the houses were required to bear identifiable markings. Except for the shame of

---

by living in North Africa during the war, the larger portion of my family, which had not migrated to the American continent, was fortunate to escape deportation to Hitler's death camps.

being seen entering a bordello, the loss of my virginity was uneventful and not particularly pleasurable. It was a reassuring experience, nevertheless, which convinced me that sex is necessary, but unimportant, and that it certainly had no relationship with love as I romantically imagined it.

The summer holidays were always very special and joyous times. In France, the major concern and topic of conversation are the plans for the next vacation or the memories of the last vacation. The French enjoy their vacations and endlessly prepare themselves for them.* My parents' idea of summer vacations was to travel to fashionable spas, to drink the mineral waters, and to take advantage of the famous thermal treatments. They stayed for weeks in luxurious and, I suspect, very expensive hotels where they rented suites to accommodate the family. We traveled in style, in our own chauffeur-driven limousine: Father, Mother, Paul, his nanny, and me.

My parents were incredibly naive about medical matters and sincerely believed that they would be benefited by the "magic waters." Moreover, they shared the prejudice of the French that everyone suffers from liver ailments. We therefore went first to Vichy, a thermal station prescribed for patients with liver disease

---

*In contrast, most professional Americans I have known, either because of guilt or fear of distancing themselves from their current responsibilities, have never taken real vacations and do not know the meaning of breaking away from their daily routine. My French upbringing has accustomed me to take one or preferably two months of summer vacation. I have reasoned, after the fact, that these yearly breaks, when I tried to cast away the work-related concerns and worries, have been extremely useful to recover from the intensive efforts, tensions, and concentrations inherent in the life of a competitive research scientist. They also provide a critical opportunity to reassess one's priorities periodically and to foster imaginative creativity.

and a lovely little city, beautifully located in the mountainous Massif Central. Of course, none of us suffered from liver disease, and I always suspected that our yearly visit to Vichy—better known today as the wartime seat of the Petain government—was rather motivated by my parents' desire to be in a glamorous and fashionable resort with a renowned gambling casino. Both my parents, but particularly my mother, enjoyed gambling at baccarat for small stakes.

After Vichy, we went to a nearby spa, the Mont d'Or, this time for more serious medical reasons. Both my mother and I suffered from mild but unpleasant asthma. The Mont d'Or, a picturesque little station nestled in a valley between easily accessible wooded mountains, was renowned, probably without scientific basis, for the treatment of asthma. Both Mother and I followed the "cure" under medical supervision, without any evidence of beneficial results. The "cure" was a serious and sometimes exhausting experience. Early in the morning, before breakfast, we went to the thermal establishment, dressed in white woolen suits with hoods, and spent a long time in steamed rooms, inhaling the vaporized magic water, to treat our bronchi. Fortunately we were free the rest of the day and I enjoyed myself tremendously hiking up the mountain trails in search of wild blueberries.

When I was sixteen, in 1937, my parents finally tired of spas and hotels and bought a summer home in Montmorency, which was then a sleepy suburban village, on a hill overlooking Paris. Although you could drive from our apartment to Montmorency in barely half an hour, the consensus was that the "air" was cleaner and healthier there. The house, built of stone in the early 1900s, was of classical French bourgeois architecture. It was a narrow four-story structure that took advantage of the unfettered view of Paris to the south, and provided privacy. It was set in a beautiful French style of manicured mini-park with a separate fruit and vegetable garden, which required the attention of a full-time resident gardener. I was delighted by my parents' decision. I loved my room

on the third floor, but spent very little time in Montmorency since
I traveled abroad, the last two summers before the war.*

Returning to real life, I was soon back at the lycée, in October
1937, to prepare for the first of two major national examinations,
the bacalauréat degree that concludes French secondary education. The examination, which I took in June 1938 after the school
year, consisted of written and oral tests. I did very well in all the
written tests except for French literature, where my defective
spelling earned me a very low grade. Fortunately, the top grade of
my math test pulled me up into the passing range, and the oral
examination presented no problem. I was officially qualified to
enter my last year of schooling. I needed to choose between the two
official programs, philosophy or mathematics, which prepared the
student for a graduate education in Letters and Law or Science and
Engineering respectively. Since the career plans my father had
made for me directed me toward law school, I registered in the philosophy class. Meanwhile, as a reward for passing the first bacalauréat examination, my parents offered me a trip to Caracas to
visit my uncle Fortunato and his family and to learn about the
business, where I was eventually destined to work. I embarked in
Marseille for a two-week boat trip to Venezuela on the Italian
steamship *Virgilio*. After a boring and uneventful crossing, I
arrived in La Guayra, where I was greeted by my uncle Fortunato
and family. They drove me back to their home in Caracas.

After more than a decade, I was again in my native land! I was
sad that the only country of which I was a citizen felt very foreign and
unfamiliar. Although I spoke Spanish fluently, no memories
remained of my early years in Caracas. I looked at everyone and

---

*This house was sold after the death of my mother but was nevertheless
destined to play an important role in our lives when we returned to France after
the war.

everything with curious eyes. Venezuela of the 1930s had not yet been seriously affected by the oil boom that later brought a large source of new revenues to this underdeveloped, tropical country. Yet, the climate was beautiful, the vegetation luxuriant, and the people gentle and very friendly. This was a big difference from the Paris I knew. No one was in a hurry. "Mañana" (tomorrow) was the standard answer to all challenging questions, and appointments were not regularly kept, particularly if it rained! Everything there depended very much upon personal relationships and friendships, which were taken very seriously. Caracas had been built in a valley, at an elevation of 3,000 feet, and enjoyed a very pleasant climate, even in the summer. It still had the appearance of an old Spanish colonial city, very different from the modern metropolis it has become.

Fortunato, my father's lifetime partner, was just as tough and shrewd as Abraham, but had a very different personality. He was not as buoyant and open, but was better at long-term planning and developing schemes to transform worthless properties into money-making propositions. However, he could be guarded and secretive, even with his family.* But at that time, he was a warm and generous host to his brother's adolescent son and made every effort to introduce me to life in Caracas. He was, indeed, well-integrated in business and traditional Venezuelan societies, the only Jew accepted in the exclusive "Venezuelan Clubs." Fortunato's family consisted of his wife, Sete, and three children, all younger than me. I had considerable interactions with Moisses, Margot, and Enrique throughout the years.

Father's business was located in a huge warehouse at Madrices a San Jacinto, No. 11 in the center of the city. Caracas addresses had the quaint custom of not referring to streets but to street corners. A given address was, therefore, formulated as "Corner X to Corner Y." The warehouse stored our accumulated stocks of textile

---

*These traits of character would be important to me when, more than ten years later as my father's representative, I would need to discuss family business matters with him.

goods to be sold to buyers from all over the country, either directly or through our traveling salesmen. In the front of the warehouse were the offices of the numerous clerks, accountants, and salesmen, as well as Fortunato's private office. In the back was the packing and shipping section. I became very friendly with the employees, all of whom knew my father and were warm and extremely hospitable. They tried to teach me the business in the short time I was there. I watched closely the performance of the salesmen and learned the secret of pricing which my father had devised. The cost of every item was boosted by an arbitrary 30 percent before it was entered into the salesmen book as "our cost." It was then further increased by an additional 30 percent to determine the selling price!

The summer passed very rapidly, and it was soon time to return to Paris. It was agreed that I should travel by way of the United States, a route that was not appreciably longer. This would give me the opportunity to see New York and to cross the Atlantic on the *Queen Mary*, an exciting prospect for a seventeen-year-old!

I embarked on the *Santa Rosa*, an American cruise ship on its return trip to New York. The highlight of the crossing was a romantic, but largely platonic friendship with a blonde American girl, tall and athletic, who impressed me all the more since I am only 5 feet 6.

I was overwhelmed and awed by New York City. As a typical tourist, after registering at the Lexington Hotel, I spent my short time visiting the Empire State Building, Rockefeller Center, Radio City Music Hall, and buying jazz records. When, at last, I was in my room packing, preparing to leave the next day on the *Queen Mary*, I received a phone call from the Cunard steamship company informing me that the departure of the ship had moved up in an attempt to avoid a major storm scheduled to hit New York and the upper East Coast the following day. I rushed to the pier and embarked immediately.

On board, I had a drink and went to bed. The *Queen Mary* left that night and, indeed, avoided the worst hurricane to hit America's East Coast in this century. Little did I know that I was going from storm to storm! Throughout the summer I had not followed developments in Europe and had not realized, as I danced my way across the Atlantic on that huge liner, that we were scheduled to arrive in Europe just at the time of the Munich crisis.

When I arrived in Montmorency, I found my parents and the whole country, for that matter, convinced that war was imminent. Reading the French newspapers and listening to the radio for the first time in weeks, I learned that Hitler, pursuing his grandiose plan of territorial expansion, European domination, and racial supremacy stated in *Mein Kampf,* had issued an ultimatum to Czechoslovakia to give up the Sudetenland. France and the Soviet Union were committed by treaty to guarantee the integrity of Czechoslovakia against German aggression. The stage was set for a new European war. But, France was in no condition to fight, morally or physically. The country was politically divided. There were pro-fascist groups with strong ideological kinships with Hitler and Mussolini. They were more worried about the political consequences of an alliance with the USSR than about the aggressive plans of Hitler. Moreover, nobody wanted to fight for the Czechs. I also found that a feeling of panic prevailed, which had affected my family as well. Everyone feared that within hours of the beginning of a war the Germans would unleash their air force on Paris with bombs and lethal gas. The fact that we were in Montmorency, far from any reasonable targets, did not reassure my parents, who decided, as many others did at that time, to leave their home and drive south. The day after I arrived from New York City we left for Tours, a lovely town in the center of France. We were at the Grand Hotel de Tours when we learned of the Munich conference, where Daladier for France and Chamberlain for England, capitulated shamelessly to Hitler's demands and forced Czechoslovakia to yield its vital, fortified territory in exchange for a worthless guaranty of no aggression.

As an indication of the lack of national resolve and confused thinking that prevailed at that time in France and England, the majority of the people and their governments accepted these shameful terms with immense relief. They entertained the illusion that Hitler could be trusted and that they had, for the price of Munich, preserved peace for a generation.

Maybe because we were Jews, both my parents and I knew better. We were absolutely convinced that tragedy had only been postponed. It would be experienced later under even more onerous circumstances. Sadly, we returned to Paris and I started my classes in philosophy.

I was fascinated by the new knowledge. I learned about psychoanalysis, the unconscious, the ego, the id, and the superego. I read Sigmund Freud, which opened a new world to my imagination and sensitivity, a world which I had perceived existed, but had never known how to reach. I was also greatly impressed by Henri Bergson, a contemporary French philosopher who wrote admirably but whose ideas, I realized many years later, lacked scientific basis. His books, *Matter and Memory* and *Creative Evolution,* were my bibles. I also enjoyed Aristotle and Kant but disliked Plato and his *Republic,* which I felt was very much a fascist work.

Hitler and the rapidly evolving political situation in Europe were very much on my mind but preoccupied my father even more. The annexation of Czechoslovakia in early 1939 demonstrated to everyone the dangers of the Munich agreement and the threat Hitler posed. War appeared to us inevitable. The only uncertainty was precisely when it would break out. Father decided that it was foolish and imprudent for him and his immediate family to remain in France any longer. In March, within a few months of my final examinations for the bacalauréat degree, to my great distress, he took me out of school. We packed our trunks, closed our apartment and our house in Montmorency, and sailed from Le Havre for

Venezuela. Both my mother and I were deeply saddened to leave our home and our family and friends without any idea of when we would return. I also felt ashamed to be running away at a time of danger. I could not mention the reason for our sudden departure to any of my friends. At school, I attributed it to an urgent business crisis in Venezuela. But I was truly devastated. In spite of being nominally a foreigner, Paris was my home and France my country, and I wanted to stay and defend it against the evil barbarians. These deeply rooted feelings would recur with considerable vigor again and again in the next few years as the tragedy unfolded. Meanwhile, I cursed the fact that I was underage and forced to obey my father's orders.

I was too depressed to remember much of the boat trip to Venezuela. Father rented a comfortable furnished house in Caracas and was pleased to attend once again to his business. All I can recall of these few months was that I could not stop thinking of Paris, the political situation in Europe, and my own bleak future. I managed to convince my mother, who was an ally under the circumstances, that I had to continue my education and that, if I could not return to France, I should be allowed to study in the United States. At least, I felt, it was closer to Europe. Considering my father's plan that I join his textile business some day, I argued that I could learn about textiles in the United States. Business associates of my father in New York recommended the Textile Engineering School of the Philadelphia Museum of Art. I agreed to study there; it was the best that could be achieved at the time. I departed in July for New York.

3

New York, Columbia University, and Meeting Annette

If someone had told me the previous September, when I departed on the *Queen Mary*, that I would return to America as a student within less than a year, I would never have believed it. Yet here I was, in New York trying to cope, materially and emotionally, with major changes in my life, in a world destined to enter a cataclysmic war.

I was totally unprepared to face the issues and opportunities of a graduate education. I never imagined that I could challenge my father's wishes for my future. I had not seriously thought of alternative plans or of the extensive possibilities offered by modern universities. I had foolishly committed myself to learn textile engineering without any idea of what it was. Classes were to begin in September at the Textile Engineering School in Philadelphia. Meanwhile, my priorities that summer were to enjoy myself, to adapt to life in America, and, most important, to learn English, which I understood poorly and spoke even less well.

I booked a room at the Hotel Commander, near Broadway and

40

Seventy-second Street. From the hotel, a single express stop of the subway would take me to busy Times Square, where I spent a considerable time in movie theaters. I decided to learn English by seeing double-feature films practically every day. The other major activity of that summer was my regular visits to the World's Fair. I was, of course, fascinated by the "Vision of the future through technology," conveyed by the General Motors exhibit, and greatly impressed by the wealth and power that emanated from the fair. Another aspect of my introduction to America that summer was my recently acquired taste for fattening junk food, frankfurters, hamburgers, and milk shakes.

When September arrived I moved to Philadelphia and registered for the first semester at the Textile Engineering School. It only took a short time for me to realize that I had made a major mistake. I did not like the school, the subject matter was uninteresting to me, and it was not challenging intellectually. I could not have cared less about the machines, the yarns, or the patterns that were the major topics of the curriculum. Nor could I relate to the other students who were genuinely motivated. It took me all of a couple of weeks to convince myself that I could never accept spending my life working with textiles.

My sense of desperation and alienation were deepened by the news from Europe. The tragedy, which we had been expecting for a year, had finally been provoked by Hitler's attack on Poland. France was at war with Germany and I was alone in a strange city, far from what I felt was my country and my friends, at their time of need. One evening, I went to a bar and ordered some whiskey to calm my nerves. I do not recall ever being drunk before that night. As the evening progressed, however, and I was feeling better, I remember making some drinking companions. One of them opened a bottle of tequila. It tasted strange but pleasant and not particularly strong. I must have drunk quite a lot, because the next thing I remembered was waking up, the next morning, on the floor of a strange apartment. No matter how hard I tried, I could not recall how I had gotten there or what occurred after the tequila. If I had been told that I had killed someone that night or that I had paraded naked in the street, I could not have denied it. It was a very scary experience. Very much sobered, I decided: (1) never to drink tequila, (2) never to get drunk again, and (3) to quit school immediately and return to New York. My career in textiles had terminated before it had even begun.

The collapse of my honest attempt to prepare myself for a business career and the evolving events in Europe convinced me that I was not ready to make career commitments at this time and that I must adapt to circumstances while I learned better what I really wanted to do and what I could do. Accordingly, I registered for a special course at the University Extension program at Columbia University designed to teach English writing and composition to foreigners.

Meanwhile, my parents had decided to join me in New York. Mother had never been comfortable in Caracas and Father had realized that, with the start of the war, the pattern of trade would radically change. He felt that he could best perform his task as buyer for Hermanos Benacerraf in New York, the only remaining trade center not yet affected by the war.

Our family reunited, we made plans to reside in Manhattan for the duration of the war, which we knew could be a long time. We rented a comfortable furnished apartment with full kitchen (an important consideration for my mother) at the Croydon, a residential hotel on East Eighty-six Street. The Croydon occupied a whole block on Madison Avenue, between Eighty-fifth and Eighty-sixth streets, and was admirably located, close to fashionable Fifth Avenue, Central Park, and the Metropolitan Museum of Art, which were to play important parts in the next years of my life. It was a plush and majestic residence in those days, with every luxury imaginable, impeccable maid and valet services, excellent restaurant and coffee shop. We rapidly, and effortlessly, adapted to the new life.

Surprisingly, my father was not angry with me for my decision to quit the Textile Engineering School, and as the excitement of my parents' arrival and of our settling in had passed, the news of the war indicated a long and protracted conflict. As a first priority we needed to address the issue of school for both myself and my brother. I discovered, to my delight, that there was a Lycée Français in New York, located close by on Ninety-fifth Street, near Fifth Avenue. This presented a unique opportunity to finish the last year of my studies for the French bacalauréat degree, which had been dramatically interrupted when we left Paris. I would be able to take the final examination, in June 1940, and finally earn my degree. Paul and I were both accepted for admission to the Lycée: I started in late 1939, while finishing my course in English composition at Columbia.

It is strange that after all the turmoil I had experienced in the previous months, my year at the Lycée Français proved to be a most wonderful, happy, formative year for me, during which I matured considerably and finally focused on realistic goals for my life. I also made valuable friends to whom I would remain attached for many years. The philosophy class was taught by a Canadian Protestant minister who was bright, enthusiastic, and sincere. It was a very small class with only six students of whom three were girls. It was the first time, indeed, that I had girls in my class. I immediately fell in love with one of them, a dashing blonde called Katenka. She was the daughter of Georges W. and Molly Bakeman. Mr. Bakeman worked for the Rockefeller Foundation and had headed their office in Paris before the war. In a sense they were refugees like myself. Georges Bakeman was a serious, yet kind and generous man, who was to influence my life at a critical time. I dated Katenka on several occasions, taking her to dinner and the movies, but alas, my romantic crush was not reciprocated and, as it is often said, we remained close friends.

I date my life-long interest in science and music from the close relationship I developed with my science teacher, Paul Weil. Paul Weil was a professional chemist who had taught at the University of Paris and had come to New York with his family (I do not remember why). He was a brilliant and charming man with a delightful sensitivity and a marvelous sense of humor. He was immensely cultured in all fields. I admired him enormously and he took a fancy to me. He made it his responsibility to fill all the existing gaps in my cultural education. He imparted to me a respect and love of science and learning. In addition, he introduced me to classical music: beginning, appropriately for a novice, with Tchaikovsky and Beethoven, to be followed later by Mozart, and lastly Bach. He also taught me about art, particularly painting, and encouraged me to visit the Metropolitan Museum regularly.

The month of June and the end of the school year arrived much too rapidly, terminating this most happy period. I was ready to take the final examinations, which again consisted of written followed by oral tests. I was immensely fortunate to be examined by two outstanding scholars: Jacques Maritain, the renowned Thomist philosopher, and René Dubos, the microbiologist from Rockefeller University, who later discovered the first antibiotics and who, in my opinion, should have received the Nobel Prize in medicine. They were my examiners in philosophy and biological sciences, respectively. It was an exhilarating experience. I can still feel my immense joy when I learned that I passed the examination with "mention très bien" which is equivalent to "Summa cum Laude." I was privileged, many years later, to become a close friend of René Dubos, whom I admired tremendously and who remained one of my role models.*

My French bacalauréat made it possible for me to be accepted

---

*It is also an interesting coincidence, for those who want to compute the odds, that the Fabyan Chair of Comparative Pathology, which I have occupied at Harvard Medical School for twenty years, had René Dubos as its previous incumbent, for the time, during the war years, when he was away from Rockefeller University.

in an American university. By then, I had developed, thanks to Paul Weil, a strong interest in science and particularly in biology. I convinced my father that it would be appropriate for me to study medicine. It was a profession of which he approved even if, in his own estimation, it was not as desirable as the law. I made plans therefore to enter a university to satisfy the requirements for admission to medical school. In my innocence I had no idea of the problem that admission to a medical school presented for a foreign Jewish boy at that time in the United States.

I toyed for a short time with the option of entering Harvard College, where I was offered admission, but only as a freshman. Then I found that Columbia University would accept me as a candidate for their bachelor of sciences degree in the School of General Studies and would, in addition, give me two years of credit for my French degree. According to their offer, I could easily complete my premedical requirements in two years and enter medical school in 1942. Moreover, while attending Columbia I could continue living with my parents. I liked very much what I had seen of the university as a foreign student of English composition. I registered as a candidate for the Bachelor of Science degree at Columbia University, to start course work in September.

The most important events of June 1940 were the invasion of Holland and Belgium and the offensive of the German Wehrmacht against the Anglo-French forces. The German Panzers broke the thin French line at Sedan and trapped the main Allied forces against the sea, resulting in the evacuation at Dunkirk, the fall of France, the advent of the Petain government, the armistice with Hitler, and the isolation of England. We were bewildered to see our worst fears materialize so rapidly. The France we loved had bowed to Hitler's will. Yet all was not lost; one gallant Frenchman vowed to fight on. We applauded Charles de Gaulle's speech of June 18 calling on France to continue the war until final victory. Convinced of the evil of Hitler and the Nazis, we were amazed that American public opinion did not share our alarm. But we saw clearly that

President Roosevelt understood the dangers facing America and was using all his skill to prepare the United States for the unavoidable conflict. We were convinced that it was only a matter of time until the war would reach America. This reasoning and the defeat of France tended to relieve the intense guilt I had experienced for having fled from the fight. With the certainty that America would bring on the eventual defeat of Hitler, I could go on with my studies without regrets.

That summer my kind and generous father bought me a car, a handsome new Packard, as a gift for my French degree. I was ready to start my life as an undergraduate at Columbia.

An American Ivy League university is truly a paradise for its students, particularly when compared with many foreign universities or even American high schools. Students enter an isolated, magical island with very different rules from those of the outside world, where everything is done for their benefit and every opportunity is opened to them, provided they pay the tuition or they win a scholarship. Universities are truly the hallowed institutions of this era. Traditionally, they have been given the responsibility by society to preserve the precious human heritage of painfully acquired knowledge, which is our most valuable possession, and to expand it through research and scholarship. This requires that everything be debatable and open to scrutiny by anyone, and that dogmatic attitudes and secrets not be tolerated.

At Columbia, for the first time in my life I had the feeling that there were no limits to my curiosity and imagination. I was free to roam through the stacks of the main library. I could ask the attendant for any book I wanted, and I was free to register for practically any course, within reason. I found the advisor responsible for my program both solicitous of my needs and desirous to satisfy with considerable flexibility my thirst for knowledge. When the requirements of the premedical curriculum were met by courses in chemistry, organic chemistry, zoology, and physics, there was ample opportunity to take additional courses in unrelated topics of interest to me, such as calculus, philosophy, or literature. I also discovered that students in American universities have a social life and that the university cares very much to make it a happy, creative, and fruitful experience.*

I do not have many comments to make on the courses required by the premedical program, except that they were well organized, adequately taught, and always informative. I did uniformly well scholastically and earned high marks without much effort. However, my greatest pleasure was to be free to read as I pleased. I recall my excitement when I read Einstein's work on the theory of relativity, for instance, and the modern French playwrights.

The active social life and numerous personal friendships, which I soon experienced, were a most important aspect of that period of my life. They were novel experiences for the sensitive twenty-year-old I was, who had lived a sheltered life with limited romantic relationships. My strong attachment to French culture and my foreign status oriented me toward those organizations where I could hope to find students with kindred experiences. I discovered the Cercle Lafayette, an undergraduate club for students interested in French culture and literature, and also La Maison Française, which was, indeed, a house on the campus where tea was served and talks and lectures were organized on French topics. I also visited the International House, an impressive structure on Riverside Drive which housed foreign students and had an excellent cafeteria and comfortable reception rooms.

---

*I was surprised and saddened in 1968 during the height of the student revolts that took place at Columbia when my daughter was a college student at Barnard. I felt that Columbia had been such an ideal environment for me, in every respect, that I could not understand the basis for this revolution, which, I believe, has weakened standards by undermining respect for scholarship and achievement.

I met a number of interesting students through the Cercle Lafayette of which I was elected president. As a consequence, I learned of the successful student production by the Cercle Lafayette, the previous year, of a French play, *Les Jours Heureux*. This awakened my latent interest in the theater and I formulated the project to direct the production of another French play in the 1940–1941 academic year. I spent days in the library reading all the plays that had been produced in Paris, in the past years, to identify a drama or comedy which could be successfully staged by amateur actors in our age group. I reasoned that such a play should illustrate the life of young people in a dramatic context, in such a way that it could be easily cast by choosing actors whose personality most closely approached those of the characters they were meant to portray. The critical issue for success would be the selection of an appropriate cast, rather than the ability of actors to impersonate characters.

Fortunately, the French periodical *L'Illustration* published all the plays produced on the French stage, and numerous issues of *L'Illustration* were available in Columbia's main library. Reading through stacks of issues I finally selected a play which met all the prerequisites. It was entitled *Altitude 3200*. The first act depicted a group of six young men on a ski trip in the Alps who stop to rest at a mountain hut, where they find themselves isolated by a sudden avalanche. By the end of the first act someone knocks at the door, and out of the storm appears a group of six young ladies, similarly stranded. The stage is set for the complex interactions, conflicts, and relationships that evolve between these young people with strong personalities. During the succeeding acts, over the next few days, critical interactions take place, motivated by love, jealousy, or friendship, and are rendered all the more dramatic and intense by the isolation of the group. Finally, in the last act, rescuers arrive and the emotions, feelings, and romances of the past few days are perceived by everyone in the more realistic context of the continuation of their lives.

Having chosen the play, my next task as director was the selection of the cast. I drafted notices, to be posted throughout the university, announcing the future production of *Altitude 3200* by the Cercle Lafayette and setting dates for meetings where anyone interested in a part in the play could come and read for it. I was pleasantly surprised by the large and enthusiastic response from a variety of sources. Most of the interested students were from Columbia University or Barnard College, and some were from the School of General Studies like myself. Many were French or had lived in France for considerable periods. Enough of them spoke perfect French and appeared to have personalities and appearances that fitted the characters in the play. I described the play and the parts to the group and I asked for volunteers willing to read for them. We were fortunate to be able to cast the play in just a few meetings. Moreover, the actors were so well cast that over the many months of rehearsals, a similar set of relationships developed in real life among the actors as had been depicted in the original play. One of these relationships is still going strong, as one of the actresses I selected is my wife, Annette.

Claudine Lutz, Denise Hahn, and Annette Dreyfus were all Barnard students. Claudine was dark blonde, provocatively beautiful and sexy, and knew it. She dressed and groomed herself in a manner designed to attract attention. She was appropriately cast in the part of the prettiest girl in the play who enjoyed her power over men. It is not surprising that I found her very attractive and dated her several times. I was amused by her and probably felt proud, in my manhood, that such a glamorous girl paid attention to me. But I soon realized that we shared few common interests, and our relationship never matured.

Denise and Annette were both good-looking, serious, darkhaired girls. They were very close friends, who were always seen everywhere together. They had attended the same school in Paris for many years and had lived in the same fashionable sixteenth arrondissement as myself. Both were Jewish and had fled from the Germans during the fall of France.

Annette was an elegant, tall, shy, and tense girl, with beautiful long wavy hair. She was a fanatic admirer of the French writer André Gide and of the Epicurean philosophy described in his book *The Fruits of the Earth*. She wanted, then, very much to be an actress and a writer or a journalist, in that order. Other important traits of her character were a whimsical sense of humor, a subtle and sophisticated natural charm, and an extraordinary determination to pursue her goals against all odds. She was also capable of absolute loyalty and naive selflessness. In addition, I was to learn that she would be far more apt to follow her own uncanny intuition than to be swayed by practical or logical considerations.*

Her friend Denise was a radically different girl. She was neither pretty nor charming, but impressed everyone by her generosity, the intensity of her emotions, and the strength of her logical intelligence. She had a strong inclination to mysticism and a deeply religious nature. Contrary to Annette, there was no fantasy to her character. At first my relations with both Annette and Denise were simply friendly without any particular intimacy, as would be expected with any of the members of our interesting group. However, a coincidence of fate brought the three of us more closely together. Denise resided at the Croydon Hotel, as I did, and Annette and her family lived in the Hotel Adams, located next to the Croydon on Eighty-sixth Street. Being the proud owner of a car, and going to the same university, I proposed to drive them, and they accepted enthusiastically. We would see each other every day and share experiences and thoughts.

After a few months, the situation radically changed. One of my friends reported that Annette had complained to him sadly that I had been cold and inattentive toward her. As evidence of my naiveté and inexperience with girls, I had not sensed that Annette was attracted to me. I was both flattered and astounded when, in a conversation we had that evening, she revealed her feelings toward

---

*It is remarkable that after fifty-seven years of intimate relationship and mutual devotion, my perception of her has not changed in any of these respects.

me and her unhappiness at my apparent lack of response. I tried to explain that I had gone through a period of introspection, and that I had been very much focused on myself. I assured her that I liked her very much.

As I reflected in the next few days, I had become very attached to Annette without realizing it. I enjoyed her company immensely. Meeting her every day for lunch or coffee, I could not conceive of life without her. We had fallen in love some time ago, but it took Annette's forwardness for me to realize it. There were nevertheless several complicating issues that affected our otherwise perfect happiness. We were very young, twenty and eighteen, respectively. In my own highly moral and naive world, love between a man and a woman led to marriage and a life of happiness ever after. Realistically, I could not see how we could envisage marriage any time soon, considering the war, our studies, and the potential hostile reactions of our respective families. Annette had a very different reaction, very much in keeping with her character. She said, "I don't care about marriage, all I care about is to be with you always!" I answered, jokingly, "But we are not Siamese twins; we must envision a strategy that will lead us to marriage." We agreed to say nothing to our parents for at least a year, and to attempt to educate them eventually to the idea of our marriage.

The other major problem was the fact that Denise, for whom I felt only warm friendship, had also fallen in love with me, without any encouragement on my part, and had confided her feelings to Annette. We were both very concerned not to hurt her feelings in any way, but did not know how to handle this difficult problem.

From that day on, the rest of my life was to be shared with Annette. It is imperative, therefore, that much more be said about her, her family, her background, her previous life in Paris, and about the circumstances that brought her to America after the fall of France.

Annette, the eldest daughter of Ado Dreyfus and Suzanne
Bruhl, belonged to a prominent French Jewish family, whose
ancestry in Alsace could be traced, on her mother's side, to the era
of Louis XIV. Her maternal grandmother, Berthe Bruhl, whom I
was to know and appreciate, was the daughter of Zadoc Kahn, the
"Grand Rabbin" of France at the time of the Dreyfus case. Annette
was indirectly related to Captain Dreyfus. She was also related to
a prominent American family who sponsored and facilitated her
admission and that of her parents to the United States. Berthe
Bruhl was a first cousin of Eugene Meyer, the former president of
the Federal Reserve Bank and the owner and publisher of the
Washington Post. One day, I was to have the pleasure and privilege
to meet Eugene Meyer; his wife, Agnes; and, particularly, their
daughter Katherine Graham with whom we continue to have a
warm relationship. As if this was not enough to impress and over-
whelm the unsophisticated Spanish Jew, who traced his own
ancestry to the ghetto of Tetuan, Annette's paternal grandfather,
Eugene Dreyfus, had been president of the Appellate Court of
Paris, the most prestigious judicial position in France.

Her immediate family in New York consisted of her father, Ado
Dreyfus, a tall, impressive man, who had fought in both world wars,
and whom I grew to love and appreciate for his kindness, enormous
wit, and original sense of humor. Her mother, Suzanne Bruhl, a
tense, energetic, and elegant lady, was chronically bothered with
insomnia. Annette's younger teenage sister was named Brigitte.
Living with them were also two of Annette's cousins, Bertrand and
Dominique Dreyfus, who had fled from France with them.

Annette had lived in Paris within a couple of blocks of where
I resided myself. She had attended the Lycée Molière where she
received an education identical to mine and passed her bacalauréat in philosophy the same year I did. Moreover, by a strange twist
of fate, she had known many of my school friends. We also realized
that Annette and I had attended the same student subscription
series at the Comédie Française, for which we had season tickets.

After the war started in 1939, her father, who had piloted a reconnaissance plane in the First World War, was called to active duty as an infantry officer. Fearing the possible bombing of Paris, he arranged for his family to move to Dinard, a resort town on the coast of Brittany, where Annette attended the local lycée. Accordingly, she spent the first year of the war with her mother, her sister, her grandmother, and her aunts and cousins at Dinard. This is precisely where they were when they learned that the German troops were approaching at the time of the fall of France, in June 1940. Annette, determined not to remain under German control, convinced her mother to drive her, her sister, and her two cousins to the nearby Atlantic port of St. Malo in an attempt to escape. They found a small Belgian cargo ship willing to take them to England, so they embarked on the evening of June 18, each with a small suitcase, having left their car on the pier. The next morning they were in England where they were immediately taken to a refugee camp, under guard, pending verification of their papers. Fortunately, Annette and her sister had been brought up by an English nanny, Joan Woodward, with whom they had kept a very close relationship. Joan, a warm and dependable friend, came to the camp and vouched for them with the British authorities, who released them into her care. After a short time with Joan, Annette and her family moved to London where she learned that her father had been taken prisoner by the Germans.

As soon as Annette and her mother had recovered from the shock of the flight from Brittany and the news of the capture of Ado Dreyfus, they discussed what to do next. They heeded the advice of a trusted friend of Ado, René Mayer, who was in London, and who would, after the war, eventually become premier of France. He strongly recommended that they leave for the United States where he knew they had relatives. Annette's mother contacted her distant cousin Eugene Meyer who instructed his friend, Ambassador Joseph Patrick Kennedy, to issue visas for Annette and her family and arranged for their passage to the United States. They left for Montreal on a Canadian ship, and in July 1940, looking very much like refugees, arrived at the Plaza Hotel in New York with their duffel bags. They were greeted by their most generous and hospitable cousin, Eugene Meyer, who financed their stay in the United States, installed them at the Hotel Adams, near the Croydon, and arranged for Annette to be admitted to Barnard College (where I met her) to continue her studies. Toward the end of that dramatic summer, Annette was overjoyed to receive a cable from her father revealing that he had miraculously escaped from the German prison camp and that he would soon join his family in New York.

Many years later, the unique relationship I have developed with Annette caused me to reflect on what I mean to convey when I say that I love my wife, my daughter, or my grandchildren. I discovered a simple answer to this question. Love for me means caring more for them than for myself, being more concerned with their welfare and happiness than my own. Love requires a complete abdication of one's naturally selfish reflexes to be replaced by an overwhelming dedication to the loved one.

The experience of love as a feeling of selfless devotion is the surest path to happiness if it is mutually experienced. It tends to shut out the world around us and to provide a recipe for self-sufficiency. It is precisely in that blissful state that Annette and I spent the next two years at Columbia until graduation. This is not to say that we did not have heated arguments, since we had to learn to adapt our personalities to each other, but they were of no lasting significance. We spent as much time as we could manage together, sharing meals, studying, or even walking in Central Park.* We also

---

*It is an indication of how much New York has changed in the short span of a lifetime that we used to meet often in Central Park, after midnight, when we had finished studying, without any sense of danger. When we were to live in New York in the late 1960s, we were already afraid to walk the streets at night.

spent much of our free time at the Metropolitan Museum and going
to concerts. Annette is an excellent musician who at one time had
toyed with the idea of becoming a concert pianist. She took over
my musical and artistic education where my science teacher Paul
Weill had left it, and also introduced me to whole segments of the
French and international literature that I had neglected. Of course,
I had to read Gide, but also, Martin du Gard, Courteline, and
Labiche (whose plays she knew by heart). But I could never
manage to read Proust. Thanks to her I became fascinated by the
Russian novelists and read Dostoevsky, Tolstoy, and Gogol. She
also introduced me to the English novelists Morgan and Huxley.
But more important she undertook the gigantic task to educate me
as a human being and to civilize me. Before knowing Annette, I
had never been exposed to fantasy, whimsy, humor, or even simple
fun; I was not even very polite. Mine had been a serious, meaningful life. The example of my parents had never encouraged
joking or the lighter aspects of life. Whereas, Annette, and particularly her father, Ado, considered fun, jokes, and irony not only
important but essential. Left to my own instincts and inclination,
without the joyous stimulation of Annette, I would tend to drift into
depressive moods.

We floated through those two years at Columbia in a cloud of
happiness, which was occasionally marred by the concern for my
career, the war, and the need to convince our respective parents to
allow us to marry.

Before I address these important aspects of our lives, I will
return to the play *Altitude 3200* which was responsible for bringing
us together and to the acting group. After numerous rehearsals and
a lot of personal dramas among the actors, the play was performed
on several successive evenings at the MacMillan Theater of
Columbia University to the applause of enthusiastic audiences. We
were delighted by the excellent reviews and surprised that the play
produced a substantial profit, which we proudly donated to the
Free French relief. The quality of the performance was so good

that we received an offer to tour in the summer, but the individual commitments of the actors made it impossible.

Within a year after our private engagement, Annette introduced me to her family as her fiancé. I was deeply grateful for the warmth and affection with which I was rapidly accepted. I was particularly attracted to Annette's father, Ado, who shared many of her traits of character and more particularly her mischievous wit and contempt for conventions. I also liked her cousin Bertrand who studied physics at the University of Chicago, and his younger brother, Dominique. I became equally fond of her sister, Brigitte, who attended the Lycée Français. She was very pretty and had an overwhelming crush on Yehudi Menuhin, the renowned violinist, who was the focus of her life.

The task of revealing our marriage plans to my parents and of convincing them of the wisdom of our decision appeared to me insurmountable. My fears provoked a typical joke from Ado, which Annette related to me. Looking out the window of his apartment overlooking Central Park, he would say, "There, I see Baruj, flying past us; his father must have kicked him in the pants when he spoke of marriage!" Indeed, among the strong prejudices which my parents had inherited from generations of inbreeding in Tetuan was their conviction that we were not only Jews, but Sephardic Jews with a tradition of marrying only our kind. When I introduced Annette as my future fiancée, they objected not only on the ground that we were much too young and had to wait several years to test the strength of our attachment, but also because, as they expressed it, Annette was not *de las nuestras* (our kind). I pleaded strongly that she was Jewish and belonged to a highly respectable family, that we were both mature and dedicated to each other, and that I was willing to wait one or at most two years but not more. Mother was intractable but, surprisingly for me, my father showed more understanding. He liked Annette and recognized the depth of our attachment. With his characteristic generosity, he was unconcerned with the fact that the Dreyfuses were presently impecunious refugees, and proposed to support us provided we wait until graduation from Columbia before announcing our engagement and an additional year before marrying. I was deeply grateful for his understanding and support.

The summer of 1941 was a most happy time for Annette and me. The Dreyfus family together with their friends Jacques and Vera Lindon rented a summer cottage in Hampton Bay on Long Island, where I was invited to visit. I was delighted to share a dilapidated cabin in the garden with Bertrand and a large colony of mice. Annette and I spent our time swimming, boating, fishing, kissing, and talking. There was almost no time for sleeping, and I remember lying on the beach most of the night, close to Annette, looking at the stars.

The major tragedy of December 1941 was, of course, Pearl Harbor and the entry of the United States in the war, an event for which we had been prepared for some time and that would influence all our lives in an unknown fashion.

In my last year at Columbia, I completed both my premedical requirements and the prescribed curriculum for my major in chemistry. I obtained from my teachers excellent letters of recommendation for admission to medical school. As prescribed by my advisor, I applied to at least ten medical schools, among them Harvard, Johns Hopkins, Chicago, Columbia, Cornell, New York University, and Yale, although I much preferred going to a New York school. In my naiveté, I had not realized that my grades, which were excellent, were in no way sufficient to ensure my acceptance to medical school. No one had warned me of the importance of ethnic considerations for admission, of the existence of quotas restricting the acceptance of Jews and immigrants, and of the critical importance of interviews often dominated by the bias of the interviewer. I was worried when I received postcard rejections from Harvard, Hopkins, Cornell, Chicago, and Yale where my application seemed not to have merited serious consideration.

But I did not become desperate since I had interviews scheduled at Columbia and New York University (NYU), where I would have been delighted to go. Both interviews proved disastrous. At NYU I met with Donal Sheen, Professor of Anatomy. He was an Englishman who, I learned later, prided himself on his command of the language. I realized immediately that he was disturbed by my strong French accent and by my occasional usage of the wrong phraseology. Otherwise, there was little substance to the interview and he did not encourage me to expect a favorable answer.

I was interviewed at the College of Physicians and Surgeons of Columbia (P&S) by Associate Dean Vernon Lippard, a typical establishment physician who, among other things, asked me what proved to be the determining question of the interview: "I see you come from Venezuela. Do you propose to return to your country when you finish your medical training or to stay in the United States?" I did not realize the significance of the question and answered truthfully that I had not decided and that I might not return to Venezuela. As soon as I spoke, I felt as if a door had suddenly closed in front of me. I had moved from one quota into another far less favorable for admission. Indeed I was soon informed that I was not accepted. I was fortunate to have the perfect scientific control to substantiate my conclusions concerning what had happened and the prejudicial reason for my rejection. There was another Venezuelan premedical student at Columbia, my friend Hidalgo, who had also played in *Altitude 3200.* He was nice and personable but his scholastic record was inferior to mine. He was also interviewed at P&S and asked precisely the same question, to which he answered that he planned to return to Venezuela. He was accepted. The result of this controlled experiment on the usefulness of the interview system for admission to medical school is that Hidalgo did not do well at P & S and eventually dropped out and returned to Venezuela, but much earlier than foreseen.*

---

*It is some consolation for me today that I have been appointed to the faculties of NYU and Harvard and offered positions at Cornell and Yale Medical Schools, which would not have me as a student, and that my daughter was accepted at both Columbia and Harvard Medical School. Right does eventually triumph!

My inability to secure an acceptance to medical school disturbed me very much and raised fears that I was a failure and would be unable to obtain a medical education. I was very depressed and disheartened.

In May 1941, I was desperate. All my applications had been rejected and the future looked bleak. Annette was not discouraged, however. She pointed out to me that I had neglected to consider that admission to medical school in the United States was very much affected by personal considerations of who you know and who knows you. Furthermore, she reminded me that Georges Bakeman, the father of my friend Katenka, had been appointed assistant to Mr. Sanger, president of the Medical College of Virginia (MCV), in Richmond. She insisted that I write to him immediately explaining my difficulties, which I did. Within a week, Mr. Bakeman wired me to come immediately to Richmond for an interview, stating that there were still two slots open in the entering class. I immediately left for Richmond where Mr. Bakeman arranged for me to be seen by several of the clinical chiefs. The next day I was accepted as a medical student at MCV.*

When I returned to New York, Annette and I celebrated and prepared for graduation from Barnard and Columbia. Our joy was tempered, however, by the sadness that we would be separated for the first time when I would move to Richmond in September.

---

*I am totally indebted for my career in medicine and for whatever I have accomplished over the years to Annette, who advised me; to my dear friend Georges W. Bakeman, who had confidence in me; and to the generosity and fairness of a southern school, the Medical College of Virginia Commonwealth University.

4

──◦─❦─◦──

Medical School and Marriage

I moved to Richmond in July 1942, eager and excited, but apprehensive about being alone in an unfamiliar environment. I
rented a furnished room in the home of a hospitable middle-class
elderly couple, the Knapps. The room was pleasant and clean, and
a Bible had been placed on the dresser for my spiritual guidance.
The Knapps, who were devoted Baptists, did not seem concerned,
however, when they learned that I was Jewish. They were far more
impressed by the fact that I was a Venezuelan who spoke impeccable French.

I soon realized that Richmond and the South were very different, particularly in 1942, from any of the societies I had experienced. They still bore the deep scars of the Civil War and of the
consequences of their defeat. It was a totally segregated land where
blacks and whites were expected to live apart in separated, but
unequal facilities. I was all the more shocked by this inhumanity
because I had known a society in South America where blacks,
although an impoverished minority, were nevertheless assured

60

equal rights. I would be particularly outraged by the segregation of black patients in a separate, less modern hospital to be cared for by black nurses and white doctors. Coincidentally, most of my clinical rotations* would take place in the hospital for blacks and therefore most of my first patients were black. In all honesty, however, I never detected any difference in the quality of the medicine that was practiced on black and white patients. Black nurses were dedicated and excellent and the patients had the same doctors who exercised identical high standards, in spite of the fact that the buildings were old and cramped. In fact, the quality of medicine that I was taught at the Medical College of Virginia in Richmond and the uniform standards of clinical practice for both the white and black communities were excellent and, indeed, considerably higher than the standards I would see practiced on a predominately white population at Queens General Hospital in New York when I interned there. This clear difference, however, is not geographical; it should be ascribed to the fact that MCV was a teaching hospital with a splendid tradition of excellence.

In 1942, MCV was almost solely a clinical institution dedicated to the care of patients with very little clinical research† and practically no basic research activities. However, the quality of clinical care and the clinical acumen, teaching ability, and ethical standards of the physicians were exceptional. I have never wavered in the belief that I received an outstanding clinical education under the leadership of great practitioners.‡

Another important aspect of my experience as a medical student is the fact that it took place in wartime. Physicians were

---

*During the last two years of medical school, students learn clinical medicine by being put into intimate contact with individual patients assigned to them. The students rotate through different clinical specialties: medicine, surgery, pediatrics, obstetrics, etc.

†Clinical research is research carried out on patients. Basic research is performed in the laboratory.

‡Drs. William Branch Porter, Isaac Bigger, and Lee Sutton, heads of the Departments of Medicine, Surgery, and Pediatrics, respectively.

urgently needed for the war effort. As a consequence, many physicians from the faculty had already volunteered or had been called to active duty, and there were shortages in every specialty. The medical schools themselves were put on an accelerated schedule. Summer vacations were abolished for the duration of the war, and the normally four-year medical program was taught in three breathless years. In addition, by 1943 all physically fit male medical students would be drafted and inducted into army or navy units set up for this purpose at the schools.

The entering class in July 1942 was comprised of eighty students, almost all of whom were from southern states. There were only seven women, a smaller number of "Yankees," and three Jews. (There appeared to have always been a Jewish contingent at MCV. During the Civil War, the father of the financier Bernard Baruch graduated from MCV.) There was another Hispanic besides myself, the Puerto Rican son of an alumnus of the school. After the first two years, we were joined by an additional group of students from West Virginia who had attended a two-year school in their state. Medical school is a stressful and competitive experience at the best of times. It was even more so under the accelerated program of the war years.

Contrary to my previous experience at Columbia University, where there were few constraints on my innate curiosity and a lot of freedom, the curriculum at a medical school, particularly in those days, was rigidly defined and permitted no elective work. The first two years, defined as preclinical, were designed to provide the student with the basic information to practice scientific medicine. Human anatomy, histology, biochemistry, and microbiology were first-year topics, whereas physiology, pharmacology, pathology, and parasitology were taught in the second year. A course in physical diagnosis given as an introduction to clinical work was part of the second year's curriculum. We were, therefore, continuously exposed to new information throughout the day from series of lectures and laboratories, with only the nights and weekends free to commit this complex material to memory.

Strong friendships developed among my fellow students in medical school. By the first months I had already made several valued friendships that have lasted a lifetime. As I stated earlier, most of the students were from Virginia or neighboring southern states, and they were suspicious of "Damned Yankee" Northerners. Moreover, the social life was organized around highly selective fraternities, where many of the students lived. There was, indeed, a Jewish fraternity, but I had no interest in joining. There was never a chance that I would be invited to join one of the Christian fraternities. I never let this bother me a bit, since I have always been a loner. In all fairness, I was never considered a Yankee by my southern friends. They saw a foreigner, born much farther south than themselves, and felt that I was entitled to all the benefits and considerations accorded foreign visitors from faraway lands, and that is the way I was indeed treated.

Most of the memories of my first year of medical school are of learning anatomy and how to dissect a cadaver. Groups of four students were assigned a cadaver to dissect with the help of our manual, while we learned human anatomy in Grey's Textbook. During the complex process of cadaver dissection, I became desensitized to the shock of death and the unpleasantness of skinless human flesh and organs. I rapidly overcame this natural repulsion and was soon oblivious of the pernicious odor of formaldehyde that clung to me and my clothes during all the months of anatomy.

The professor of anatomy, Dr. H. L. Osterud, was dedicated and enthusiastic. To this day, it is hard for me to understand how one can become enthusiastic about such a topic. Either because I was scared or because I was impressed by Dr. Osterud's dedication, I studied much harder than I needed to, and earned the highest grades in anatomy, histology, and embryology. The other two first-year courses, biochemistry and microbiology, were comparatively easy tasks. I particularly enjoyed learning about viruses and bacteria and their pathogenic* properties.

*Pathogenic means capable of causing disease. Typhoid bacteria (*E. typhosa*) are the pathogenic organisms responsible for typhoid fever.

When I was not busy studying or sleeping—which occupied nearly all my time—I was very lonely and missed Annette tremendously. She visited me in Richmond a couple of times, always chaperoned by my mother or another senior family member. Although my landlady, Mrs. Knapp, could have arranged for Annette to have a room in her house, it was not thought proper. Instead, she rented a room with my mother in a neighbor's house. We were both impatient to get married, and a date was finally set for the ceremony to take place during the short week of recess between the first and second year of medical school.

We were married on March 24, 1943, in New York City by Rabbi de Sola Pool, head of the Orthodox Sephardic congregation in their temple on Central Park West. The selection of the rabbi and the religious ceremony was made by my parents. Annette's father was an agnostic, and her mother, in spite of the many prominent rabbis in her ancestry, was not religious either.

I associated three trivial events with this most important ceremony in my life. It is, indeed, remarkable the number of unimportant but conventional matters that must be decided and settled for a wedding. For example, sometime before the wedding, Annette, my father, and I met with Rabbi de Sola Pool to plan the details of the ceremony. We were explained the deep religious significance of the various rites and words to be used by us and the rabbi, and the symbolic meaning of the shattering of the glass at the end. Then, the rabbi asked what music we wanted played by the organist when the bride marched down the aisle. Thoughtlessly, Annette answered, "The 'Ave Maria' by Bach-Gounod." An embarrassed silence followed, as the rabbi looked at me not believing what he heard. I hastily said any music by Bach would do.

Another issue was the formal attire of the bride and groom. Annette was to wear a beautiful white satin wedding gown which has been saved ever since. I was to wear a formal suit with striped pants, tails, and a hard collar, which made me look like the proverbial stuffed penguin and feel very uncomfortable as well.*

The major drama of our wedding day, of which I take full responsibility, occurred at 11 A.M. in the rabbi's office, just before the ceremony. I was asked to produce the rings and the marriage license. I was shattered; I had the rings but had left the marriage license at the Croydon Hotel. I rushed across the park in a cab, my coattails fluttering in the wind, and returned breathless with the essential document. We were married half an hour later than scheduled and were overjoyed after two years of waiting. After a luncheon for the immediate family, followed by a reception at the Croydon attended by close friends, we finally changed to sensible clothes and left on our honeymoon.

Since we had only three days for our honeymoon before my return to school, we boarded a train at Grand Central Station for nearby Rye, where reservations had been made for us at the plush Westchester Country Club. The club was deserted but we had a lovely room.

Three days later we were in Richmond where, as husband and wife, we entered the apartment I had rented for us for $40 a month in a new housing development. We were overjoyed to be the first to occupy the tiny apartment, but we had to wait for several days for the furniture that my father had bought at bargain prices to arrive from New York. We were delightfully happy in that apartment, except for the dreadfully hot Richmond summer in an apartment without insulation and cross ventilation. We spent many a night that summer outside on the lawn. Having learned our lesson, we later moved to an old house with tall ceilings, big windows, and good ventilation.

---

*The next time I wore rented tails was in Stockholm nearly forty years later.

The second year at MCV was much more exciting than the first; I was enrolled in physiology and pathology. I was particularly impressed by Dr. Frank L. Apperly, professor and chairman of the Department of Pathology. He was an Englishman and a true scholar. He taught me that pathology is not simply the morphological* diagnosis of tissues, but rather the study of the mechanisms of disease, not only by morphology but also by the use of any suitable techniques such as physiology, biochemistry, immunology, or, as I learned later, molecular biology and genetics. Stimulated by his teachings, this has been one of my life's goals.

I was very fortunate that in the junior faculty of Apperly's department there was a remarkable young assistant professor named Dr. Bernard Black-Shaeffer, who had an irreverent, iconoclastic, and enthusiastic personality with a thirst for research. I was fascinated and attracted by Black-Shaeffer. In fact, I date my lifetime interest in research to the initial experiments I carried out under his direction. Trained as a classical pathologist, he unfortunately lacked experience in any of the basic sciences. I realized later that this made his approach and our experiments unlikely to succeed. His strong interest was in the effects of bacterial endotoxins, the fascinating toxins of Gram negative bacteria,† and in their capacity to induce hemorrhagic necrosis in man and rabbits in certain tissues and particularly in tumors. These phenomena were known as the Schwarzman reactions, and had been described initially by a pathologist by that name at Mount Sinai Hospital in

---

*Pathology was initially and traditionally the study of anatomical changes of tissues, detected by microscopic examination, which are characteristic of disease, and permit definitive diagnosis to be made. With the progress of medical science pathologists became increasingly also concerned with the mechanism of diseases as revealed by bacteriology, biochemistry and immunology, and genetics.

†Gram negative bacteria stain negative when treated with Gram stain in the laboratory. A typical Gram negative bacterium is Salmonella, which is responsible for severe gastrointestinal inflammation. Many Gram negative bacteria produce a toxin called endotoxin which can cause multiple symptoms, including vascular shock, a collapse of blood pressure.

New York. Black-Shaeffer enlisted my help in carrying out laboratory experiments designed to elucidate the mechanism of these reactions. Although I must give him credit for his enthusiasm, energy, and uncanny intuition in spotting an important problem as well as the general direction where the answers probably lay, we carried out numerous experiments that were generally inconclusive, technically immature, and always unpublishable. I nevertheless profited greatly from our work and relationship, which aroused my sustained interest in experimental pathology and got me hooked on laboratory work for life. It is historically relevant that the questions we were investigating in 1943 were only resolved in the last twenty years, as a consequence of the critical discovery of tumor necrosis factor (TNF) by one of my most gifted students Lloyd Old. TNF is a molecule capable of killing tumor cells. It is secreted by activated macrophages exposed to endotoxin. Old's experiments had been motivated by the studies he and I carried out together on tumor cells in 1961 which, themselves, have roots in the 1943 experiments I conducted with Black-Shaeffer.

Now that medical research has justifiably become both fashionable and very prevalent in universities and institutes, thanks to the generous and wise support of Congress, it is appropriate to recall that when I started in the laboratory with Black-Shaeffer, we were the only ones in the department doing experimental work. The experimental projects in the whole of MCV could be counted on the fingers of one hand at that time.

Another major event of 1943 was my induction into the U.S. Army. As a foreign citizen, I would be drafted unless I specifically and in writing objected to it. Such an objection would carry with it the loss of the right to apply for U.S. citizenship. My own personal involvement in the war, both as a Jew and a refugee from occupied France, made me support it all the more. I was very desirous to participate in it at the appropriate time. I was therefore ready and willing to join up when called to do so. Sometime in 1943 the decision was made to draft all eligible male medical students into the armed forces and to train them to serve as medical officers upon graduation. How long the war would last was uncertain, but it was clear that the urgent need for trained medical personnel would continue for an unforeseen period, even beyond victory over Germany and Japan.

For approximately a week or two, school was suspended and we were drafted into active duty. I was inducted as a private at Camp Lee, Virginia, a basic training camp, and processed with the other draftees through the system. I went through the first phases of basic training while I waited for orders assigning me to a new unit created at MCV for the medical students. It is interesting that, when I went through the battery of tests to determine my aptitude as a soldier and to ensure an appropriate assignment, I was told I was best suited to operate a tank!

Even more remarkable was how much drilling, KP duty, and other routines could be done during my week or ten-day stay at Camp Lee. I was introduced to rows of toilets where everyone is expected to defecate together without any privacy.

The order assigning me to the MCV army unit finally came through and I was sent back to Richmond as a private first class, proud to wear the uniform in wartime. Being in the army did not change our life very much, except that the government paid my medical school tuition and provided me with a comfortable allowance. I no longer needed to depend on my father's support. Our unit was assigned to reside at home as before and only required to do a little drilling on Saturday afternoon. Of course I had to wear my uniform at all times, to which was later added the good conduct medal, the highest army decoration I was ever to earn.

Three months after my induction I was called into the captain's office and told that since I was expected to be commissioned as an officer in the American army upon graduation in less than two years, and since only citizens could be commissioned, I should apply for American citizenship, which I was pleased to do. On November 19, 1943, together with a large number of other foreign draftees, I was "marched" into court, sworn in by the judge, and granted my citizenship papers without the need to pass a civics examination. I reflected that a lot had happened in these short months: I had married Annette, started research in the laboratory, was drafted and promoted to PFC, and granted American citizenship. At last, I was ready to enter the clinical years and to learn what medicine was really about.

At the beginning of my third year of medical school I was astonished to learn that I had been elected with three other students to membership in Alpha Omega Alpha, the medical honorary fraternity, which indicated that my grades in the first two years had put me in the top 5 percent of the class. This unexpected news tended to relieve, at least temporarily, the fear of failure, which I have always, unreasonably, entertained.

The life of a medical student undergoes a total change at the beginning of the third year. Memorizing the sciences basic to medicine is assumed to have been accomplished. The student is given a white coat and thrown headfirst into the clinic and onto the wards, as a "doctor." There are still some lectures and clinics to attend but most of one's time is spent in patient contacts in an attempt to teach the art of medicine by watching and doing. The burden of teaching medical students is unequally shared by the professors and attending physicians,* who review the cases with the students, and mostly by the interns and residents, who are effectively treating the patients on a twenty-four-hour basis and making most of the clinical decisions. Most house officers† were

---

*Attending physicians are doctors who are granted attending privileges by a hospital and are responsible for deciding the patient's treatment.

†House officers in a hospital are the interns and residents who are directly responsible for the care of patients. Interns and residents reside in the hospitals and are on duty for patient care often for thirty-six hours before they get twelve hours off to sleep and relax.

kind and helpful with the students in spite of being harassed and exhausted from sleep deprivation. They remembered that they had been students themselves with identical ignorance and bewilderment only one or two years before.

Taking care of the sick is both a stressful and emotional experience. It is difficult to limit one's personal involvement and empathy with the critically ill patients under one's care. This is a problem that I was to be faced with more and more, particularly when as an intern I was given sole charge of patients. Yet, to exercise reasoned judgment when managing a patient requires the ability to detach oneself from emotions. Identifying with patients can reduce a doctor's ability to give them and their families the benefit of his professional expertise. The matter has gotten even worse nowadays when, because of the constant threat of costly lawsuits, doctors are forced to practice defensive medicine and have to deal with yet another emotional parameter, fear, affecting the doctor-patient relationship. The advent of managed care and modern HMOs has further compromised the traditional intimate patient/physician relationship.

My most vivid memories of clinical training relate to my rotations in medicine, surgery, pediatrics, and obstetrics. As I recall some of my salient experiences as a medical student, I realize that my involvement in American medicine over a period of fifty critical years has enabled me to witness the major advances in scientific knowledge which have transformed the practice of medicine from a discipline capable of providing sound diagnosis but limited care in the 1940s to a complex specialized system capable of delivering sophisticated definitive therapies today. It was my good fortune to be a student when penicillin was an experimental drug and sulfa drugs had just been introduced, before the discovery of the effectiveness of streptomycin in treating tuberculosis, and before the development of a preventive treatment for hypertension. But the list would be too long if I were to mention all the advances that have occurred in the last half century. It is, however, a measure of the past successes of American medicine and research that the public becomes impatient because a cure for AIDS has not been found in the relatively few years since this dreadful disease was identified.

My first patient during those years of medical rotations was a young black male severely ill with acute lobar pneumoccocal pneumonia. He had a high fever and was in an oxygen tent. As soon as the diagnosis was made he was treated with sulfonamides, a relatively new drug at the time, which cured him in three days. His pneumonia was a textbook case. Although I felt guilty intruding on a sick man, I was required to examine him and could verify by auscultation the presence of consolidation in his lung as well as its resolution after treatment.

The second patient I would like to mention was a very sad case. She was a black middle-aged female who suffered from severe progressive glomerulonephritis.* She would die eventually from kidney failure. Hers was also a textbook case, which, according to the medical history I elicited from her, had begun with what appeared to have been strep throat and eventually resulted in progressive renal damage. It is sad that little could be done for her at the time. Today, her life could be prolonged indefinitely by dialysis and her disease cured by kidney transplantation.*

My most important surgical patient was an adult white male who had suffered a ruptured appendix and had developed generalized peritonitis (infection of the peritoneal cavity) as a consequence. He was critically ill for weeks with fever, anemia, and weight loss, all symptoms of severe infection. Unfortunately, we did not have the antibiotics in those days which would have helped

---

*Glomerulonephritis is an acute inflammation of the kidneys, often occurring as a complication of streptococcal infection. Glomerulonephritis can progress to eventually destroy all kidney function and to death unless treated by dialysis or kidney transplantation.

†In 1960, I would carry out experiments with my associate Robert McCluskey that contributed to the further understanding of the pathogenic mechanism of acute immune complex glomerulonephritis, the disease that killed my patient.

considerably in the treatment of his case. He was eventually saved, first by repeated transfusions which helped bolster his defenses, and then later by surgery. I was proud to be the first to detect that his infection had localized in a large abscess under the diaphragm, which was confirmed on X-ray. The abscess was surgically drained and the patient made a complete recovery thereafter. When asked by Dr. Isaac Bigger, Chief of Surgery, to present the case at the Clinical Surgical Conference, I was proud as a peacock. For a short time I even entertained the fancy of becoming a surgeon, but the calling was really not there.

I always loved children, with whom I feel a personal kinship. Moreover, children generally like and trust me. It is not surprising, therefore, that my most enjoyable rotation was in pediatrics and that I chose to spend my elective on the pediatric ward. Much of pediatrics is concerned with the normal growth and development of healthy children, and is therefore very gratifying.

Most sick children recover rapidly and those who are chronically ill or who do not do well never lose courage. In spite of my sadness at being powerless to cure very sick children, a feeling I would experience repeatedly during the 1945 polio epidemic, my interactions with children, even sick ones, were always uplifting and rewarding. The major drawback to pediatrics was dealing with the parents who neither shared the charm of their offspring nor their patience and fortitude.

The most vivid memory of my pediatric rotation was my experience with the poliomyelitis epidemic that hit Richmond and our hospital during my senior year. My feeling of helplessness before the suffering and the irreversible paralysis which were the inevitable results of the disease, was overwhelming. It was heartbreaking to work in isolation in these wards and realize that we were doing nothing for the patients beyond attempting to relieve the muscle cramps and the pain. Here again is a vivid example of what has been accomplished by medical science in a relatively short time. The polio vaccines developed by Jonas Salk and Albert

Sabin have wiped out this disease. We owe the possibility of these vaccines to John Enders, who discovered how to grow the poliomyelitis virus in the laboratory, an enormous contribution for which he received the Nobel Prize in 1954.*

My last clinical experience at MCV, which is etched in my memory, is my performance in obstetrics and my delivery of babies. There was a program at MCV whereby patients with uncomplicated pregnancies, who already had several pregnancies, were delivered at home. Home-delivery teams, consisting of a fourth-year and a third-year student, were on call to go to the home of women in labor with an appropriate kit and were required to stay on-site until the baby was born, or the patient was brought in by ambulance if a complication arose. I went out to impoverished communities and successfully delivered my share of babies. I gathered from this experience a healthy respect for nature and the process of childbirth. I discovered that nothing is really expected from the doctor in these uncomplicated cases except to catch the child, repair the tear on the mother when needed, and cut the umbilical cord. I told Annette that the parents of one of the babies I delivered insisted on naming him Baruj Benacerraf Brown, but I might have invented this tale to impress her.

My clinical responsibilities, however, did not stop my experiments in the laboratory with Dr. Black-Shaeffer. Annette would accompany me when I spent my free evenings working on research projects. In addition to the study on endotoxin, we started a second study, also with rabbits, on the pathogenic mechanism of serum sickness. These experiments were just as unsuccessful as the ones on endotoxin, but I was not discouraged and, when my medical education ended, I was even more curious and addicted to research

---

*It was my privilege to have known and greatly admired John Enders, who headed the laboratory of infectious diseases at Children's Hospital in Boston for many years. It is one of those strange coincidences that I was offered by John Enders a position in his laboratory to work on the techniques for growing viruses when I looked for a research position in immunology in 1947.

than ever before. I was to work on serum sickness again in 1957, when I was an assistant professor of pathology at New York University. At that time, Robert McCluskey, Fred Miller, and I were fortunate to explain the mechanism of the lesions of serum sickness.

I would like to return, now, to my life with Annette in Richmond. We were, indeed, always very much in love and overjoyed to be together. Annette would reassure my unreasonable fears of failing my examinations by making fun of me. The standard joke was that I kept a bag packed and ready to join a tank brigade in case I failed a critical test and got thrown out of school. We did not mind that entertainment was limited in wartime Richmond. We owned a Steinway upright piano (a wedding present) and Annette would play Bach's preludes while I studied. We also loved going to the movies. Sunday evenings we became addicted to listening to Jack Benny, Fred Allen, and Edgar Bergen.

Annette, looking for an occupation, was offered and accepted a position teaching French literature in the Collegiate School, a fashionable high school for girls. She very much enjoyed this experience and was proud to earn $900 per year.

Graduation was rapidly approaching. After receiving my M.D. degree I would be discharged as a private first class and immediately commissioned as a first lieutenant in the Army Medical Corps. Then I was to be placed on inactive duty for a period of nine months during which I was expected to train as a house officer. The major concern in my last year of school was, therefore, to secure a suitable internship, which presented a problem, although not as serious as the one I had when I was applying to medical school. Annette and I, after years in Richmond, were both eager to return to New York, which we loved very much. I decided to apply only to New York hospitals, although I was aware that this decision diminished my chance of securing a good internship in a teaching hospital.

I should, at this time, explain what happened to our respective families during the critical war years, from 1942–1945, while we were in Richmond. Starting with the Dreyfus family, Ado was employed initially in New York by the Office of War Information (OWI). Then, when Charles de Gaulle's Free French government was, unofficially and later officially, recognized by President Franklin D. Roosevelt, a French purchasing commission was established in Washington to channel the Lend Lease aid to the French forces. This commission was placed under the direction of Jean Monnet, who was to be better known for his essential contribution to the creation of the Common Market and the European Community after the war. Jean Monnet knew Ado and liked him. He asked Ado to work for him directly in Washington. Annette's father accepted enthusiastically. Ado moved to Washington and would often come to visit us in Richmond on weekends.

Meanwhile, my father was urgently needed in Caracas where critical decisions had to be made as opportunities created by the war had to be exploited. Father decided to move back to Caracas and eventually my mother followed him. They nevertheless maintained an apartment at the Croydon and my brother, Paul, entered the Peddie School, a private boarding school in New Jersey. During the war years, Abraham and Fortunato, working as a team, were to expand their business interests considerably into a variety of new enterprises. They started a shoe factory, a retail chain, and most important, together with business friends and associates, they founded a new bank, the Banco Union, with which I was to have considerable involvement one day and which is still one of the most important banks in Venezuela.

Selecting an internship in New York was not an easy task. I knew I would not have any chance at New York Hospital or Columbia's

College of Physicians and Surgeons. I thought, however, that my
record at MCV and my election to Alpha Omega Alpha would
make me acceptable to the Mount Sinai Hospital, which had an
excellent clinical reputation and where I wanted very much to
intern. I applied to Mount Sinai and also to Montefiore Hospital in
the Bronx. Just to be safe, I also applied to one of the New York
City hospitals, Queens General, although it was not a teaching
hospital. I was very excited when I went to Mount Sinai for my
interview. I was seen by one of the senior administrators, who was
very smug and, I might even say, unnecessarily contemptuous. He
said: "I see you want to intern at Mount Sinai. Do you know the
types of applicants we have? The top students at P&S, the top two
at NYU, and so on." I replied: "I am also at the top of my class."
He retorted: "Yes, but what does it mean to be at the top of the
class in Virginia?" He had, in a single sentence, insulted both me
and my school. I thanked him courteously for his time and
departed crestfallen. I had to come to terms with the realization
that I performed poorly in interviews in New York. Shortly after
this, I received an acceptance letter from Queens General Hospital
and decided to spend my nine-month rotating internship there. I
was proud to receive my M.D. degree from the Medical College of
Virginia. I took this occasion to express my gratitude to Georges W.
Bakeman who had been responsible for my career.

There was practically no time to rest between graduation and
the beginning of my internship. Annette and I moved back to the
familiar Croydon Hotel in New York, into the furnished apartment
which my parents had rented for their occasional visits from
Caracas, and we put our furniture in storage.

5

Internship and Army Training

Q ueens General Hospital had 900 beds and was one of the
newest of the city-owned. It served primarily the borough of
Queens. I was one of twenty-four interns who, with a set of ten residents, would be responsible for the care of 800 to 900 acutely ill
patients. The stresses of medical school would be child's play compared to what I experienced as a rotating intern in the next nine
months. Throughout this period I was to be on duty every other
night, which meant literally that I worked, or was effectively on
call, responsible for the care of a ward of fifty very sick patients for
thirty-six hours straight. Then, I was off and could leave the hospital for twelve hours. A room was assigned to me in the doctor's
quarters, but never in those months could I sleep in it for more
than a few hours a night, if at all. During my internship I developed a physical aversion to the ringing of the telephone, particularly at night, which has remained with me all my life and has permanently prejudiced my attitude toward this essential instrument,
which my wife and daughter both adore.

It is not surprising that this kind of sustained stress has damaging effects. It is common knowledge that the frequency of nervous breakdowns and pulmonary tuberculosis is much higher among interns than in the general population of doctors. Indeed, an intern in my group developed active tuberculosis during this period.

Although I must admit that the pressures at Queens General Hospital in 1945 were worse than usual, because of the wartime shortage of doctors, the conditions under which I worked as an intern have been traditionally those which, until very recently, were deemed appropriate to train physicians. When my daughter, Beryl, was a surgical intern, over thirty years later at the Peter Bent Brigham Hospital in Boston, she had a similar experience. I recall an instance when, after a thirty-six-hour period of continuous duty, mostly in the operating room, she called because she did not feel competent to drive her car back home. Her husband had to fetch her. It is only in the last few years, under the pressure of public opinion, which realized that the judgment and efficacy of physicians working under that kind of stress are likely to be impaired, that hospitals have agreed to put some limits on the working hours of their house staff.

It is undeniable, however, that the complete immersion in clinical medicine and the constant stress caused by the immediate responsibility for patient welfare are a unique education for a starting physician. It is only as an intern that I really learned medicine and developed the judgment, medical reflexes, knowledge, and ethical standards that make me a doctor and that have stayed with me all my life, in spite of a career spent mostly in the laboratory.

Unfortunately, clinical competence does not come all at once with the issuance of the intern's traditional white suit; it takes time and practical experience to acquire the necessary proficiency. Anyone who has knowledge of our teaching hospitals is aware that if one has any choice as to when to be hospitalized—for elective surgery, for instance—the months of July and August are to be avoided at all cost in order to escape being under the care of a new set of as yet inexperienced house officers.

I felt very inadequate when, starting my internship on July 1, 1945, I was assigned a medical ward and realized that I was directly responsible for the diagnosis and treatment of patients. There were two extremely able, experienced, and dedicated residents from whom I could seek advice. But both made it clear that the immediate responsibility for my ward was mine. Unlike medical school, there were no students to help, nor professors to teach us. The attending physicians were in general marginally competent and provided little if any support. I was very much on my own. The same was true of my rotations in surgery, traumatic surgery, and obstetrics, except that in none of these other services were the residents as competent as the medical and pediatric residents. The surgical residents were primarily interested in operating, whereas the obstetrical residents were inept and lazy. In contrast, I was fortunate that the interns, with a couple of exceptions, were uniformly excellent and dedicated physicians. One of the first lessons I learned was that all doctors are not equally knowledgeable or dedicated and that an M.D. degree is no assurance of competence. It is therefore extremely important to select one's physician carefully, a very difficult task for the uninformed public. Fortunately the traditional myth, harmless when medicine was generally powerless, that deified both priests and physicians has not resisted the advent of modern medical practice. As the tools and medicines have been provided by science to intervene effectively and sometimes to cure diseases, the decision of how to treat and when to treat becomes critical. It is essential, therefore, to choose one's physician wisely and to insist on openness and accountability, which is now the practice in the best medical centers.

Compared to my balanced opinion of the physicians with whom I dealt as an intern, the nurses were absolutely superb. The nurses in charge of the wards, the emergency room, or the operating rooms were all, without exception, extremely competent, dedicated, and compassionate. I admired them tremendously and, as a very inexperienced physician, I learned a lot from them. I understood very quickly that both nurses and physicians have an equal stake in healthcare and must form an intimate partnership, based on mutual trust and respect, to treat patients successfully. I would like to speak with equal warmth, also, of the student nurses who, although not as experienced, were just as dedicated and warm.

As was the case with my clinical experience as a medical student, my memories as an intern are primarily concerned with those special patients who particularly impressed me. I was deeply distressed by a young and beautiful nurse who was suffering from active miliary tuberculosis,* which was slowly but progressively suffocating her. During the time I spent talking to her when she could be out of the oxygen tent, I tried to hide my distress at the thought that she would soon die and that I could do nothing for her.

Another very tragic experience was my realization that a young child I was examining probably had tuberculous meningitis,† a uniformly fatal infection before streptomycin. My tentative diagnosis was sadly confirmed by the laboratory examination of the spinal fluid. It is to the credit of medical science that these patients would be saved today, thanks to the discovery of streptomycin, an antibiotic effective against the tubercle bacillus, made by Selman A. Waksman, whom I was privileged to know.‡

Another distressing experience occurred during my surgical rotation. In the course of a month we were to admit three patients suffering from cancer of the head of the pancreas, a lethal tumor for which even today medical science has not produced a successful therapy. The tumor is usually undetected for a sufficient time to invade much of the surrounding tissues. The first symptom

---

*A form of tuberculosis where the tubercle bacillus spreads through the bloodstream causing multiple small lesions which eventually grow and invade the lung tissue and asphyxiate the patient.

†An infection of the central nervous system with the tubercle bacillus. It was uniformly lethal before the discovery of antibiotics.

‡Waksman was to receive the 1952 Nobel Prize for this major contribution. I was to become a very close friend of his son Byron, a distinguished immunologist.

of trouble is the appearance of painless jaundice due to the blockage of the common bile duct. Surgeons have devised a major operation to remove the tumor. The three patients were all operated on. None of them survived very long after surgery and I could not help but ponder, sadly, whether it would not have been more humane to spare them the added trauma of surgery, in the absence of better odds. But not all the surgery cases were as disastrous. I remember a white middle-aged male who had a large tumor high in his esophagus. We operated, removing the tumor as well as most of the esophagus. We moved the stomach into the chest cavity to maintain the digestive tract. The operation lasted five exhausting hours. The postoperative course was difficult, but the patient recovered and walked out of the hospital without symptoms.

Another strange case was that of a young white male who had tried to kill himself by hanging. He was brought in unconscious after an emergency laryngotomy* had made it possible for him to breathe. The brain had been deprived of oxygen for too long. For several days he was unreactive and unconscious but surprisingly he recovered completely and did not remember a thing, not even the reason why he had wanted to commit suicide!

As in medical school I very much enjoyed my pediatric experience, and in obstetrics I became an expert at performing circumcisions on scores of newborns.

As I reflect on my experience as an intern, the useful message I want to convey is that the type of medicine we practiced in 1945 in pediatrics, cardiology, and obstetrics, for instance, has been very much improved by the manifold advances contributed by scientific medicine, as the increased life span of our population attests. Further improvements are still forthcoming, as more and better research provide more definitive ways to treat as yet incurable diseases. But we begin to appreciate the emergence of important new socioeconomic issues that concern the unequal access to

---

*Surgical incision into the larynx to provide an opening for respiration.

the best care, the increasing cost of care, and the inefficiencies inherent in the complex system of the delivery of care.

Near Queens General Hospital, sharing the same administrative structure was another major city hospital, Triboro Hospital for Chronic Pulmonary Diseases, which specialized in the treatment of tuberculosis. The chief surgical resident at Triboro was a remarkable physician named Dr. Klopstock. He was a middle-aged immigrant from Prague, very cultured and highly introspective, which is unusual for a surgeon, even for the skilled chest surgeon he was. Klopstock was a keen researcher, who, when working at the Massachusetts General Hospital with Churchill, its famous chief of surgery, had introduced the technique of lobectomy* for the treatment of localized pulmonary tuberculosis. Klopstock's prestige increased in my eyes when I learned that he had been a close friend of author Franz Kafka, whom he had treated for tuberculosis, and that he was at Kafka's bedside when the famous writer died. Klopstock and I were to become close friends and I am very much indebted to him, as you will see.

When we returned to New York, Annette was able to fulfill her lifetime dream of becoming an actress at last. She registered at a dramatic school in Rockefeller Center. Of course I was only able to see her on my nights off when I was exhausted from the previous thirty-six-hour ordeal. She was happy, therefore, to have an activity which fulfilled her basic interests. Possibly because of my Spanish roots, I have always been extremely jealous of any friendships or even familial attachments when Annette is concerned. I was disturbed, therefore, at the thought that she was rehearsing with other young men when I was away. She took my concerns very lightly and said that I was very fortunate that there was a high proportion of gay

---

*Surgical removal of a lobe of the lung.

men in her school. I could verify for myself, indeed, that the attractive and talented student she was rehearsing with was unquestionably gay. In fact, maybe because of Annette's strong interests in music, dramatics, and art, many of the friends we made, over the years of our life in New York, would be talented and, as it happens, homosexual.

By the end of the summer, when we had barely begun to adjust to our new life, disaster struck. Annette had been accepted as a full-time student at the famous Neighborhood Playhouse, and was required to take a physical examination. She went to her mother's physician for a checkup, a French internist with a highly fashionable Park Avenue practice. She was tense and anxious when I saw her that evening. She revealed that the doctor told her that he thought that the fluoroscopy had detected a suspicious shadow in the upper lobe of the right lung. I was alarmed and incensed that the doctor had not taken a chest X-ray, the only way to surely confirm or rule out the diagnosis.

I immediately took Annette to Triboro and to my friend Dr. Klopstock. We took chest plates which revealed that Annette had effectively a typical small tuberculous lesion. But, it was located in the lower lobe of her left lung and not in the right upper lobe as her doctor had suspected. Because of the suspicions raised by an erroneous finding, improperly made, we had discovered that Annette had active pulmonary tuberculosis. I was shattered. The only treatment prescribed, at the time, was extended bed rest, until one could verify that the infection was arrested and the lesion had calcified.

This unexpected discovery started one of the most unhappy periods in both our lives. Annette had to stop her classes, give up her ambition of a dramatic career, and for months spend all her time in bed, in our apartment. It is not surprising that I found her sad and depressed when I came home every other night, exhausted from my own stressful life. Klopstock, who helped me manage her case, recommended that we treat Annette with high doses of intravenous ascorbic acid (vitamin C), which, he had discovered, appeared to promote healing of the lesions. I followed his advice, since it was a nontoxic therapy, although to this day I honestly do not know whether intravenous ascorbic acid contributed to the arrest of Annette's infection. I decided, indeed, to manage my wife's treatment myself, and in doing so, I disregarded the myth that doctors should not treat themselves or their families. I have, in fact, always done the opposite all my life and never regretted it. I do not see how doctors, with the knowledge they have, can avoid using their judgment, at least as consultants, on their own illnesses and those of their immediate family, even though it can often be a painful experience.

For many months we waited anxiously for the next X-ray examination, and hoped that the lesion would indeed stabilize and not progress. I was adamant about complete bed rest, even if it depressed Annette's usually happy disposition. We were fortunate, in our misery, that Annette's mother and sister had remained in New York, while Ado was in Washington. After a while we decided that Annette would move to their apartment in the Hotel Raleigh, on West Seventy-second Street, where she would be better cared for and we hoped more cheerful. I would join them there, on my nights off. After six months of this routine, we were enormously relieved to find that the lesion had stabilized. Annette, who had always been underweight, had gained fifteen pounds, and we felt that the end of our ordeal was in sight. She was allowed to resume partial activity, with afternoon rests, and we could look at the future with more optimistic eyes. But Annette was immensely disappointed that the possibility of having children, which she wanted very much, was relegated to the distant future, as pregnancy is a known activator of tuberculous infections.

Meanwhile the nine months of my internship were coming to an end and a new chapter of our life was ready to unfold.

⚜ ⚜ ⚜

In the short period of my internship, many important world events had occurred. First and foremost, we celebrated V-E day and the defeat of Hitler that summer. Times Square was electrified in glorious happiness. I was fortunate to have been off that evening. At that time, everyone assumed that war with Japan would continue, as bloody as ever, until the final invasion of the Japanese main islands and the assault on Tokyo. These battles were expected to take a long time and cause many casualties, since there was every indication that the Japanese would fight rather than surrender. I expected to be involved in that final onslaught, when called on active duty in a few months. The atomic bombings of Hiroshima and Nagasaki and the immediate surrender of Japan that followed changed the pattern of my future, together with that of millions of young men, who could have been involved in these deadly battles that never took place.

By April 1946, when I left Queens General Hospital, it was clear that the only army duty I would perform would be with the occupation forces in Europe or Japan. I received my orders placing me on active duty as a first lieutenant in the medical corps and assigning me temporarily to an army hospital on Staten Island, where I was not needed and there was nothing for me to do. After years of frenetic and exhausting activity, these few weeks of idleness seemed unreal. I would rush, early in the morning, to catch the ferry, report for duty, and spend most of my time reading, until it was time, in the evening, to catch the ferry back to Manhattan. I learned my first army lesson: there is no apparent reason for what one is asked to do, or for being there at all. Shortly after these few weeks, I received my orders to report to Fort Sam Houston, Texas, to take a training course, organized for all the physicians of the graduating classes of 1945, after which we were to be shipped out, immediately, to Europe or Japan.

When he learned of these plans, Ado, who by now had made important friends in Washington, intervened, without my knowledge, with his contacts in the army and requested that his son-in-law be assigned to Europe, rather than Japan, and preferably, to a unit in France. He gave as reasons for his request, the still critical health of Annette, who was soon to leave for Paris to be with her parents, and my command of the French language, which would make me an asset to the army in France. Surprisingly, he was successful and I would be, in due time, stationed in Paris where I would join Annette.

Before I left for Texas, arrangements had been made for Annette to sail on the *Ile de France* to join her parents who had just returned to Paris. It is remarkable how soon after the end of the war normal travel had been reestablished to France. The liner had not yet been reconverted from a troopship to its customary luxury, but Annette, nevertheless, had a pleasant crossing, and was greeted at Le Havre by Ado, who managed to surprise her by coming on board with the pilot. When the Dreyfuses returned to Paris, they found that they had lost their apartment and that all their belongings had been looted by the Germans. However, except for a great-uncle of Annette, Leon Zadoc Kahn, and his wife, who had been deported and gassed by the Germans, all the rest of their large family survived the German occupation. Leon Zadoc Kahn, a brother of Annette's maternal grandmother, Berthe Bruhl, had been a distinguished physician and director of the Hôpital Rothschild in Paris. The Nazis in their wicked thoroughness had managed to locate them in a little village near Paris, where they had been hiding.

Since much of our life in the next few years was to be spent in France, and Annette and I were to have frequent interactions with her family, it is useful to learn more about the Bruhl family. Annette's grandmother, Berthe Bruhl, then seventy-five years old, had miraculously survived the war. She had lived in her own apartment during the German occupation and had worn, dutifully, the yellow star of David as required of the Jews. She was a spunky old lady, always on the move, interested in everything and everyone. Throughout the war, she managed to safeguard a magnificent collection of impressionist paintings that had been bought by her late husband, Henri Bruhl, a diamond merchant with a rare taste for art. Among these were several oils by Renoir, Degas, Pissaro, Sisley, Mary Cassat, Boudin, Fantin-Latour, and Guillaumin, to mention the most important ones. It is remarkable that these treasures on the wall of her small, dark apartment escaped the greedy hands of Hermann Goering and his agents. Two of these paintings, the Boudin and the Guillaumin, are hanging in our living room today. Annette's grandmother traded one of the Degas during the war, according to Ado, in exchange for chocolates of which she was very fond.

Berthe and Henri Bruhl had five children: daughters Suzanne, Madeleine, Lise, and Odette and a son named Etienne. Annette's mother, Suzanne, and her sister Madeleine had married two brothers, Ado and Jacques Dreyfus. Annette's cousins, Bertrand and Dominique, who fled to England and then to the United States with Annette, were the sons of Madeleine and Jacques.

Lise and Odette had married non-Jewish scientists who made it easier for them to escape detection during the German occupation. Lise was the wife of the well-known zoologist Georges Tessier, who directed the French Marine Laboratories in Roscoff. Odette's wedding to Jacques Monod took place just before the war. Jacques Monod, with whom I would become very close, was to be a worldfamous molecular biologist and would receive the Nobel Prize for medicine in 1965.

The Bruhl sisters and their mother were very attached to each other, and the family always focused on them. Around the turn of the century, Berthe and Henri Bruhl had purchased a huge country house with a beautiful garden and a tennis court in Le Vesinet, near Paris, where the whole family—the Bruhl sisters, their husbands, and children—spent every summer before the war. Like many others, the house had been looted by the Germans, but was again available for occupancy. It was into this house that Ado decided to move his family when they returned to France in the summer of 1946, and it was in this same house that I would find Annette when I myself arrived in Paris several months later.

✠ ✠ ✠

When Annette left for France, I departed for San Antonio, Texas, to learn to be a medical officer in a few short weeks. The barracks were taken over by hundreds of young, recently graduated physicians there to learn about army organization, procedure, and discipline. The classes and the drilling, under the direction of professional army personnel, left little impression on me except for one of general boredom. One memorable night, however, we were taken out in the country in trucks, and dropped off, two by two, with only a compass and general instructions to find our way back. This exercise was fun, although I did not know how such a drill could prepare a medical officer to discharge his duties.

Toward the end of the six-week training period I received my orders: I was to be stationed in Europe. I was to report to Camp Kilmer, New Jersey, and sail on the troop transport ship *George Washington*, a couple of weeks hence.

Just at that time I received the disturbing news from Caracas that my father and my uncle Fortunato were both critically ill. Apparently, Fortunato suffered a massive coronary thrombosis in the middle of the night. My father was awakened by a phone call informing him of his brother's heart attack. He was very much shaken and immediately suffered a severe stroke rendering him completely paralyzed on the left side and unable to speak. As for Fortunato, his massive attack seriously compromised his left ventricle and provoked severe bouts of pulmonary edema, which affected his ability to breathe. My presence in Caracas was urgently needed. I was also requested to arrange for the best cardiovascular specialist in the United States to come to Caracas for consultations.

With the help of the International Red Cross I secured compassionate leave to visit my father and uncle in Venezuela, and arranged to fly to Caracas via Miami. In the meantime, I contacted a friend of my father in New York and asked him to reach Dr. Samuel Levine, the famous heart specialist and head of cardiovascular diseases at the Peter Bent Brigham Hospital, in Boston, and to convince him to come to Caracas for twenty-four hours to examine the patients and propose a course of therapy. I did not know Dr. Levine personally, but greatly admired him, because of his authoritative work on heart disease. His book on the subject was the bible of all medical students. Dr. Levine was unwilling to go to Caracas, but upon my friend's insistence that he nevertheless quote a price for his services, Dr. Levine mentioned the absurdly high fee of $10,000—a huge sum in 1946, equivalent to more than $150,000 in current dollars. He was greatly surprised when I accepted his terms and arrangements were made for me to meet him in Caracas.

Although I was familiar with the appearance of patients who suffered massive strokes, I was deeply shocked by the sight of my father, whom I had always known as strong and awe-inspiring. Lying in his bed with tears in his eyes was a speechless cripple, unable to move or speak. He had also aged tremendously. I kissed him and hugged him. He laid there so helpless and in such misery. As a physician I realized that my father was no longer in critical condition and that he would survive. But, it was also obvious that he had suffered a major cerebral hemorrhage, and that recovery would be very slow and extremely limited. He would never regain the normal function of his left arm or leg, and his speech, when it did eventually return, as the swelling in his brain diminished, would be forever impaired.

Even though I had never been really close to my father, I always admired him for his intelligence and courage and I was deeply grateful for his generous and understanding attitude toward my marriage. I knew that I had depended on him all my life. I reflected, sadly, that the era when he was the head of the family and provided for all of us and protected us was definitely over. The mantle of responsibility for the family's welfare, for the defense of our assets, even for his own health, had suddenly fallen upon my weak shoulders. This occurred at a time when I was least able to discharge this responsibility, being committed to serve for two years in the American army and to a career in medicine.

My mother was well and as usual behaved admirably under stress. She took excellent care of my father, supervised the nurses, and slept on a couch in the same room. She was with him day and night.

Dr. Pifano, the Venezuelan physician treating Father, was an excellent internist and had done all that was required. He had prescribed a treatment recommended to limit the brain damage. He assured me that, besides his stroke and high blood pressure, Father was in excellent condition: his heart was strong, there were no complications, and he was expected to recover at least some of his speech. I realized also that there was little Dr. Levine could contribute to Father's care, when he was scheduled to arrive in a few hours.

Later that day I went to see my uncle Fortunato. He presented a totally different picture. He was acutely ill with obvious left heart failure as a consequence of the extensive myocardial infarction he had experienced. Dr. Levine might be able to prescribe a treatment to improve his condition. But beyond the immediate problem of heart failure, which needed to be managed, Fortunato was mentally alert and just as sharp as ever. He, in contrast to Father, could recover and be able to manage his and even our business interests.

It was extraordinary to return as a U.S. citizen and army officer to my country of birth. The city of Caracas, and Venezuela in general, had already begun to experience the enormous change that would transform this tropical land into a modern oil- and iron-ore-producing country. There were new buildings and new highways sprouting everywhere. I wore my uniform at all times, as required by army regulations, and to my surprise I found that I rated military salutes from every policeman directing traffic, as I passed in my car. I had forgotten the extent to which the military, who have often ruled Latin American countries by force, demand and are given respect from the population.

The next day I met Dr. Levine's plane and drove him to the Hotel Avila, where my father lived and where we had reserved a room for our consulting physician. Dr. Levine was an impressive, articulate, no-nonsense physician, with apparently few outside interests besides cardiology, but clearly a superb practitioner. He seemed to be in good spirits and not too tired from his long flight. I took him first to see my father. He examined him carefully and, after meeting with Dr. Pitano, concluded that the treatment had been correct and did not require any changes. Furthermore, he confirmed our assessment that my father was unlikely to recover normal motion and would be permanently impaired in his speech.

We later went to see Uncle Fortunato. Again Dr. Levine made a thorough study of the case and this time made a critical suggestion. He said: "Elevate the head of the patient's bed by six inches." This simple procedure promotes the collection of blood and fluids in the lower extremities and relieves the venous return to the right heart and therefore the congestion in his lungs. It is remarkable that this small change was probably responsible for the disappearance of the attacks of pulmonary edema that had plagued the patient. Dr. Levine volunteered that he was willing to see Fortunato in Boston when he recovered completely.

The next day I obtained from the office of Hermanos Benacerraf a check to cover Dr. Levine's fee. As I gave him the check, I reflected, "This makes it $1,666 an inch; it's a bargain." In any case neither my father nor my uncle ever complained about Dr. Levine's fee, and Fortunato continued to consult him regularly in Boston.

Having accomplished the purpose of my trip, I came to the end of my leave and sadly left my parents to cope by themselves with the long task of rehabilitation ahead. After we made tentative plans for them to come to Paris as soon as circumstances and my father's health would permit, I departed on my flight to New York.

6

━━►◦◄━━

Army Medical Officer in France

Upon my return to New York, I reported to Camp Kilmer to sail
for Germany on the USS *George Washington*, a troop transport
designed to carry a couple of thousand men across the Atlantic.
The major difference in this trip, compared to previous crossings
of the *George Washington*, was that a large group of the men were
medical officers, just graduated from Fort Sam Houston, who were
hurriedly shipped abroad to relieve the physicians who served
during the war. I had the opportunity, therefore, to appreciate life
on a crowded troopship with the important difference that there
were no U-boats to worry about. My bunk, as luck would have it,
was in the bottom of the hold and the bedding consisted of a single
woolen blanket which infected me with crab lice.

When a ship is as crowded as ours was, life must follow strict
rules. Two meals a day were served at scheduled times. They were
to be eaten rapidly standing up to make room for the next group.
Access to toilets was a real problem and there were always long
lines. Of course there was no place to sit except on the decks, if a

92

place could be found between the poker games. Apparently, gambling is the major activity that young men resort to under these crowded and boring conditions. Naturally, no alcoholic beverages were allowed. We were fortunate that the crossing, which lasted ten or eleven days, was smooth and the weather very pleasant. When we arrived in Bremerhaven, Germany, we were taken by train to Marburg, a small university town, green and beautifully landscaped, which had escaped damage from the war. There, we waited for our permanent assignments. I was overjoyed when the officer in charge said: "I regret to inform you that orders from Washington assign you to go to France." It appeared ironic to me, but everyone considered Germany to be a better assignment because better quarters and facilities were available to the American army in occupied Germany than in Allied France.

I arrived in Paris on a beautiful August weekend in 1946. It was a gorgeous day, the sun was shining and my heart was singing. Paris was even more beautiful than I remembered. I was billeted at the Grand Hotel, a stylish palace near the opera house. I had a spacious room with the luxury of a private bathroom. What a change from the primitive conditions of my ocean voyage. I phoned Annette in Le Vesinet and boarded a commuter train at the Gare St. Lazare for the twenty-minute ride to her grandmother's country house. I can still experience our joy at being reunited after our short but eventful separation. She looked wonderful and felt well. The house where Annette and her parents were living was a huge mansion located in a beautiful garden, with an orchard and a tennis court across the street. The house had been occupied by the Germans who looted it and by the American army who finished the job. Much of the house was empty but habitable. The Dreyfuses had fixed for themselves an apartment on the second floor, and invited Annette and me to stay with them, at least temporarily.

The next day I reported to Colonel Evans, chief of Medical Operations at army headquarters, at the Hotel Astoria on the Champs Elysées. As I sat in his office overlooking the Arch of Triumph, I could not believe my eyes. Here I was back in Paris after so many tragic years and wearing the prestigious uniform of the victorious army. Recent events had taught me to avoid planning more than a few months ahead. The immediate future looked very pleasant. I promised myself to make the best of the present. I was much less certain what the distant future would hold.

Colonel Evans was an elegant, highly cultured physician who had been trained as a psychiatrist. He very much appreciated being in Paris and was pleased that I spoke fluent French. He felt that I would be most useful at the local army hospital, the 50th Field Hospital located in nearby Villejuif.

As I recall, the 50th Field was a 400-bed general hospital serving the numerous American units still stationed in France. It was located in the old buildings of a French mental hospital, a few kilometers south of Paris. When I reported to the hospital I met the chief of medicine, Captain Thomas Kirmse, a dedicated and considerate man who welcomed me to the 50th Field and put me in charge of two wards which were not yet assigned: the female ward and the prison ward. My duties at the 50th Field resembled very much those at Queens General, since both were general hospitals equipped to handle all types of cases, with the exception that the pace was much more relaxed at the 50th Field. The patients, with rare exceptions, were not as seriously ill and the night duty was only every fourth or fifth night. In addition, I was supposed to help in the clinic or cover the other wards when on night duty.

My experience at the hospital was most interesting. First there were large numbers of patients undergoing treatment for syphilis with penicillin. This was before the development of long-acting penicillin. They were given an intramuscular injection of penicillin every four hours, for eight days, until 8 million units had been administered, which was the recommended curative dose. To illustrate the importance and rapidity of the benefits of the discovery of antibiotics, and particularly of penicillin by Sir Alexander Fleming, I had been treating syphilis in the Medical

College of Virginia clinic only a couple of years earlier with arseni-
cals and bismuth injections with less satisfactory results.

The number of army personnel with syphilis in Paris was very
high for two reasons: prostitution was prevalent in Germany and
France at the time, and all soldiers AWOL from Germany tried to
get to Paris and were usually infected with syphilis by the time
they were caught. The Treponema* was not respectful of rank or
gender. I treated both female dependents and officers as well as
enlisted men for the disease.

As an indication of the times we were living in, penicillin,
which was used by the millions of units to treat American military
personnel with syphilis, was extremely scarce in France and was a
favorite black-market item. I was told that unscrupulous black
marketeers would fill empty penicillin bottles with urine, which
had the color of the drug used then, and sell it to the unsuspecting
public. To avoid feeding the black market, every empty bottle of
penicillin had to be accounted for and destroyed by a team of
enlisted men under the supervision of an officer.

Another important group of patients under our care was suffering from viral hepatitis, of which there was a serious epidemic
at the time.

As an example of the hazards of army practice, I had a strange
experience with a patient under my care in the female ward. A
WAC sergeant was admitted to the ward. When I elicited a history
from her, she volunteered that there was a conspiracy in the WAC
detachment where she worked. She stated that all the members of
her unit were lesbians except herself and that they were perse-
cuting her. Upon questioning, she admitted that she had been
hearing voices when no one was in the room. She presented a typical case of paranoid schizophrenia, but she did not seem violent
at the time. I decided to request a psychiatric consultation and to
sedate her heavily in the meantime to ensure that she would not

---

*Treponema pallidum is the organism which causes syphilis.

harm herself or others. I went off duty after this case and joined Annette.

When I returned the next morning I found an impressive and severe-looking colonel in my office. He started by saying: "I am from the Inspector General's office. I must warn you that everything you say can be held against you. You have been accused of suppressing criminal evidence." I could not have been more bewildered; I had no idea what he was referring to. He continued: "You have admitted a patient to this hospital, who made statements to you concerning sexual perversions in the WAC detachment, and you immediately gave her a shot to make it impossible for her to give evidence." Apparently, someone had accidentally watched my examination and treatment of my patient and, believing she had witnessed a major crime, had alerted the Inspector General's office. I had visions of being carried off in chains to Leavenworth after my first month in Paris! I tried to explain to the skeptical colonel that the patient he was referring to was a paranoid schizophrenic, that I had requested an expert examination by the hospital psychiatrist, and that her rambling accusations were without any basis. I justified sedating the patient by the need to prevent her from harming herself in her tense condition. Fortunately for me, the psychiatrist confirmed my diagnosis and approved my handling of the case.

The patient was evacuated to Heidelberg, Germany, for treatment. I fear that the Inspector General, who dropped the case for lack of evidence, continued to suspect me of some obscure conspiracy nonetheless. This experience made me feel as paranoid as my patient!

France in the summer and fall of 1946 was trying desperately to recover from the war and the German occupation, which had left both its industry and agriculture in terrible shape. There were shortages of everything, and essentials such as gasoline, coal, and even food were rationed. There were unexpected cuts in electrical power. Food, traditionally an important item for the French, was not yet plentiful. French bread was yellow because of its content of corn flour. Not enough wheat had been grown to feed the population. Of course, the shortages made the black market flourish. The trains and public transportation, however, functioned efficiently. In spite of the shortages, every one was cheerful and optimistic.

My father-in-law had been given a most important and interesting job by Jean Monnet, who was impressed with his dedication and impeccable honesty. Ado was put in charge of an agency of the French government entrusted with the allocation of the huge surplus stocks that the American army had accumulated and which remained after the war. The American government had generously donated these extremely valuable materials to the French to help fuel their recovery. It was Ado's task to ensure that they be utilized efficiently, judiciously, and above all, without graft. It is both a miracle and a credit to his integrity and cheerfulness that he managed to accomplish this goal perfectly and to the satisfaction of everyone in that climate of intense shortages.

Annette and I were enormously privileged in many ways. We had enough money to indulge our taste for gourmet food in the best three-star restaurants. As an American army officer I had access to the Post Exchange (PX) that stocked every desirable item from food to clothes and, most importantly, cigarettes, chocolate, and coffee. Since I have never enjoyed smoking myself, except for a pipe and an occasional cigar, I was astonished by the immense value that American cigarettes commanded in postwar Europe, considering the harmful effects of tobacco on health widely recognized nowadays. So many were addicted in those days that anything could be gotten for a pack of American cigarettes. We were also allocated a generous ration of precious gasoline coupons that permitted us to drive in a Paris free of traffic jams.

As soon as I had some free time, I visited my parents' apartment and our country house in Montmorency. Unlike the pilfering that had taken Annette's family possessions, everything we owned survived the war and the German occupation, intact, thanks to my father's foresight. When the Benacerraf family left Paris in 1939, Father had requested a close friend, who was a member of the Spanish diplomatic corps and a physician to the Spanish embassy, to look after our affairs and to list them as Spanish assets. I had strange feelings of both pleasure and guilt when I found our personal belongings, undisturbed after all these tragedies. One item, namely my parent's six-passenger Chrysler limousine, was a most valuable find. It was a miracle that after tuning and greasing, it was in perfect working condition. Although it was a gas guzzler, we had all the gas coupons we needed. I would soon drive the old Chrysler with Annette, through the relatively empty streets of Paris, and also back and forth between Villejuif and Le Vesinet, nearly an hour's ride.

I also had the pleasure of meeting the rest of Annette's family. I was particularly impressed by her tough grandmother, who greeted me warmly, and by Annette's uncle Jacques Monod, with whom I would play tennis on Le Vesinet's family court.

Time passed rapidly and happily that summer and fall of 1946. Annette and I enjoyed our daily life and I found my work interesting. The news of my father and uncle was good. Fortunato had recuperated and Father was very slowly recovering some motion in his left leg, and could speak, although it was labored.

Meanwhile, the American army units in France were rapidly being transferred back to the United States or sent to Germany, where a permanent force would remain. Soon the only army personnel in France would belong to the Army Graves Registration Corps (AGRC) with headquarters in Paris, charged with the repatriation of the bodies and the creation of the permanent American military cemeteries. Such cemeteries were to be located close to the battle sites, in Normandy, the south of France, and Alsace-Lorraine.

By the fall of 1946, the 50th Field Hospital closed and I was assigned temporarily to look after an army dispensary in one of the last American staging camps, at Genevilliers, north of Paris. It was almost winter and the temperature was falling rapidly. Annette and I decided to leave Le Vesinet and rent a furnished apartment in Paris. We located an attractive studio, shaped like an artist's atelier, with high ceiling and picture windows on the Rue St. Simon, in the Left Bank.

The winter of 1946–1947 was unusually cold and there was no central heating anywhere. Since coal was scarce, wood-burning stoves were the only sources of heat. We had a single such stove in our studio apartment which was unable to keep us warm except when we practically sat on it. Never in my life have I been as cold as I was that winter. Stupidly, we did not realize that the large picture windows which gave the apartment such an open feeling and attracted us were the source of bitter cold. They were continuously covered on the inside with a thick layer of ice, which never melted. To make matters worse I developed acute tonsillitis with high fever, which required treatment with penicillin. Fortunately Annette was hale, healthy, and cheerful. She was impervious to the cold under her several sweaters. A highly competent French otolaryngologist kindly made a house call on his American colleague and efficiently cauterized each and every herpetic sore in my throat. This treatment relieved the discomfort and I recovered sufficiently to be able to discuss with Colonel Evans the possibility of a more permanent assignment in France.

He explained that the only assignments in France open to me would be with the Army Graves Registration Command, which were the only army units to remain in France. There were no possibilities at headquarters in Paris and the only two positions open, with any permanency, were at Carentan in Normandy or at Nancy in Lorraine. I chose Nancy as the larger and more cultured of the two towns.

Annette and I closed our apartment and departed for Nancy, in the Chrysler on icy roads, in the middle of winter. We arrived in Nancy, and I took command of my own medical unit, located in the

French military hospital. We rented a comfortable room with bath at the Hotel Thiers on the Place Thiers across from the railroad station and next to the Hotel Exelsior, where the headquarters of the American army unit I was assigned to was located. We were to spend the next twelve happy months in Nancy and at the Thiers.

The American unit of the AGRC centered at Nancy was commanded by Colonel Burrit, an old-fashioned gentleman, courteous and considerate, with a great respect for army regulations. The unit had the responsibility for the cemeteries at Epinal in Lorraine, in Alsace, and also in the south of France, near Aix. The major task of the unit was the repatriation of bodies and the establishment of the permanent cemeteries. The main base of the unit and especially its essential motor pool were located in Nancy. I was assigned, as the senior medical officer on Colonel Burrit's staff, the responsibility for the health of the personnel and also of the numerous dependents of the officers and enlisted men, wherever they were, in this extended command. This meant that for a year I was going to practice what is now known as community medicine on a small community. Of course I was on call all the time. And, although the true emergencies were very rare, I was called at odd hours of the day or night sometimes for little or no reason. I recall a particular embarrassing time when, in the best movie theater in Nancy, the film stopped at the most gripping moment, and the light went on. As I commented to Annette about the poor working condition of the equipment, a loudspeaker barked: "On demande le Dr. Benacerraf d'urgence a l'hotel Exelsior!" (Dr. Benacerraf is urgently requested to go to the Hotel Exelsior). I rushed out red-faced to find that I had to tend to a minor injury which did not even require stitching. Another night I received an emergency call to see a patient in Strasbourg, two hours away, to diagnose a simple viral infection.

My main base was a five-bed minihospital in a wing of the

French military hospital. This unit comprised a well-equipped emergency room, a portable X-ray unit, a dental unit, two ambulances, and a jeep. Annette rented a piano, installed it in our mini-hospital, and accompanied our dental surgeon, Lt. Berman, as he sang. He was an opera fan and an excellent singer.

I confess that during that period, besides the administration of routine care, which took a fair amount of my time, I had few medical emergencies requiring experienced medical skill. But, a medical officer in the field has many other important duties. I ran an effective anti-venereal-diseases program involving surprise inspections. I was responsible for the health and morale of the troops, which required occasional on-site inspections that took Annette and me several times to Strasbourg, Epinal, and to the French Riviera. Another one of my duties concerned the general health and morale of the command and the quality of the food served in the messes.

Everybody complained with good reason that the eggs served for breakfast were moldy and rotten. I made an inspection of the stock of eggs, which were shipped from Germany in huge refrigerated trucks, and on the strength of my authority, as the local health officer, condemned the whole truckload and had it destroyed. My triumph did not last very long. The bad shipment was immediately replaced with another just as rotten and moldy as the previous one. I advised the use of powdered eggs and tried to buy fresh eggs from the local French farmers.

Because of my command of French, and my understanding of French customs, Colonel Burrit asked me to help him with his relationship with the local French military command and occasionally to act as an interpreter in his meetings with the French commander, General de Linares. This was fun since General de Linares, commander of the French forces in Nancy, was a general in the style of de Gaulle or MacArthur, with plenty of dash and a primary concern for the spectacular aspects of soldiering. He had been one of de Gaulle's best generals and would eventually command the French troops in Indochina. When I met him he was an impressive, handsome soldier who could organize spectacular parades and beautiful balls in the gardens of his military head-quarters. But, as I recall, there were no substantive issues to be discussed between Colonel Burrit and General de Linares.

A few months after my arrival in Nancy, I was promoted to the rank of captain and Annette proudly pinned my captain's bars to my shoulders.

Annette and I enjoyed our time in Nancy. It was my first real opportunity to observe life in a French provincial town. Nancy is a lovely city with a jewel of a square, the Place Stanislas named after Stanislas Lesczynski, Duc of Lorraine and former king of Poland who was the father-in-law of Louis XV. His statue stands in the middle of the square surrounded by buildings designed in the most elegant Louis XV style. Nancy had superb restaurants such as Le Capucin Gourmand, which compensated for the drab cooking of the army mess.

As spring arrived, we loved driving in the surrounding coun-tryside and enjoyed my inspection trips to Strasbourg, where I heard General de Gaulle give a speech, and those to the Riviera, the Vosges, and the Jura, where I visited Louis Pasteur's birthplace.

Occasionally I went on business to Heidelberg and Frankfurt, but those were not enjoyable trips. Until now I have avoided writing about the way I felt about Germany. As a Jew and because of my French cultural background, I had been extremely uncomfortable in Germany from the moment I set foot there until I left for France. The same acute discomfort would recur every time I returned to Germany on army business. It took several decades for this feeling to weaken. In 1946–1947 I could not sort out my strong feeling of hatred for the recent past from that of compassion for the obvious suffering, misery, and humiliation of the German people. I deliberately chose to avoid confronting the issue and my feelings as much as possible. It was most fortunate for me, therefore, that my army service in Europe was spent in France, which I have always loved, and that my contacts with Germany were limited to occasional day trips.

In the summer of 1947, my parents returned to France. I went to fetch them at Le Havre in the old Chrysler. I was overjoyed to hug them and particularly to see that Father had sufficiently recovered to be able to walk slowly by himself with a cane. I had to accustom myself, however, to the realization that he was forever an aged, diminished man, who spoke slowly and with visible effort and who needed the constant care of my mother. I drove them to their country house in Montmorency and did all I could to make them comfortable and to restore the pleasant life they enjoyed there before the war. My father revived his interest in the orchard and the vegetable garden, which remained his main source of pleasure in his final years.

To give a complete account of that period of my life, I need to express my feelings about serving in the army. I have always had a problem with authority. Contrary to Annette, who is not very law-abiding, and enjoys getting ahead in waiting lines, I am scrupulously respectful of rules and of persons in authority, particularly if they wear uniforms. But this respect imposed upon me by others is associated with a strong resentment and a desire to escape authority as rapidly as possible. Since childhood, I have been distrustful of authority and I have always hated to be responsible to anyone above me. I strongly suspect that my ambition, which has led me to positions of authority myself, has been largely fueled by my desire to escape the authority of others.

It is only with time that I have discovered that my quest for freedom from authority is a neurotic trait that never can be realistically satisfied, since no matter how high I rose in the academic or administrative structure there was always another layer to report to, here or in Washington. I might add that I do not enjoy the exercise of power over others, which I have learned is always associated with the responsibility for their welfare and their actions.

The army, even for a medical officer, is the most evident instrument of authority in society. I was naturally resentful and anxious, therefore, at being subject to military regulations and, possibly, arbitrary orders from superior officers, although my life was extremely pleasant, comfortable, and much less stressful than when I was a civilian, and my commanding officer was one of the kindest and fairest men I had ever met. My latent anxiety was fed by unreasonable fantasies that Colonel Burrit could be replaced by a sterner, less reasonable officer, or that by some absurd bureaucratic error I would be transferred to Germany or even Japan. My experience with the Inspector General's office at the 50th Field Hospital went a long way to provide fuel for my imagination of what could happen.

In spite of our happy and pleasant life I could not wait for the day I would be discharged from the army. Foolishly, I did not appreciate that these eighteen months had been a time of mental peace when I was relieved of the necessity to face the problems of career, family, and responsibility for the family financial assets, which I had set temporarily aside and which I would have to confront again as a civilian.

Considering the political situation in Europe generally and in France particularly in the months I was stationed there, the wartime alliance with the USSR had rapidly evolved into hostile confrontation focused on the fate of Germany and Western Europe. It was clear to us that the Soviets were then determined to extend their domination to the segment of Europe they did not occupy. They already had control of the relatively strong Communist parties in France and Italy. The American military and atomic power were the only deterrents against a large and well-armed Soviet military. We were acutely aware of the ridiculously weak condition of the American armed forces in Europe at the time, and of the fact that we in the army were pawns to guarantee that the invasion of Western Europe would trigger a conflict with the United States. To be part of a defenseless contingent did not make us comfortable.

Those of us who were in Europe at the time could best appreciate the great wisdom and generosity of the American diplomatic efforts, which resulted in the Marshall Plan and in the economic and eventually political integration of Western Europe into the European community. Because of the strong friendship of Ado Dreyfus with Jean Monnet, the wise old man who pioneered the European community, we were very attuned to the critical importance of rebuilding the European economy and of creating the political structure of a united and prosperous Europe, as the best and safest way to keep the Communists out.

We followed closely the political situation in France. The right-wing parties responsible for the policy of collaboration with the Germans had been discredited. Power was initially shared by a coalition of the Christian Democrat, Socialist, and Communist parties and there were Communist ministers in the French government. While I was there the Communists, who opposed the policy of European integration of the other two parties, left the government and initiated a violent opposition, associated with a sustained policy of labor unrest. It was clear by then, however, that the Communists would lose in the face of the economic recovery fueled by American aid.

For the first time in my life I had occasion to meet real dedicated Communists. One of Annette's uncles, Georges Tessier, a professor at the Sorbonne, and his daughter Marianne were card-carrying members of the French Communist party. When we met at family reunions, we always endeavored, by mutual agreement, to avoid political discussions.

After a year's service in Nancy, having satisfied all my obligations, I was eligible for discharge from the army. I chose to remain in Europe temporarily, and was discharged in Frankfurt. I was offered promotion to the rank of major if I accepted a reserve commission, which I refused for obvious reasons. I took the overnight train back to Paris. I was a civilian again and had to decide what to do with my life.

7

Introduction to Science
in Kabat's Laboratory

Annette and I decided to stay a few weeks in France before returning to the United States to resume my medical training. This would give us some time to enjoy Paris and also to visit with my parents, who were spending the winter months in Nice. We stayed first with the Dreyfuses in the lovely duplex apartment they had moved to at Rue de Boulinvilliers, in the sixteenth arrondissement, my boyhood home area. Then, we took the night train to Nice and visited my parents at the Negresco, the most famous hotel on the French Riviera. There was little to do in Nice except for the casino, the legal gambling establishment. I have never enjoyed gambling, but I was willing to lose a few francs at the Boule, which is a form of simplified roulette with ten numbers. Annette discovered that she could predict the winning number, but only upon entering the room. She kept going in and out and guessed correctly more often than warranted by simple chance. I was much too scared of being married to a witch to pay serious attention to her claim of extrasensory perception.

Finally we traveled back to Paris and began packing to sail to New York on the SS *America*. I had to return to the United States to consider the options, not yet clear in my mind. My problem was made infinitely more complex by my father's stroke and his inability to manage the extensive assets which he had built in Venezuela, and which were intricately enmeshed with those of his brother and partner, Fortunato.

These assets were the sole resources of my parents and would need to be managed at some time. It was my judgment, however, that the situation was not yet critical since Fortunato, who had recovered from his heart attack, could look after the business for the time being. But I knew that our long-term plans were likely to differ from those of Fortunato, and that he would not feel the same loyalty to me as he did to my father. At some time in the not too distant future, therefore, I had to be prepared to become directly involved in the management of my father's assets. The time available to complete my medical training was limited, and the circumstances required that I restrict my options to alternatives that would leave me some flexibility and freedom to respond to a possible emergency from Caracas.

Two major career choices were open to me. I could complete my clinical training and seek a residency in pediatrics or medicine, or, if I decided that I had learned all the clinical medicine I was ever going to need, I could seek a fellowship in a first-class laboratory to determine whether I liked research.

Soon after our arrival in New York we returned to Richmond as I tried to make up my mind. Dr. William Porter, the chief of medicine, offered me a position in his residency program, which required a commitment of three years for intensive clinical training. Faced with this opportunity, I realized that I lacked the motivation to spend additional years in clinical training. I did not see myself as a practicing internist all my life. I opted to look for a research position instead.

I had to decide: In what field, where, and with whom? I knew

that my work as a medical student with Dr. Black-Shaeffer had
been amateurish and unproductive. This time I had to train with
an established and experienced scientist. I had a long-lasting
interest in immunology and particularly in the mechanism of
hypersensitivity, because of my experience with asthma as a child.
Moreover, in medical school I had already carried out some unsophisticated experiments on immunopathological problems, such as
the mechanism of serum sickness or the Shwartzman reaction. I
decided to look at immunological laboratories, preferentially but
not exclusively. The most attractive laboratories were either in
Boston or New York. My professors in Richmond gave me strong
letters of recommendation for Dr. Edwin Cohn, a famous bio-
chemist at Harvard Medical School, and Dr. John Enders, the well-
known virologist at Children's Hospital in Boston, with whom they
had good relationships. I decided also to contact René Dubos, the
brilliant French microbiologist at the Rockefeller Institute, who
had been my examiner at the Lycée Français.

Entering excellent research laboratories in those days was
much less difficult than it would become in later years with the
awakening of strong interest by graduates of medical schools in
research careers. It was then, indeed, a buyer's market where the
laboratories tried to convince the applicants of the relevance and
interest of their research programs. I was given a warm welcome
by both Drs. Cohn and Enders in Boston.

Dr. Cohn impressed me as a forceful scientist who directed a
large research enterprise involving many investigators and geared
to isolating and identifying human-serum proteins. He introduced
me to his associate John Edsall, whom I found much more accessible. I declined their offer of a position because I wanted to be in
a smaller laboratory and the problems they were working on didn't
interest me.

I was from the start enormously intrigued by Dr. Enders, who
was obviously a man of great intelligence and culture. I learned
much later, when we became friends in the 1970s, that he had

earned his doctorate in English literature at Yale before becoming interested in microbiology and particularly virology at Harvard. He was a tall gentleman with the natural elegance and restraint of the native New Englander. He had a small laboratory where he worked with few students. He made a real effort to convince me to give up immunology and go into virology with him, complaining sadly, as he played with his Phi Beta Kappa key, that it was difficult to convince students to go into virology. I left his laboratory very much interested, but still committed to try initially an immunology laboratory. I could not help wondering, many years later, what would have been my career as a virologist if at this critical turning point in my life I had wavered in my resolve and decided to work with John Enders, who was to win the Nobel Prize in medicine in 1954 for his "discovery of the ability of the poliomyelitis virus to grow in culture," a prerequisite for the eventual development of antipolio vaccines.

René Dubos, whom I saw next, was able to direct me to immunologists. He recommended that I consider working with either Dr. Elvin Kabat, a young immunochemist, associate professor of microbiology at the College of Physicians and Surgeons of Columbia University (P&S), or more senior classical immunologist Jules Freund, who was at the New York Public Health Research Institute. Dubos spoke very highly of Dr. Kabat as a most productive and dynamic scientist, able to teach me immunology and to emphasize its essential biochemical basis.

I visited, first, Dr. Jules Freund who regretted that he had no room in his laboratory at the time but also strongly encouraged me to work with Kabat, if he would be able to accommodate me.

Dr. Elvin Kabat saw me in his tiny office on one of the upper floors of the Neurological Institute of P&S, where his crowded laboratories were located. He impressed me immediately as a tense young man, not much older than I and always on the move. In contrast to Dr. Enders, there was nothing gentle or elegant about Kabat, who, during the Depression, had to fight his way to obtain an education at City College and a Ph.D. at Columbia University with Michael Heidelberger, the founder with Karl Landsteiner of modern immunochemistry. But Kabat was obviously bright, determined, methodical, demanding, and, above all, painfully scrupulous. I realized immediately that because he and I differed very much in character and intellectual approaches, there was much he could teach me that I sorely needed to learn to work effectively in the laboratory. Although he would set impossible standards of accuracy and quantification, these were precisely what I needed at this early phase of my training. I would have to pay a very high price for that training, however, in terms of my sensitivity. Elvin, who was mercilessly opposed to loose thinking and idle speculation and was totally impervious to one's feelings, could express devastating criticism delivered in a shrill, rasping voice. But, I must admit that he imposed on himself the same exacting standards that he expected of others.

He offered me a position in his laboratory, or, to put it more accurately, he offered me a slot on a bench in a 200-square-foot laboratory where four others were already slaving full-time. I accepted enthusiastically, feeling that now I would really learn what science was about under such a hard taskmaster. I am deeply grateful to Elvin Kabat, who took a green physician into his laboratory and taught him the critical importance of accuracy and the need to evaluate data with total objectivity before indulging in speculations.

Immunology was a relatively new field when I entered Dr. Kabat's laboratory. The enormous extent of our ignorance of this subject was even stimulating. We knew, thanks to Heidelberger and Kabat, that antibodies were proteins and gamma globulins. Landsteiner had produced the best analysis of antibody specificity. But, nothing was known of the structure of antibodies, of their classes, of the genes that code for them, or of the genetic mechanisms which generate diversity among these antibodies. There was no information on the cellular basis of immunity. We did not know that B lymphocytes and plasma cells made antibodies. Cellular immunity was not understood and the essential role of T lympho- cytes, the key player in immunology as demonstrated by the AIDS epidemic, was not known as yet. Transplantation antigens had not yet been discovered. The important phenomena of antigen pro- cessing and presentation by macrophages to generate the immuno- genic peptide remained to be demonstrated. Immunopathological phenomena had been scarcely investigated, and the immunolog- ical basis of allergic diseases had not been worked out yet.

It is both gratifying and a testimony to the enormous advances that have been made in this important field of medicine in the span of forty years that these questions have been answered in my lifetime as an investigator. It is a source of personal satisfaction that I have been able to witness the emergence of these discoveries and occa- sionally contribute to them. It indicates, also, that my curiosity about immunology in 1947 was either a wise choice or a lucky one.

Considering my personal interest in hypersensitivity and Dr. Kabat's obsession with quantitative measurements, he proposed that I investigate the amounts of rabbit antibody required to sensi- tize guinea pigs passively for systemic anaphylaxis and for the Arthus reaction (a hemorrhagic phenomenon caused by immune complexes), as a prerequisite to developing an understanding of the mechanism of these hypersensitivity reactions. This approach would have the added advantage of teaching me the techniques of immunochemistry.

In addition to learning how to measure antigen and antibody concentrations by the precipitin technique and to perform quanti- tative nitrogen analysis by colorimetric titration, a feat for a color- blind investigator, I was able to accomplish our experimental goals well within the two years of my fellowship. Moreover, I was fortu- nate to follow a few independent leads that resulted in my dis-

covery of new relationships. For instance, I noted that the amount
of antibody required to sensitize guinea pigs for anaphylaxis
varied inversely with the time of passive sensitization, an indication that the antibody had to be fixed to some as yet unidentified
cell to sensitize. Many years later the cells to which the anaphy-
lactic antibody fixes were shown to be the mast cells. In other
experiments I discovered evidence that the vascular damage of the
Arthus phenomenon is caused by circulating antibodies reacting
with antigens in the blood vessel wall.

For the first time, I experienced the exhilarating feeling that
accompanies making a discovery. I was hooked for life as surely as
if I had become addicted to heroin. I was delighted also that Dr.
Kabat thought my data worthy of publication and asked me to prepare three manuscripts, which appeared, eventually, in the prestigious *Journal of Immunology*. It was a thrill to see my name in print
for the first time. But I found, in time, that publication is much less
pleasurable than discovery. After nearly fifty years, I am still just
as excited when I discover something new or verify a research hypothesis—i.e., Nature yielding its secrets—as I was in 1948.

When looking for a place to live in New York, we automatically
went to the Croydon Hotel, moved by habit and memories, in spite
of my need to drive to work uptown every day. We loved that old
hotel and particularly the surrounding upper East Side, Central
Park, and the Metropolitan Museum. We were offered a small two-
room apartment overlooking the park, which could accommodate
our furniture. We had a home again among our familiar belongings.
To finance our life in New York, I arranged, with my father, to
receive $750 a month from the business in Caracas. I started my
scientific career, therefore, on a generous Benacerraf fellowship,
as Kabat would jokingly comment. Needless to say we were extremely happy to be back in New York. Annette, particularly, has

always had a passion for the city and the exciting life it offers to young people with sufficient means.

There was, however, a cloud on the horizon. For nearly a year Annette very much wanted to become pregnant. The periodic monitoring of her tubercular lesion had revealed that it had healed and calcified. The lung specialist we consulted in France had assured me that Annette could now safely sustain the stress of pregnancy. For nearly a year we had tried unsuccessfully and I began to suspect that either I or Annette had a fertility problem. One of our first priorities in New York was, therefore, to consult Dr. Isidor Rubin, the famous gynecologist, who specialized in fertility problems. He found that I had a normal sperm count, but Annette's Fallopian tubes were blocked. Fortunately, Dr. Rubin had devised a procedure, which bears his name, whereby compressed air is blown through the cervix to open the tubes. A sharp pain in the shoulder caused by the irritation of air penetrating the peritoneal cavity is the indication that the tubes are now open. Annette was successfully treated by Dr. Rubin, who assured her that she would become pregnant within a few months. I strongly suspected that his ability to convince her of this was as material as his unblocking of her tubes in facilitating Annette's pregnancy. Dr. Rubin had a charismatic way with his patients. In any case, by August when we flew to Paris for a month to visit our respective parents, the pregnancy test was positive. The return plane trip to New York in September (which in those days was made in propeller-driven Lockheed Constellations) was long (twenty-three hours) and difficult. The flight was bumpy and Annette was sick both from motion sickness and from the nausea associated with pregnancy. She was also deathly afraid of losing the baby.

When at last we reached the Croydon I put in an emergency call to Dr. Rubin, who came immediately, reassured her that everything was normal, and convinced her that she was in no danger of miscarrying. Annette's months of pregnancy were probably some of the happiest of her life. She was at last fulfilled, and a smile never left her face.

In the spring of 1949, I chose to take the New York Board of Medicine examination. With all the rush of the war years, the internship, and army service, I never had the time or opportunity until then to take the examination that confers the legal right to practice medicine. It is ironic that I was never to practice again after I secured the right to do so, except on my immediate family.

My daughter, Beryl, was born on April 29, 1949, at Flowers and Fifth Avenue Hospital after an uneventful delivery. We very much liked the name, which was also the name of Georges Bakeman's lovely younger daughter. As I have said earlier, I am inordinately fond of babies and children. I was deeply conscious that Nature, in addition, stimulates in the father of the helpless infant a sense of pride and responsibility, which compensates for the inequality that childbearing imposes upon the mother. I was proud as a peacock and enormously protective of my daughter.

The birth of Beryl also influenced my professional plans. I had just about accomplished my goals in Kabat's laboratory, which were to learn immunological technics and to determine whether I had both a vocation and an ability for medical research. Under his stern tutelage I had been able to answer these questions in the affirmative, which meant I had to choose my next laboratory if I was to conduct more complex and detailed research. I received attractive offers from Harold Baer and Marianne Ropes in the rheumatology division of Massachusetts General Hospital and from Beatrice Seegal, one of the few lady scientists who worked in the department of microbiology at the College of Physicians and Surgeons of Columbia University. A few months earlier, however, I had met a French pharmacologist, Dr. Bernard Halpern, who visited Kabat's laboratory. Halpern had contributed to the discovery of the first clinically effective antihistamine and had an active research laboratory in Paris concerned with the study of hypersensitivity phenomena, which was precisely my area of interest. His laboratory was located in the Broussais Hospital in the medical department headed by Professeur Pasteur Vallery-Radot, Louis Pasteur's grandson.

Halpern offered me a year's appointment in his laboratory, which I accepted eagerly. I felt this would give Annette and me an opportunity to show Beryl to her grandparents, to watch after the health of my father, and to come to some decision about what to do about Caracas while still pursuing my scientific career.

When Beryl was three months old, we closed our New York apartment, put the furniture in storage again, and embarked on the *New Amsterdam* for Le Havre.

8

Broussais Hospital, Paris

Mother was very jealous that we chose to stay with my in-laws at Le Vesinet first. Characteristically for her, she was unwilling to accept the need of a mother, who has just given birth to her first child, to be with her own parents. She was sullen and cold until we moved to her house in Montmorency after the second week. I suspect that she was also very jealous of Annette. As I mentioned earlier, she had always wanted a daughter herself and felt very possessive toward Beryl. Soon, however, she became completely enthralled with my daughter and her spirits and behavior improved appreciably. Fortunately for me, Annette was not jealous; she was delighted to let her mother-in-law bathe and feed her daughter. She knew that Mother was reliable and knowledgeable and very attached to Beryl. Over the years, we depended much more on Mother to look after Beryl, when we had to travel, than on Suzanne Dreyfus, in spite of the fact that Beryl was more attached to Suzanne, with whom she had more fun.

Before the summer was over we settled in a lovely furnished

116

apartment, on the Rue du Ranelagh, practically across from the Dreyfuses, and I was ready to start my experiments in Halpern's laboratory, at the Broussais Hospital, where I was to work for several years.

Neither the hospital nor the laboratory made a good impression
on me. The hospital was not as modern as the American hospitals to
which I had grown accustomed. I was shocked that the permanent
staff of interns and attending physicians was on duty in the morn-
ings only. After one in the afternoon, every day, only the house
officer on call was available. Moreover, since the hospital did not
have a paging system, he could be very hard to find. I am convinced
that Brigitte, my sister-in-law, who would die tragically of ascending
paralysis (Guillain-Barré-Strohl syndrome*) a few years later in
Hôpital Cochin, was not attended to as rapidly as her emergency
warranted, in that inefficient system. But, I was not to have clinical
responsibilities and my work was to be solely in the laboratory.

I was to realize shortly that, in spite of my poor initial impression, I was in one of the most prestigious departments of medicine
in Paris. The chief of medicine, Professeur Pasteur Vallery-Radot,
Pasteur's grandson, who I would eventually know well and appreciate, was the most influential internist in France, at the time, with
an international reputation, which would take him to King Ibn
Saud's bedside in consultation.

Halpern's laboratory consisted of a very large room of approximately 800 square feet, equipped as a classical physiology laboratory, with a small operating room, a tiny animal room, and a personal office. No facilities for chemistry, microbiology, or tissue culture existed. I was introduced to Halpern's laboratory technician,
Mlle. Bourdon, a tough, acerbic lady who had an obvious crush on
Jean Hamburger, Professeur Pasteur Vallery-Radot's assistant, and

---

*Following severe infections such as acute hepatitis, some patients develop
progressive muscle paralysis that gradually ascends and finally reaches the
muscles concerned with respiration. Unless put in a respirator, these patients
die of asphyxia. If saved by a respirator, the patient survives and the paralysis
progressively disappears.

I was told that she would provide me with all I would need. I was fortunate that my innate charm must have had an effect on her because, contrary to her uncooperative behavior toward many others, she always tried to be helpful to me.

A flock of ambitious and bright young French physicians, former house officers of Pasteur Vallery-Radot, were attracted to Halpern's laboratory, either to learn some physiology or to foster their academic careers. Some have, indeed, made it to the top in the French medical hierarchy. All of them worked in the laboratory, where they carried out physiological or pharmacological experiments on dogs and rabbits. A couple of highly gifted Swiss physicians, Samuel Cruchaud and Antoine Cuendet, with whom I would become very friendly, trained there also.

The head of the laboratory, Bernard Halpern, had had a very tough life. He was born in the Ukraine in 1904 and escaped, as a penniless teenager, to Poland, where he attended high school. By the time he was twenty, he moved to Paris. To finance his studies he worked as a technician in the physiology laboratory of the Faculty of Medicine while he went to medical school. Upon graduation, he obtained a position with the major French pharmaceutical company, Rhone Poulenc. Just before the war, he was chosen to head their pharmacological research laboratory. In the meantime he married an attractive Polish art student, Renée, who was always very devoted to him.

While working at Rhone Poulenc in the early years of the war, Halpern described the pharmacological properties of the first clinically effective antihistamine. The first compound with the properties of an antihistamine had been discovered by Daniel Bovet, a Swiss pharmacologist working at the Pasteur Institute. Bovet investigated a series of compounds, initially studied by Fourneau, the brilliant chief of the laboratory of pharmacology at Pasteur, and found that one of them had interesting properties as a histamine blocker, but that drug was too weak for clinical use. Bovet received the Nobel Prize in 1957 for this discovery and for his development of curarelike muscle relaxants.

Soon after his discovery of the first clinically effective antihistamine, Halpern escaped with his family to Switzerland, where he remained throughout the war. After the liberation of France he accepted an offer from Pasteur Vallery-Radot to head the research laboratory dedicated to the pharmacological study of hypersensitivity reactions, at Broussais Hospital. Since this position carried an inadequate salary, Halpern also initiated a successful practice as an allergist. In the French medical tradition, he worked in the laboratory in the morning and in the afternoon saw his patients in an office in his apartment.

Halpern was a clever scientist, a highly competent pharmacologist, but a very ambitious man. I would learn, in due course, that there were no limits to his ambition, including his insistence on signing all papers from his laboratory, often as first author, regardless of his contribution to the work.

In September 1949, my goal was simply to learn pharmacological techniques applicable to the study of hypersensitivity phenomena, and Dr. Halpern was an ideal teacher. In the year that I was planning to spend in his laboratory, I proposed to investigate the effects of antihistamines on a variety of hypersensitivity phenomena. Halpern had recently described the strong activity of a most interesting new antihistamine, Phenergan, the first of the promethazines. The chlorinated derivative of promethazine would eventually prove to have powerful psychopharmacological properties and to be effective tranquilizers in psychiatric patients.

I began by a study of the treatment of guinea pigs with high doses of Phenergan, to determine the effect of the drug on the pathological lesions of the Arthus reaction and serum sickness.

As I have repeatedly experienced, science is an unpredictable activity. The results of experiments are seldom foreseen and more often than not point the work in other directions. I made the unexpected observations that high doses of Phenergan were eventually lethal for guinea pigs, who died of systemic infections from their own bacterial flora. This effect was not observed in rats or mice. I needed to explore the changes caused by Phenergan on antibacterial defense mechanisms in guinea pigs.

To answer this question I initiated some experiments with Dr. Guido Biozzi, a young physician from Italy who had joined Halpern's laboratory at the same time I did. Little did I know at the time that these pilot studies would evolve into a major project which would occupy our attention for the next six years.

Guido Biozzi was a highly cultured Florentine physician who had trained in internal medicine in Rome. He was about my age, and his experience in research had been very much self-taught. He appeared very bright, enthusiastic, and well-informed. In Rome, he had studied the effects of histamine on capillary permeability in the skin of rats, and had described an interesting phenomenon, whereby histamine caused the uptake of intravenously administered carbon particles by endothelial cells of small blood vessels behaving as phagocytes. He proposed that we use his carbon suspension to measure the clearance of particulate material from the blood by the phagocytes of the liver and spleen as a measure of natural phagocytic defense mechanisms. We could then explore the effect of Phenergan on such a clearance.

This project was to be carried out initially on rats but was eventually applicable to other experimental species, including humans. Initially, the development of the technologies to sample blood at fixed times and to measure rapidly and accurately the concentration of carbon particles in the blood and the organs was required to establish the pattern of clearance.

At this time I should suspend my account in order to introduce some basic physiology. A system of fixed phagocytes (macrophages) lines the small blood vessels of the liver and the spleen. These cells are responsible for collecting particulate material from the blood, such as infectious bacteria or viruses, dead-cell debris, and effete red cells, to destroy and digest them. This distinct group of phagocytic cells, which was named the reticuloendothelial system by the German pathologist Jurgen Aschoff, is the scavenger of the body and a very important defense mechanism, which keeps the blood sterile. It is immensely efficient: the liver phagocytes, for example, can effectively clear the blood in one pass, provided the concentration of particles to be phagocytosed is not too high.

At the time we started our experiments very little was known concerning this important phagocytic system. Its capacity had never been measured or challenged. The properties of these particles, the intimate mechanism of phagocytosis, or the origin of the phagocytes themselves had not been explored. It was an open field. We raced through it happily and successfully.

Over the next six years my collaboration with Dr. Biozzi would generate twenty-seven publications and establish a general method to study the phagocytic capacity of the reticuloendothelial system. We derived the mathematical equations governing the physiological clearance of particulate matter from the blood by the phagocytic system. In addition, our work with experimental tuberculosis in mice would illustrate the enormous stimulation of the phagocytic system brought about by infections such as Bacille Calmette Guérin (BCG)* vaccination, and the importance of activating macrophages to increase resistance against intracellular pathogens.† Some of

---

*Bacille Calmette Guérin is an attenuated tubercle bacillus which has been developed at the Pasteur Institute as a specific vaccine against tuberculosis. Its efficacy against tuberculosis has been questioned, but it is harmless. BCG treatment is currently used successfully against bladder cancer.

†There are two types of infectious organisms: those that infect and multiply outside cells, such as Staph, strep, or *E. typhosa* of typhoid fever, and those that only grow inside cells. The latter are called intracelluar pathogens. Among these are the tubercle bacillus and all viruses.

these experiments were carried out in collaboration with the Pasteur Institute which was far better equipped than we were for experiments involving immunological technic or microbiology. I pursued several of these themes in my research in later years.

Modern biomedical science is technically so complex that it has become very much a team effort involving partners as well as students. This creates opportunities to build lasting and meaningful relationships, and also creates difficult human problems. As for myself I found these relationships not only tremendously enriching but also stimulating of ideas and creativity. My partnership with Guido Biozzi was my first experience of such an intense collaboration where one shares every thought and competes with an intimate friend to contribute the most inventive approach and the brightest idea. I was very fortunate that Guido was a highly creative scientist and a most gifted experimenter in addition to being the wittiest of dedicated friends. He was endowed also with a critical mind that accepted nothing at face value and had an immense respect for Nature's trickiness.

The conditions of our work in the laboratory were very primitive and required a lot of improvisation and self-teaching. Instruments were scarce and not sophisticated. This had such beneficial consequences that all my future laboratories appeared well equipped by comparison; I was to be forever convinced that technical problems never resist imagination and dedication.

The carbon suspension we used initially was the commercial India ink made by the German manufacturer Gunther Wagner in their Hanover plant. Biozzi had used it in his experiments in Rome. It had a particle size of about 250 Angstrom and was very well dispersed and stable in the blood. The first experiments performed in rats were very successful, the clearance proceeded regularly: the carbon particles were taken up by the phagocytes of the liver and spleen in about sixty minutes. However, there was a radical change when a dose above 16mg of carbon per 100Gm of body weight was administered, the clearance was over in a matter of minutes and all the carbon lined the endothelial cells of the lung, but the rats did not appear inconvenienced nor was their circulation affected.

Based on these observations, we thought (erroneously) that the challenge with a large number of particles had stimulated the release, from the spleen or liver, of a "hormone" which enlisted the activity of endothelial cells in the lung to help in the removal of the particles. We proceeded to try to extract from the spleen such a hormone that, when injected, could cause even low doses of carbon to be taken up rapidly in the lung. After months of effort we isolated an active molecule with the desired properties. It was the well-known clotting enzyme thromboplastin! Apparently, there was a material in commercial India ink which, above a critical dose, caused the release of thromboplastin from platelets and the submicroscopic carbon particles were enmeshed in microclots of fibrin that coated the endothelial cells of the lung. We were shattered; we had rediscovered blood clotting!

It was imperative, if we wanted to continue our work, to obtain a carbon suspension stabilized with only harmless gelatin and free of the ingredients in commercial ink that were toxic for the platelets. Annette, Biozzi, and I drove to Hanover and convinced the Gunther Wagner Company to prepare for us a carbon suspension stabilized solely with gelatin for biological use in our experiments. We were back in business with a safe and well-controlled product. This episode taught me to be forever suspicious of my hunches, and to remember that the old adage about Occam's razor is right: the simplest explanation of phenomena is the first one to be considered before invoking more complex or ambitious mechanisms.

A year or so later we made the puzzling observation that the injection of rats with serum that had been heated to 56 degrees centigrade for thirty minutes, a standard procedure to destroy complement activity, caused the clearance of carbon particles to decrease markedly. This time we came to the correct conclusion that heating to 56 degrees had denatured and aggregated some of the serum proteins and made them attractive to the phagocytes. The denatured serum proteins were competing successfully, we thought, with the carbon particles for receptors on the surface of phagocytes. We repeated our observation with a pure serum protein, human serum albumin (HSA), and noted that, whereas injections of native HSA did not affect carbon clearance, injection of heat-denatured HSA completely blocked it. We needed to measure the clearance of the denatured HSA itself to verify that our hypothesis was correct. But this required labeling of the material with radioactive iodine with which neither we nor the laboratory had any experience. We contacted a laboratory at the Hôpital Nestlé in Lausanne, Switzerland, willing and able to train us in the use of radioisotopes and to help us initiate the first experiments. We spent three weeks in Lausanne and very much enjoyed our short stay in Switzerland. Our work at the Hôpital Nestlé was successful; the experiments worked. Heat-denatured human serum albumin was indeed phagocytized by the liver's and spleen's macrophages, even more avidly than carbon particles.

We established the capacity to work with radioactive iodine in our own laboratory at the Hôpital Broussais at a time when working with radioisotopes was very rare in France. In the early 1950s such work was neither regulated nor supervised as it has become. No one instructed us concerning the potential hazards of gamma-emitting isotopes to others or to ourselves. No one would monitor us or our thyroids for contamination, but we were nevertheless as careful then as I would ever be later under regulatory supervision. There was no provision for the disposal of radioactive waste. The iodine was bought from Amersham in England and sent to us without any license. The situation is very different today in both France and the United States.

Our experiments were successful and we were able to duplicate with denatured serum albumin labeled with radioactive iodine all the data we had generated with our carbon suspension.

Moreover, this material could safely be injected intravenously in trace amounts to volunteer patients. It was effectively cleared by their liver phagocytes in one passage, which made such a test useful as a measure of liver portal blood flow, a test that is still being used today.

These studies were carried out in Halpern's laboratory without his involvement in any tangible way. Biozzi and I conceived of the experiments, planned them, and carried them out. We also wrote all the papers. Nevertheless, Halpern signed all publications from his laboratory, a tradition in French medical circles. For our work, we had agreed that we would rotate the privilege to sign as first author among us three, regardless of whether Biozzi or I wrote the paper. Of course, Halpern neither contributed to these studies, nor wrote any of the papers he signed. By 1956, the situation between Halpern and myself was to become so tense and unpleasant that he forbade me to continue to collaborate with Biozzi. I decided that I could no longer work in his laboratory. In a private conversation we had in his office before I left his laboratory, he said cynically: "Benacerraf, you and I know how the work was done and the real contribution of everyone, but for history and the world outside, the only record which remains is the way the papers describing the work have been signed."

Biozzi and I were appointed to the Centre National de la Recherche Scientifique (CNRS), which is the French organization that supports French research personnel. However, the CNRS could not afford to pay both of us. Biozzi, who needed financial support much more than I, was paid a full-time salary, whereas I was appointed as a part-time scientist on a one-quarter salary. This gave rise to a catch-22 situation. All foreigners in France who are employed need a work permit from the ministry of labor. Dutifully, I applied for such a permit and was told that I needed a certificate of employment from the CNRS, my employer. When I went to the CNRS to obtain this document I was confronted with the usual bureaucrat who said: "We cannot give you a certificate of employment since you work for us only part-time. Get the certificate from your other employer." I protested that I had no other employer since I worked full-time at Broussais Hospital even if they were only willing to pay me part-time. He finally agreed to give me the certificate, but was very careful not to mention any salary.

When the situation became critical in 1956 and I decided to leave Halpern's laboratory, I looked seriously into the possibility of working in another laboratory in Paris. I sought the advice of Professor Bugnard, the director of the CNRS. He was very frank and told me that, as a foreigner without a French medical degree, I had no hope of ever being able to direct my own laboratory. He made it clear that as a foreigner I had no future in France. Jacques Monod, Annette's uncle and by then a dear friend, sadly agreed with Professor Bugnard's conclusions and advised me to return to the United States.

Forty years later, after having trained many French immunologists in my laboratory, including the director of the CNRS, my good friend François Kourilsky, the French government has very much compensated for this temporary lack of hospitality by awarding me the medal of the Legion of Honor.

In 1956, Biozzi and I presented our research results at a major international meeting on the reticuloendothelial system, held at Gif-sur-Yvette in a lovely French castle near Paris. This meeting was attended by scientists from England, the United States, and Switzerland. Among the American scientists was Lewis Thomas, a bright and charming experimental pathologist, chairman of the department of pathology at New York University. Dr. Thomas had done distinguished work on both the reticuloendothelial system and the Schwarzman reaction. We sympathized immediately, and knowing my problem and uncertainties, he offered me an appointment as an assistant professor of pathology in his department at New York University. Kabat advised me to accept this excellent offer. I made the critical decision of my life to return to New York and to start my career as an academic scientist in the United States.

9

⟫⟩•⟨⟪

I Am a Businessman in Venezuela

After the first year in Halpern's laboratory, I decided that I needed to become better informed about my father's business interests, which had been for nearly three years left in the sole control of my uncle Fortunato. Father insisted that I make an effort to understand and manage his assets on which the whole family depended for their financial security. He gave me general power of attorney to act on his behalf. I took a leave of absence from science and the laboratory during which Biozzi generously promised to manage our project without me. Annette, Beryl, and I left to spend eight months in Caracas.

This time I entered the office of Hermanos Benacerraf as an equal partner to my uncle but, alas, a completely ignorant one. My first task would be to make a complete inventory of our assets and of their market value. This was rendered difficult by my lack of training and business experience and by the obvious reluctance of Fortunato, who was naturally secretive, to share information, let alone the control of our common interests, with a green upstart. In addition, all these discussions had to be conducted in Spanish, a language I spoke well but with which I had less experience than with French or English.

I was most surprised and reassured when I discovered that, in spite of my lack of experience and training as an accountant, I was able to understand a balance sheet almost instinctively. The assets of Abraham and Fortunato were substantial. But, they were totally integrated in a partnership and were not accessible as ready cash. All of the company's assets were located in Venezuela, except for a couple of hundred thousand dollars which my father had deposited in New York.

Our oldest enterprise and the one from which everything arose, was the textile import and wholesale business. Well over one million dollars was invested in it, when stocks and the receivables were factored in. I found that we also owned other businesses. A chain of highly successful retail stores had been started in partnership with an extremely able and honest businessman, Salvador Salvatierra. Salvatierra was to be elected president of our bank, the Banco Union, which had been started during the war by Abraham and Fortunato and some of their business associates. My family owned 10 percent of the shares of Banco Union, and we had an investment in an insurance company, Seguros Caracas. We also owned several pieces of generally undeveloped real estate in Caracas.

In addition to these well-managed and prosperous enterprises, there were also a couple of poorly administered investments, which were to give me considerable headaches but valuable business training. The largest one was a shoe-manufacturing company, managed by a bright but unscrupulous associate. This business had been structured in the form of three corporations: the parent company owned the other two (a factory and a tannery) and sold the shoes to retailers. The business had reported an impressive profit, which entitled the managing partner to a substantial cash distribution as his share. Upon examining the books I realized that we had been cheated. The profit was the result of an internal juggling of the books. The factory had been selling its products at a loss to the parent company and had accumulated an internal debt, which was larger than the fictitious profits. In fact we had been operating the business at a loss. The manager had deliberately created a fictitious profit in order to be able to claim his share in cash.

I was both proud to have discovered this myself, but shattered at the lack of honesty of some of the partners with whom we were in business. In addition, we had to put up with costly strikes, which were eventually settled by labor management negotiations.

I thought that the best course was to sell the losing enterprise to the eager manager for the best terms we could get and take our losses.

This detailed description of our business interests will give the reader an idea of the problems that confronted me in my first year in business. I decided, from the start, that our long-term family interests no longer coincided with those of my uncle and his children who were to make their lives permanently in Venezuela. My main purpose, over the next years, would be to disentangle as much of our assets as possible without sacrificing value and without endangering our associates. I had no objection in keeping a major share of our investments in Venezuela, a country which had been generous and hospitable to us, which seemed prosperous, and in which we enjoyed valuable business connections. Over the next five or ten years, therefore, I planned to liquidate our participation in industrial and commercial enterprises in favor of investments in bank shares or in real estate, which are easier to manage in absentia. I also proposed to move a substantial share of our assets to the United States, as soon as free cash was available in reasonable amounts.

Fortunately, some of the long-term goals of my cousin Moisses, Fortunato's eldest son, were in agreement with my plan. Moisses graduated from Yale University, where he trained as an architect. In Caracas he had both the expertise and the interest to start a real-estate company that would begin by developing our valuable real-estate holdings in Caracas. I encouraged him to do so and promised my strong support with his father as well as our participation in the real-estate company.

The other plan was to increase our involvement with the Banco Union and with its president, our partner in the retail business, Salvador Salvatierra. I found him to be an honest and very capable man who had been an old friend of my father and who could teach me how to survive in this unfamiliar market. He would also be capable of buying us out when the time came to move completely to the U.S. capital market.

After eight tense months of daily efforts as a businessman, I felt that I had learned all that I could learn. I had initiated the first steps in the long-term plan. In the future, such a plan could be managed by coming to Caracas for about one or two weeks every four to six months. Fortunately, excellent flights had been developed between Paris and Caracas. I would become a regular traveler on these flights, which would take me from Paris to Caracas in thirty-six exhausting hours by way of Amsterdam, Madrid, Lisbon, Dakar, and Paramaribo in Dutch Guyana. In the meantime, I could return to my scientific projects and to our family.

Annette, Beryl, and I sailed happily back to Europe. I bought and brought with me, as a just reward for what I had accomplished, a yellow convertible Studebaker, with red leather seats, with which I had fallen in love. I have always been fond of fast convertibles. I loved the feeling of speed in an open and glamorous car. I suppose that even my ascetic, self-denying nature has some chinks in its armor. After a long crossing we landed at Barcelona in July 1951 and motored proudly back to Paris.

10

⇒➤◆◄⇐

Our Life in Paris, 1950–56

When we returned to Paris, the pattern of our life was set for several years. Biozzi and I worked on a research project at Broussais Hospital: it excited our imaginations and we felt free to pursue the research as we saw fit. Three times a year I would make short trips to Caracas to oversee our business plan. After making the necessary effort to take control of the family investments in Venezuela, I formulated long-term plans to liquidate some of our assets and consolidate others. Father had been very pleased with my performance and agreed with my decisions. I was deeply grateful that he never questioned my judgment on these matters. We could look forward to some stability in our lives at last, and we could look for an apartment in Paris in close proximity to our respective families.

In 1950 my parents' beautiful prewar apartment, located at 11 Rue du Conseiller Collignon, which had been requisitioned by the French authorities at the liberation of Paris (as all empty apartments were), was finally returned to my family. My parents offered us the apartment, since their lives were very much set and they no longer needed it. They were happy to stay most of the year in their house in Montmorency, where they were comfortable and where Father could enjoy his garden. They would spend the four coldest months of the year in Nice, where they preferred renting an apartment rather than returning to the Negresco.

I was delighted in September 1951 to return to the home I had left in 1939 and to recover most of my parents' comfortable but ugly old furniture. To please Annette who never liked the huge and impersonal apartment and hated the furniture, I had our original Richmond furniture, which had been stored in New York, shipped to us. Soon we were installed in our old bedroom and living room. This was to be our home until we returned to the United States in 1956 and took up permanent residence. Another source of discomfort for Annette was the need to hire and supervise a permanent domestic staff whose members had to be fed and kept happy and content. This was a novel experience for her and for me, one that we never enjoyed. I have always hated to be served and much prefer to look after my needs. From my childhood days, probably as a revolt against my mother's obsession for order and neatness, I have always resented cleaning and dusting, and I become wild when my papers and books are moved. We recognized our needs in that apartment, however, and hired a wonderful housekeeper-cook, and a competent live-in nanny to look after Beryl and to help with the housework.

We did not realize at the time how spoiled we were. Since the birth of my first grandchild sixteen years ago, Annette and I have helped our overworked daughter care for her children, on a full-time basis, in spite of the fact that they also have a nanny. Beryl's nanny in the 1950s was on duty day and night, six days per week. We were always involved, of course, but we never felt the pressure we have felt with our grandchildren. Modern nannies, generally much less competent than the ones we had in Paris, are always off duty at 6:30 P.M. and never work on weekends. As a consequence, we have looked after our grandchildren much more than we ever took care of our own daughter, particularly at night and on weekends, and we have enjoyed every minute of it.

Our daily life was both pleasant and comfortable. Having spent much of our time either in Paris or New York, we had become accustomed to an active cultural life with outings to concerts, plays, or museums whenever we pleased. In the summer we spent several weeks at the seashore at Dinard in Brittany, where we played tennis, swam, and forgot about all the cares of the world. Our summer trips to Italy were a most pleasurable experience as well. We became very fond of that beautiful country, which was to become for many years, for us and eventually for Beryl, the symbol of summer idleness and artistic treasures.

Another important feature of our lives was the close proximity of our families, which we very much enjoyed. Annette was probably far too close to her parents and sister than she should have been. This attachment would greatly magnify the loss she would soon suffer when they were to die in the next few years.

It is with a deep sense of sadness and pain that I recall those few years in Paris because of the grievous losses we both experienced; they very much marred the happiness we felt. The memory of those years is still so painful that, when we travel to Paris today, we try to avoid walking by the very street where our apartment was located. Every year for three years, beginning in 1952, we were to suffer the loss of a dear one.

Annette accompanied me on one of my short trips to Venezuela in 1952. When we were in Caracas we learned that her sister Brigitte had developed a high fever and had become severely jaundiced, indicating that she was most probably suffering from a case of viral hepatitis. Her condition, however, grew rapidly worse and complications arose. Her legs became paralyzed and she had to be hospitalized at the Hôpital Cochin. Progressively the paralysis ascended the spinal cord and she lost the use of her body and arms. She apparently had ascending paralysis (Guillain Barré syndrome), a rare but dangerous disease. Without a respirator she would die of asphyxia. We were very concerned and deeply distressed to be so far away when we were needed.

Brigitte died on January 7, 1952. I learned that she was never put on a respirator. The tragedy and our deep sense of loss were magnified by my knowledge that the paralysis in that disease slowly regresses spontaneously. It is essential, therefore, to protect the patient through the early stages of the asphyxiating paralysis by the judicious use of respirators. I am convinced that under the conditions that I knew existed then in Paris hospitals, Brigitte never had a chance.

Annette reacted to her sister's death with deep depression and profound anxiety. To this day, she is uncomfortable when we speak about Brigitte or when she sees her sister's picture, so strong was their attachment for one another. For a long time after Brigitte's death, Annette would wake up at night deeply anxious and feel paralyzed herself. It took much time, love, and effort to allay her anxieties and fears, but I could never decrease the grief she felt so profoundly.

The next year was marked with the death of my own father. On a morning in early February 1953, Marcel Santucci, my parents' chauffeur, called me from Nice to inform me that my father was in a coma. He had been well the night before, had his dinner, and went to bed as usual. When Mother woke up the next morning, she found him unconscious next to her in their bed. There was no sign that he had suffered any pain. Annette and I rushed to the airport. One hour later we were in Nice, where Marcel was waiting for us at the airport. He informed us that Father had never recovered consciousness and had died. Soon thereafter, we were in my father's bedroom. He was lying in his bed, his face peaceful, as if he had been sleeping. I hugged his dead body and was painfully aware of how cold and hard it had become. There was no way I could tell whether he had died of another stroke or of a massive coronary thrombosis, and I did not care. For a couple of weeks after my father's death, I was to experience a strange, selective amnesia that would never recur, not even after the death of my mother in 1981. I would forget trivial, recent events, such as what I did a few hours ago, or what I ate for lunch, or the first names of familiar people. These symptoms disappeared slowly and spontaneously.

The first matters I had to attend to were the burial of my father and the religious ceremonies. To respect my father's wishes and beliefs, I contacted the local rabbi and asked him to come and say prayers for my father. I then made arrangements to bury my father in Paris as rapidly as possible, because it is important in the Jewish religion to bury the dead preferably within twenty-four hours. I contracted for a coffin and a hearse to drive my father's body to Paris the next morning so that he could be buried the day after.

The evening of my father's death the rabbi and I stayed up all night. It was a strange experience because I soon learned that the rabbi had just lost his dear sister for whom he was deeply grieving. It is strange that I spent most of that night comforting the local rabbi for the loss of his sister, in the room next to where my father's body lay.

The next morning, Marcel and I, riding in Father's Jaguar, followed the hearse containing my father's body to Paris. I was very much in a daze by then. Annette and Mother returned by train.

Father was buried the day after in a new plot that I bought for him and my mother in the Jewish section of the Pantin cemetery, near Paris. In spite of my great attachment to Father when he was alive, I found it difficult to return to his tomb after the burial. I would only return to the same cemetery to bury my mother next to him nearly thirty years later.

I invited mother to live with us in our apartment. She accepted our hospitality temporarily. To satisfy her desire to live independently, I bought a very pleasant apartment for her in a new building being constructed on the nearby Avenue Paul Doumer. Within six months she moved to her new home where she resided until her death in 1981.

A month after Father's death, Annette and I left again for

Caracas so I could settle my father's estate. According to Venezuelan law, my mother inherited two-thirds and Paul and I shared
one-third of Father's assets. But the responsibility for the management of my mother's and brother's shares would always be mine. I
was now wealthy in my own right and just as involved as before in
Venezuelan businesses.

The next tragedy to strike was the death of Annette's father,
Ado, in March 1954. For several years, Ado's health had not been
good. He had both high blood pressure and atherosclerosis. Several
years before Ado had suffered a heart attack from which he recovered without the need of treatment. But his high blood pressure
worried us and there was nothing that could be done for him in
those days. Early in 1954 he suffered a massive stroke, just like my
father had years ago. But Ado never recovered. Instead of improving with time, he progressively lost more function, indicating
that the lesion had not stabilized. He was either still bleeding or
blocking progressively more cerebral circulation. This slow agony
lasted for several painful weeks, while he was fully conscious of
what was happening to him, at least in the beginning.

I felt helpless. I knew that I was powerless to stop the inevitable
outcome. I had become very fond of Ado, whom I loved dearly. He
was Annette's preferred parent with whom she felt particularly
close, for she had inherited much of his sensitivity, humor, and
imagination. The loss of her beloved father, only two years after the
tragedy of the death of her sister, contributed further to Annette's
despair and depression. She expressed anger and disbelief at our
inability and that of medicine to help her father and to save him.
Again, all I could do was offer the support of my love and affection
to help her bear the insufferable burden of her combined losses.
The pain proved tolerable solely because we were so attached to
each other that we could bear it together, and because, if anything,
adversity brought us even closer than happiness had done.

❖ ❖ ❖

What I remember fondly about this troubled period of our lives is the warm relationship we had with a small number of friends and relatives. Among the members of Annette's family, two stand out particularly: her cousin Bertrand and her uncle Jacques Monod. Perhaps because both were scientists, I felt much closer to them than to any other of Annette's numerous relatives.

Bertrand, you may remember, had fled to the United States with Annette, and had trained at the University of Chicago where he became an atomic physicist. He was extremely bright, witty, and remarkably unselfish. He had been severely ill as a child with tetanus and rheumatic fever which left him with serious musculoskeletal problems and an aura of detachment and irony that made him a precious companion in any circumstance. He worked in Joliot Curie's physics laboratory, and I loved hearing about his latest instruments and experiments.

Jacques Monod was a well-known public figure both in France and the United States. He was one of the founders of the discipline of molecular biology. He can be credited with training many of the American scientists who were to make important contributions in this field. There were always American scientists working in his laboratory at the Pasteur Institute when I visited him. In 1965, he shared the Nobel Prize for medicine with Andre Lwoff and François Jacob. But Jacques was much more than a great scientist. He was a renaissance man, a great humanist, and a born leader. He belonged to a famous Protestant family. His father, a well-known painter, had married an American and had lived most of his life in Cannes where Jacques was brought up. Jacques Monod had been attracted to biology and music and had been equally successful in both. He played the cello masterfully, and before the war he had directed a choral ensemble, which sang Bach's cantatas. He received a serious offer to tour the United States professionally but decided that biology was his vocation. Just before the war he married Odette Bruhl, Suzanne's youngest sister.

Jacques's work on bacterial inducible enzymes of *E. coli* provided the system which would permit major advances to be made in our understanding of the genetic control of enzyme expression and protein synthesis. He was also responsible for the elegant concept of allosteric control of enzyme activity, whereby proteins can take different shapes dependent upon their interactions. During the war, Monod had been very active in the resistance, and after the war he directed one of the most dynamically productive and exciting laboratories of the Pasteur Institute at the forefront of modern biology. It was always a treat to visit him in the laboratory or at home, and his advice was always precious.

His accomplishments were not limited to the laboratory. In spite of a weak leg and a noticeable limp (the result of poliomyelitis), he became a daring mountain climber capable of ascending the most difficult slopes. He also loved sailing, but not along the coast. He would leave Cannes in his sailboat and head for Corsica, Italy, or even Greece. Annette and I remained very close to Jacques throughout our life, until his untimely death in 1976.

Our most intimate friends in Paris were Raphael and Adriana Salem. They remained the closest friends we ever had, in spite of the age difference. They were, indeed, more contemporary with Annette's parents than with ourselves, but their youthful character and enthusiasm directed their interests more to the younger age group. Raphael and Adriana were highly cultured and sophisticated Sephardic Jews. He was born in Turkey and she in Italy. Raphael's father had been a successful international lawyer who settled in Paris before the war. Adriana's family belonged to the wealthy Jewish Italian aristocracy. They had both been brought up in the culture and luxury of prewar Paris. Raphael went to engineering school before becoming a banker. He rose to a prominent position with the famous Banque de Paris et des Pays Bas, the principal investment bank in France. While working as a banker, he studied at the Sorbonne and earned a Ph.D. in mathematics. Before the war, he was, therefore, a professional banker, and an amateur mathematician. The war, however, would change his career plans.

Raphael escaped with his family to the United States. By chance, he was in the same ship that transported Annette and her family to Canada. When Raphael reached the United States and looked for a job to support his family, he was surprised to find that he was well known from his publications as a mathematician. He received an offer of a faculty appointment from the department of mathematics at the Massachusetts Institute of Technology, and he accepted. He spent the war years, happily, in Cambridge teaching at MIT. After the war he was appointed professor of mathematics at the Sorbonne in Paris and gladly gave up any likelihood of ever returning to a banking career.

The numerous analogies with my own life and background are sufficiently obvious to explain why I was tremendously attracted to Raphael Salem, who became my role model more than my own father. However, we were very different in other aspects. Raphael, a highly sophisticated and cultured man, had a passion for platonic friendships with younger women. Annette was indeed among the chosen few with whom Raphael enjoyed chatting and having coffee. But strangely, I was not jealous, because I was very fond of him myself, and equally fond of his wife, Adriana.

Adriana was a lady in every sense of the word. She had class, intelligence, culture, manners, distinction, and an air of nobility about her. She was also very courageous and determined, whereas Raphael was likely to be cautious and fearful. Together they made an impressive and well-adjusted couple.

They had three children; the oldest one, Daniel, has always been one of my closest friends. He went to Harvard College and made his career in business, initially in New York. He eventually became head of international operations for Conde Nast publications. When we lived in New York, we saw him almost every day. Daniel held my hand during the birth of my daughter in New York and helped me celebrate the happy event.

Among the lessons we learned from the Salems and tried to imitate were their interest in young people, their style of life, and their elegance as hosts, whether in their sumptuous Paris apartment or in their superb country house near Aix en Provence. We were immensely proud to be invited to their magnificent old mansion surrounded by olive and cypress trees. From their grounds one could see the mountain Sainte Victoire, which was made famous in Cézanne's paintings.

Having made the final decision to return to the United States in the fall of 1956 to take up a position in the department of pathology at New York University, I decided to visit New York with Annette that summer to find an apartment and to buy new furniture. I had, in fact, been invited to speak at an international meeting that summer in Boston.

11

---⟫◦⟪---

New York University

Upon our arrival in New York, we fell in love with a beautiful three-bedroom apartment for rent on the fifteenth floor of Manhattan House, a splendidly managed building on East Sixty-sixth Street. Then we went to Knoll, a furniture company recommended by my cousin Moisses, the architect, and in one morning bought all the furniture we needed for that apartment. It is remarkable that we never regretted any of the choices we made in that hurried morning. We were to spend six happy years in that beautiful apartment, which faced both north and south and, in 1956, commanded a magnificent view of the downtown skyline. Annette had a passion for the views from upper floors. The high buildings which were to be erected, both south and north of us, would be a major reason for our move to a condominium apartment on the thirty-second floor of Tower East, a new building on East Seventy-second Street. There was no way that Annette's view of the skyline could ever be obstructed there.

Having organized our lives in New York, we sailed back to

Europe with our friend Raphael Salem. He convinced us to accompany him on the *Cristoforo Colombo,* a magnificent Italian liner and sister ship of the *Andrea Doria,* which sank off Nantucket. Life on a transatlantic liner was one of those luxurious experiences which air travel has rendered obsolete. Of all the liners I have sailed on, which include British, French, Dutch, and American ships, none was designed to indulge the whim of the traveler in as extravagant a style as Italian ships. I have always feared that this blissful, carefree atmosphere might be associated with a poorer ability to handle a major emergency at sea. On the other hand, as you may have guessed, the safe American ships were the least fun of the lot.

In keeping with the magic of this beautiful voyage, which provided a welcomed rest for Annette and me, we landed in Naples in the sight of Capri and Mount Vesuvius.

We returned to Paris and prepared to depart for the United States to take up permanent residence. As a last indulgence before the task ahead, we spent a glorious week as guests of our friends the Salems in Mont Joly, their estate near Aix en Provence.

I was ready to begin my career as a junior faculty member in a medical school. New York University School of Medicine (NYU) in which I was appointed assistant professor of pathology was a most exciting place in 1956. It had a brilliant basic science faculty which comprised Lewis Thomas in pathology; Colin Mcleod, Alvin Pappenheimer, and Bernard Horecker in microbiology; Severo Ochoa in biochemistry; and Homer Smith in physiology. Moreover, it was totally imbued with Flexner's philosophy that modern medicine is scientific medicine, and that physicians must be trained to think as scientists before becoming clinicians, a belief I have always held as fundamental. The students I would have the privilege to teach for the next twelve years were always very interested in the basic medical sciences, with a high proportion of them willing to work in the laboratory far more than the students I would encounter later at Harvard.

In spite of Lewis Thomas's warm and generous support (he financed my laboratory for over a year, until I obtained my own grant from the National Institutes of Health [NIH]), I was very apprehensive and insecure about being able to work creatively by myself without Biozzi. I was in the big leagues now, playing for high stakes in the roulette wheel of research with only my wits and ambition to rely on.

Because research is an unpredictable activity that depends heavily on chance and also on imagination, I have always said to the students who wanted to work with me that a research career is the most hazardous of all professions, and justly so. Because the work, generally financed with public funds, is done for the good of humankind, the most stringent criteria of quality and competitiveness must be maintained at all times in the manner in which support for the research is granted. This attitude is necessary to ensure that the best ideas and the most imaginative and skilled scientists prevail. It is precisely because the peer-review system, under which most biomedical science is supported in the United States by the NIH, has worked impartially that American biomedical science has been so successful.

The price, which has to be paid by the individual investigator in terms of uncertainty, anguish, and time spent in writing grant applications, is awesome. I tell my students that only those who have a very strong vocation, anchored in a deep, unrelenting, and obsessive curiosity for the workings of Nature, have the motivation and, yes, the addiction that will protect them against the disappointments and uncertainties of such a hazardous career.

Another matter of concern to me was my lack of identification with my new department. My sole qualification as a pathologist was an A in pathology in medical school. I had never trained as a pathologist and had never performed an autopsy. I was not particularly experienced with a microscope, the pathologist's key instrument. This was soon obvious to my new colleagues, most of them traditional morbid anatomists. Two of them, Robert McCluskey and Norman Cooper, who were very much interested in research, taught me microscopic anatomy as part of our collaborative projects. Others were less generous. Professor Sigmund Wilens, previously pathologist-in-chief at Bellevue Hospital, was particularly skeptical about my qualifications. He welcomed me saying, "Dr. Benacerraf, since you are now an assistant professor of pathology, would you be willing to take the gross and microscopic examinations that I have prepared for the students? It would be interesting to find out how you rank." Trapped by my vanity, I had no choice but to face his challenge, unprepared. To my and his great surprise, I received an honorable grade. I had not forgotten the material, and fortunately the field had not moved appreciably in the twelve years since I took the course. My standing among my colleagues was enhanced by my willingness to face the old curmudgeon.

In spite of my anxieties and fears, my years at NYU were to be extraordinarily productive and on the whole very exciting professionally. Lewis Thomas was a masterful chairman of the departments of pathology and medicine: his enthusiasm, his exceedingly good taste, and the wisdom of his appointments fostered a creative climate at the school. His most generous attitude toward young faculty members, which I have learned from him, favored the development at NYU of a unique community of young immunologists. This golden period coincided also with the dramatic increase in funding of immunology by the NIH, and with the attraction to our discipline and my laboratory of many of the most gifted and brightest students and fellows with whom it would be my pleasure to work. I was enormously fortunate in those exciting years to have been at the right place at the right time, when much less was known than today and much more could be discovered in our science.

❖ ❖ ❖

(From left) The author's parents, Henriette Lasry and Abraham Benacerraf, and his uncles Fortunato and Isaac Benacerraf, in Caracas, 1921.

(Above) Baruj Benacerraf, age four, in Caracas.

(Left) Young Baruj and his parents in Paris, 1926.

Benacerraf, age seventeen, returning to Paris in September 1938 on the Queen Mary.

Annette Dreyfus and Baruj Benacerraf while courting in New York City, 1941.

U.S. Army Captain Benacerraf at Nancy, France, in 1946.

Benacerraf at Harvard Medical School, 1980, where he was chair of the Department of Pathology.

Benacerraf is awarded the 1980 Nobel Prize in Medicine by King Carl XVI Gustaf.

(Top) Benacerraf receiving an honorary doctorate at Columbia University in 1985.

(Bottom) Benacerraf is awarded the National Medal of Science by President George Bush at the White House in 1990.

Initially Thomas assigned me a 200-square-foot laboratory, in which the major piece of equipment was an old refrigerator, and authorized me to hire a technician to help with my research. I complained to Annette that I felt lonely and dejected. She reassured me that I would soon be so busy I would not have time to whine and mope. Among the first applicants for the technician's position was Martha Sebestyen, a young, recently graduated, Hungarian physician who had just escaped the Budapest uprising.* She seemed enthusiastic and highly intelligent, but wanted to be hired as a postdoctoral fellow and not as a technician, which meant that she would be entitled to work on her own research with me. I agreed with her request, and we started our experiments, with the collaboration of Stuart Schlossman, a brilliant and aggressive medical student who joined our eager little group.

I must have hit the jackpot with my first throw of the dice. Martha is now a professor of pediatrics at the University of Vienna and a distinguished clinical immunologist, while Stuart is professor of medicine at Harvard Medical School and head of the Division of Tumor Immunology at the Dana-Farber Cancer Institute. Stuart was to make outstanding contributions which are the foundation of modern clinical immunology. He is responsible, among other things, for the identification of the antigen receptor of human T cells and the discovery of the CD4 molecule. This cell surface molecule characterizes the critically important helper subclass of T lymphocytes, the main target of the viral infection in AIDS, and functions as the receptor used by the HIV virus to infect these cells.

With Schlossman and Sebestyen, I continued my studies of the phagocytic function of the reticuloendothelial system (R.E.S.) and of the effect of endotoxin on macrophages, which I had begun in

---

*In 1956, an attempt was made by some members of the Hungarian Communist party to detach their government from Soviet influence and domination. This provoked the intervention of Soviet armed forces, with ensuing riots and the repression of this attempt to freedom. Many Hungarians fled at this time.

Paris. We turned our attention to the blood clearance of bacteria and viruses and demonstrated the importance of opsonizing antibody* and of complement factors in this process. Within a year, however, I was engaged in several other projects that, although related to our past experience, constituted novel areas of investigation. The themes of these studies would progressively orient my interest to immunopathology and eventually to basic immunology.

My immunochemical studies with Dr. Elvin Kabat and my experience with the reticuloendothelial system led naturally to the demonstration that soluble immune complexes in the bloodstream are phagocytized by the R.E.S., and to the hypothesis that the abnormal depositing of such complexes in the kidney and blood vessels of the heart could result in the lesion of serum sickness, the mechanism of which had eluded me as a medical student. My colleague Robert McCluskey, whose laboratory was adjacent to mine, had a strong interest in kidney pathology. With him and Fred Miller, a bright and enterprising medical student, we were able to show that the injection of soluble complexes of antigen and antibody into normal nonimmune mice produced the characteristic lesions of serum sickness (i.e., arteritis, glomerulonephritis, and endocarditis), because of the abnormal localization of these inflammatory immune complexes at these sites. We further demonstrated the role of mediators of inflammation on these deposits. My two associates in these studies, as in the previous ones, would go on to brilliant careers. Robert McCluskey became professor of pathology at Harvard and pathologist-in-chief at the Massachusetts General Hospital, and Fred Miller is chairman of the department of pathology at the State University of New York at Stony Brook School of Medicine.

Another successful research project was initiated by a phone

---

*These are antibodies capable of attaching themselves to macrophages. When such opsonizing antibodies bind to their bacterial targets, they cause the bacteria to stick to macrophages and thereby stimulate and initiate the first step in phagocytosis of the bacteria by the macrophage.

call from Lloyd Old, a young physician working in the Rye division of the Sloan Kettering Institute for cancer research; he expressed a strong interest in initiating experiments in collaboration with me on tumor immunology. Old, with whom both Annette and I would become very close, was a fascinating young man and a superb violinist. He had made a lifetime commitment to work on cancer and to finding a cure for this dreaded disease. Upon graduation from medical school in San Francisco, Old joined the department of experimental chemotherapy at the Sloan Kettering, but, sensing very early the future importance of cancer immunology, he approached me at NYU to learn immunology. He convinced me to start a project with him in his laboratory at Rye. I could not resist his charm and energy and agreed to come once a week to Rye to initiate a joint program. At that time tumor immunology had just been recognized as a fruitful area of investigation with the advances of Paul Gorer and George Snell in the field of transplantation and the development of inbred strains of mice capable of accepting homografts.*

We confirmed the earlier findings of Prehn and George and Eva Klein that tumors induced in mice by chemical carcinogens possess distinct tumor antigens, specific for each individual tumor. We attempted to influence tumor rejection by increasing the capacity of mice to mount immunological and inflammatory reaction against the tumor. Again, I took advantage of the earlier observations Biozzi and I had made that infection of mice with BCG is a powerful stimulant of the phagocytic system. Taking a cue from George Bernard Shaw, whose character had counseled "Stimulate the phagocytes," we showed that previous infection of mice with BCG increases the rejection rate of a variety of experimental tumors and decreases cancer deaths. Old† further pursued these studies until he was able

---

*These are tissue grafts among members of the same genetically identical inbred strains. Allografts are grafts from genetically incompatible donors.

†Lloyd Old, fulfilling my expectations, has a brilliant career at Memorial Sloan Kettering, where he is William E. Snee Professor of Cancer Immunology.

to isolate and characterize tumor necrosis factor (TNF), an agent responsible for the destruction of tumors by activated macrophages, and which is now under investigation as an antitumor agent. TNF has also been shown to be a major mediator of vascular shock during certain bacterial infections.

Old had also a most important part in our life outside the laboratory. His professional talent as a musician and violinist made him dear to Annette, who played sonatas with him and soon organized a warm circle of music-loving friends around her. Among these were the well-known harpsichordist Albert Fuller, oboist Mel Kaplan, and singer Robert White. Under Annette's direction we would frequently have dinner parties followed by lovely concerts.

By this time my laboratory had grown considerably from the original 200 square feet to occupy four rooms. I kept my desk in the main laboratory, however. Privacy is not compatible with the need to be aware of all the experiments performed and of the results as they are obtained. I particularly enjoyed the magnificent view of the East River from my desk. Watching the water flow and the ships go by very much favored creative thinking.

At about that time Annette decided to train as a technician to join my laboratory. She already knew and understood my work but was eager to be involved in it, as well. She soon became an active participant and has been an invaluable assistant to me ever since. She worked closely with many of my young associates, who sometimes would confide in her what they would not tell me directly, knowing that the information would reach me through this informal conduit.

Several of the projects I directed in the early phase of my NYU period, such as the ones I have just mentioned and a couple of others concerned with the study of immunological mechanisms in experimental pathology, evolved as a direct consequence of my past experience and the opportunity of collaborations.

Zoltan Ovary was an old friend of Biozzi. He was a highly cultured Hungarian physician with a remarkable knowledge of art and music who trained at the Pasteur Institute before the war. I had met Ovary in Paris. I was surprised and delighted to learn that he emigrated to the United States and was working at Johns Hopkins University in Baltimore. I convinced Al Stetson to offer Zoltan a position at NYU soon after Stetson became chairman of pathology, replacing Lewis Thomas who took over as chairman of medicine.

With Ovary I returned to my old interest in allergic mechanisms. We initiated a successful collaborative project that demonstrated that different classes of immunoglobulins (antibodies) are responsible for different biological activities. Special regions of the antibody molecule were shown to be responsible for these different activities. They determined the binding of guinea pig antibodies to specific receptors on the surface of mast cells for gamma 1, and on the surface of macrophages for gamma 2 antibodies.

These experiments were carried out with the collaboration of two dedicated postdoctoral fellows, Kurt Bloch and a French physician named François Kourilsky. Continuing the impressive list of accomplishments by brilliant graduates of my small NYU laboratory, Bloch is presently professor of medicine at Harvard Medical School and the Massachusetts General Hospital, and Kourilsky, who for many years headed the Center of Immunology at Marseilles, later became the director of the Centre National de la Recherche Scientifique, the major research organization of the French government.

Related to these discoveries was our demonstration with another postdoctoral fellow, Arthur Berken, of the presence of a receptor on the cell membrane of phagocytic cells. This receptor is responsible for the binding of antibodies and therefore of antibody-coated bacteria prior to phagocytosis. Berken became a clinical professor of medicine at Stony Brook School of Medicine.

Reflecting on the high proportion of my young associates of this period who made successful careers, I have concluded that it is more an indication of the importance of the emerging science of immunology than of the level training they may have received.

✤ ✤ ✤

I have not mentioned my role as teacher at NYU. I have concentrated on my life in the laboratory and on my interactions with postdoctoral students and colleagues. I was, also, an educator and I took my responsibility seriously. I contributed to the teaching of the classical pathology course to second-year medical students, particularly in the areas of phagocytosis and the R.E.S. My main effort, however, was in the organization and teaching of a new course in immunology which I taught year after year to highly interested students.

At first, I would prepare my lectures carefully. One day, an urgent call to the laboratory informed me that the whole class was waiting in the auditorium. I had either forgotten or not been informed that I was scheduled to lecture that morning. Hurriedly I threw some slides together and lectured unprepared. The consensus was that I gave my best lecture, which may very well show that too much time is spent in preparing lectures and that one performs best under pressure.

12

—>·0·<—

Our Life in New York, 1956–68:
I Am a Banker

In addition to my busy scientific and professional life at NYU, I still had to discharge my responsibilities as caretaker of our family's assets.

I faced a major business challenge in 1958, for which I was not prepared. Salvatierra and my other associates of the Banco Union in Caracas learned that controlling interest, i.e., 96 percent of the shares of the Colonial Trust Co., a small New York bank with headquarters in Rockefeller Center and three other branches, was for sale. The ownership of a New York bank appeared very desirable to the Banco Union group, as it would enhance both their prestige in Venezuela and their business opportunities by providing them with a New York base. Two of the Banco Union directors flew from Caracas to join me in negotiating the purchase of the Colonial Trust shares. We signed a purchase agreement for the sum of 5.5 million dollars, payable within a month, and my associates returned to Venezuela to secure the funds. The ink on the agreement was barely dry when a major revolution took place in Venezuela,

151

which resulted in the overthrow of the unpopular dictatorship of General Perez Jimenez.

This revolution, which terminated an era of military dictatorships and made Venezuela one of the first Latin American countries to enjoy stable democratic government, created uncertain conditions at the time. I was terrified that the funds would not be transferred to New York in time to meet the obligation I had assumed on behalf of the Banco Union. Fortunately the money to close the deal was wired as planned, but I was informed that, under the circumstances, no one could be spared from Venezuela to supervise the operation of our New York bank. I was told that I should do it myself and I was appointed director and chairman of the credit committee at a yearly salary of $15,000, three times the starting salary I received at NYU in 1956. On the day following our purchase of the bank, my name appeared in an article on page one of the financial section of the *New York Times* reporting that a New York bank had been bought by a Venezuelan group.

The other important events related to our purchase of the Colonial Trust Co. were an invitation to lunch by the president of the Federal Reserve Bank of New York, who was curious to see what I looked like, and an interview with the commissioner of Banks of New York State, where I was sternly warned to keep my hands off the depositors' funds. The commissioner had apparently a very low opinion of Latin American business practices and morality.

Strange as it may seem, I managed the bank competently for several years, and learned banking by doing. We had an excellent, efficient, and honest staff. They were patient with me and delighted in teaching me bank regulations and bank examinations, as well as loan and deposit theory. I learned the principal rules of successful banking: Keep your loan portfolio well secured and insist on compensating balances. I was soon totally at ease managing a bank, which I found far easier and less hazardous than managing a research laboratory.

I impressed Annette when I told her that every day I received the list of all overdrawn accounts. I warned her to be careful, that her name would be sent to the president of Citibank if she overdrew her account.

After several years the Colonial Trust Co. was sold at a considerable profit to the Meadowbrook National Bank. I negotiated the sale agreement, which had a clause requiring that I stay on as a consultant for two additional years. This concluded my formal business experience in the United States until I was to manage a hospital and a research institute starting in 1980, when I became president of the Dana-Farber Cancer Institute in Boston. My training as a banker was of much help then.

During the first years of our life in New York, I would still need to fly to Caracas at regular intervals but managed to stay only a few days each time. I would eventually achieve my final goal of complete divestment of our assets in Venezuela by selling them to Salvatierra and to my cousins with payment terms that were attractive to them.

We still had one more tragedy to experience. I neglected to mention that there was a strong history of hereditary malignancy in Annette's family and that her grandmother had been surgically cured of a cancer of the breast. In 1953, Annette's mother, Suzanne, had noticed a lump in one of her own breasts, which proved malignant and for which she had a mastectomy. She was told that she was cured, and was not warned, then, of a suspicious bone lesion, indicating that the cancer had spread. In 1959, lung metastasis were discovered and she was never well after that. Annette traveled repeatedly to Paris to be near her mother during her worst months. Each time she would leave Beryl, who very much missed her mother, with me. Within a year, Suzanne presented signs of massive brain tumors. She eventually lost consciousness and died in August 1960.

In less than a decade, Annette's immediate family, to which she had been so attached, had been wiped out. Her mother's death rekindled the feelings of depression and despair she had experienced after the loss of her sister and father, and for a few years she would be uncomfortable returning to Paris in the summer.

Faithful to my belief in the beneficial and creative effects of extended summer vacations, I would close the laboratory and send everybody on vacation, at the end of June until Labor Day. We had spent our annual research funds by then, anyway, since I always managed to do in ten months the work budgeted for twelve.

In 1961, we bought a lovely summer home on a little lake on Shelter Island, at the tip of Long Island. We had a lot of acreage which, left wild, provided welcome isolation and a magnificent view. The house was a very primitive chalet, made of California redwood. It had a large A-frame living room with a small kitchen, three minuscule bedrooms, and a shower. We loved this enchanted spot and every year spent the month of August in our little house. Fred Kantor, a research fellow with whom I was to initiate my work on the genetic control of the immune response, was a passionate amateur pilot. He would fly his own plane from New Haven, Connecticut, to Shelter Island for visits with us.

Those twelve years we spent in New York had been busy and on the whole very happy. Annette and I were in the vigor of our adulthood, in an exciting city, with ample means to live a comfortable life among many valued friends. The work was exciting and our social life an enriching experience. In addition to the concerts and parties Annette organized, our interest in art dates also from this golden period when we began to gather a modest collection of valuable art pieces. I mentioned earlier that Annette's grandmother Berthe Bruhl had managed to preserve, through the war, a collection of French impressionists which had been bought by her husband. Unfortunately, most of these paintings would be sold by her heirs, Annette's uncle and aunts. Annette inherited two valuable pieces and a few lesser works of that collection: a beautiful Boudin, which depicts a group of washerwomen on a riverbank, near Trouville, and an excellent Guillaumin, with a typical river view as a theme. There were, in addition, two lovely Constantin Guy drawings and watercolors by Jongkind and Marquet. These valuable pieces stimulated the collector's bug in us, at a time when prices were not yet outrageous. Annette convinced me to follow the sales at Parke Bernet and we enjoyed bidding on some of them. During that period we bought a beautiful Modigliani drawing, an oil by Baron Gros, and two superb Matisse drawings. But our most remarkable piece is a 1958 Picasso oil depicting a young lady from Arles. I must give Annette complete credit for this acquisition, which is the star of our modest collection. I was working in the laboratory one morning in 1960, when she called from Parke Bernet telling me that she had spotted a beautiful Picasso painting, which could be bought for a reasonable price. In the middle of an experiment, I said thoughtlessly, "Do what you want, but let me finish my work." She bought it for $8,000, which we could afford, but was still a lot of money at the time. I loved the painting, but I voiced a serious concern: "How do we know this is not a fake? There is no guarantee in auction sales, and neither you nor I can tell a real from a fake Picasso." Fortunately the painting had been sold by KahnWeiler, Picasso's dealer in Paris who, upon request, sent us an authenticating certificate. The Picasso has enlightened our living room ever since, but I have not dared to have it appraised since Picasso's death. We have over the years added many more affordable prints to our collection; among these are lovely works of Picasso, Chagall, Toulouse-Lautrec, Miró, Vassareli, Debré, and Calder. Both Annette and I derive a lot of pleasure from this collection.

After six years at Manhattan House, we moved to Tower East, a recently erected building at 190 East Seventy-second Street, where we bought a condominium apartment on the thirty-second floor. The apartment was truly magnificent with a large living room looking west and south. We had a completely unobstructed view of Central Park and of the New York skyline from any place in our living room. And of course at that height, the noise of the city could not be heard. We were the first to move into the building in 1962 when it was just completed and would spend six very happy years and entertain many dear friends there.

This period was also the golden age of our social life. I am personally somewhat of a loner who enjoys only few friends but values intimate relationships. Annette is a much more gregarious person who likes formal as well as intimate entertaining. Over the years she has trained me to enjoy this more active social life. Her talent as a hostess and her natural charm have made our home a popular one, and has fostered the development of valuable friendships with several most interesting people. We continued to see our dear friends Raphael and Adriana Salem both in France and in New York when Raphael, who traveled more, would visit us. I would be deeply grieved by their deaths, particularly Raphael with whom I felt a personal kinship.

We made many other dear friends. I developed a close personal relationship with Leo Szilard, who was the other friend I admired most next to Raphael. Leo Szilard was the Hungarian atomic physicist who convinced Albert Einstein to intervene with President Roosevelt to initiate work on the atom bomb. Szilard was one of the brightest and most unconventional men I knew. When I met him he had become more interested in biology than in physics and directed his active mind to speculations about the mechanisms of immunity and aging. He would pop up from anywhere, at any hour of the day and night, and continue a conversation he had with you weeks or months before, as if no time had elapsed. He always lived in hotels and loved to spend time in their lobbies. He had a particular affection for the lobby of the Plaza in New York. It was said about him that, if he visited a laboratory one morning, he would leave behind enough ideas for that lab to work on for a year until his next visit. Three stories will offer insight into this man's complex irreverent personality, which I enjoyed so much.

When Szilard worked on the Manhattan Project, General Leslie R. Groves, the administrative head of the project, soon tired of the unmilitary behavior of the scientists in his command and thought it would be a good idea to give all the scientists commissions in the army and make them subject to military discipline. He discussed it with Szilard. Szilard agreed that it was an excellent idea, but that it was a matter of rank. "What rank would be appropriate for you?" asked Groves. "General, of course," answered Szilard. Needless to say, this response convinced Groves to abandon his idea.

At the time of the Cuban missile crisis in 1962, Szilard had been living in Washington. He called me, in a very agitated state, to alert me to the seriousness of the international situation. He felt that the risk of an atomic conflict was very real and he arranged to fly to Geneva where he would spend a few days until the resolution of the crisis. I thought at the time that he was unreasonably panicky and went myself to Washington to attend a scientific meeting on the very day he flew to Switzerland. Now that the historic facts are known, it is clear that Szilard was right to be alarmed. The Soviet Union had missiles in Cuba, armed and aimed at Washington and New York at the time, and he knew we were very close to disaster.

In the early 1960s Szilard was diagnosed with cancer of the bladder. He told his physician that he wanted a second opinion. When asked whom he wanted to consult he answered: "Me." He spent weeks looking up all the literature on the treatment of bladder carcinoma and decided that he wanted to be treated with local radiation therapy. Radium implanted in his bladder destroyed the tumor. When Szilard died of a heart attack in California many years later, no tumor could be found at the time of autopsy. This example supports my thesis that patients, particularly when they have medical or scientific training, must never abdicate the decision-making process concerning their treatment, or those of their dear ones, solely to other physicians, no matter how learned or skillful their doctors may appear to be.

André Cournand was another of our close friends of that period. He was a French cardiologist who came to Columbia's College of Physicians and Surgeons after his training in France. He started a lifetime collaboration with Dickinson Richards who headed Columbia's Medical Division at Bellevue Hospital. Their work would introduce cardiac catheterization as a valuable diagnostic and therapeutic procedure in cardiovascular diseases and earned them the Nobel Prize in medicine in 1956. Cournand's French background and culture made him very attractive to both Annette and me, and we developed an intimate relationship with him and his lovely wife, Ruth.

René Dubos, who, you may remember, was my examiner in science at the Lycée Français and who had advised me to work with Dr. Elvin Kabat, was also a close friend of Cournand, and became a dear friend of Annette and myself. Dubos headed the important Division of Microbiology at Rockefeller University. He was a Frenchman of modest background. His father had been a village butcher. He performed brilliantly at school in France and earned a scholarship to study at Rutgers University, where he received his Ph.D. in microbiology under Selman Waksman, who would later discover the drug streptomycin. After graduation he was appointed to the Rockefeller University, where he spent all of his life, except for an interval of a couple war years, when he occupied the Fabyan Chair of Comparative Pathology at Harvard, to which I would be appointed myself in 1970.

Dubos was not only a brilliant scientist but a gifted writer and an excellent philosopher. Alexander Fleming, who observed in 1928 that the mold *Penicillium notatum* had antibacterial properties, made that discovery accidentally, and for many years did not realize its significance. Dubos, in contrast, wondered why pathogenic bacteria seldom survived in nature outside of their parasitized host, and reasoned that other microorganisms must produce molecules toxic for many pathogenic microorganisms. He deliberately attempted to identify products synthesized by soil microorganisms with antibacterial properties. Luck was not on his side this time. Although he had reasoned correctly and he was able to identify Gramicidin, an antibacterial product produced by soil organisms, this early antibiotic proved far too toxic for therapeutic use.

This is an example again of the importance of chance in discovery. In addition to his scientific contributions and to the training of generations of physician-scientists at Rockefeller University, Dubos was one of the first to perceive the importance of preserving the environment that nature has struggled for ages to evolve and that humanity can destroy in less than a generation. Dubos passed merciless judgment on those around him who did not meet his high standards, and since he was also endowed with excellent gifts of expression, he could be very much feared. I learned a lot from him—above all, never to compromise my principles for the sake of expediency.

13

———⊰•⊱———

Move to National Institutes of Health

When I arrived at New York University, I was totally inexperienced in the administrative and political management of academic institutions. In modern American medical schools, the opportunity to apply for substantial research support from government institutions, granted individually to faculty members, has given some measure of independence to the researchers. The control of space, appointments, and institutional resources, however, has remained in the powerful hands of the administrators. The power structure of medical schools varies between two typical models. In one, the power resides in a small oligarchy of permanent department chairpersons and policies are decided by a committee composed of the heads of the major departments with the dean playing a lesser role. New York University was structured after this model. In the other model, according to which Harvard University is administered, the dean is the dominating figure and the various faculty committees either have a rotating membership or such a large one that they can be easily controlled and manipulated by the powerful dean through his appointing power.

For the twelve years that I was a member of the Department of Pathology at NYU, I was supported and sheltered by my chairmen, Lewis Thomas and later Al Stetson. I was assigned adequate space and resources to mount an effective research and teaching program. With the success of our work, however, the need arose for more space and, particularly, for an opportunity to obtain faculty appointments for my younger associates.

To illustrate the problems I faced in 1966 after being a member of the NYU faculty for ten years, I need to describe the type of laboratory organization which, in my experience, is essential for successful biomedical research and for effective training of young scientists. I have found that it takes usually five years of intimate scientific partnership to train a scientist to the point that he or she can carry out an independently funded research program. This is best achieved in a pyramidal system in which starting research fellows are, without abdicating my responsibility or involvement in their projects, often assigned to senior research fellows in the group, who are promoted, eventually, to instructor and eventually assistant professor. The promotion should be coincident with the development of an independent, or semi-independent program with separate funding.

Success in such a system carried with it the necessity to find space and to secure faculty appointments for the senior members of the group, who were desirous to stay on with me. This is precisely the situation that I was confronted with at NYU in 1966. In addition, our work on the genetic control of the immune response required an appreciable increase in resources, particularly animal-breeding facilities. I thought, at first, that these could be provided at NYU and that my younger associates, particularly Ira Green and William Paul, who were to become leading contributors to American immunology, could be given the faculty appointments they clearly deserved. But, unbeknownst to me at that time, the power structure at NYU had radically changed. Lewis Thomas had accepted the position of Dean of the Medical School and had abandoned the powerful chairmanship of the Department of Medicine to Saul Farber. Several events made me understand that Farber was effectively in control of NYU and that I could not work happily and effectively under his leadership.

The chairmanship of anatomy became vacant at NYU, at that time, and I was persuaded by Dean Thomas to be a candidate for the position. He assured me that my appointment was certain. Of course, I had to appear in front of the search committee, but it was unthinkable that I should not be chosen, considering his strong endorsement. He argued, also, that as chairman of anatomy I would have command of considerable laboratory resources and appointing power to solve my problem with my younger associates. Moreover, I would have a seat on the powerful committee of departmental chairpersons. I was foolish to believe the rosy picture he painted. I appeared in front of the search committee to suffer the humiliation of a rejection which I attributed to Farber's influence. I decided that I could not stay at NYU any longer and I began to search actively for a new position in the United States or in Europe. Both Ira Green and Bill Paul assured me that they would accompany me anywhere I would move in the United States.

I spread the news in the immunological community that I was looking for a position and that I was available. I learned of several interesting opportunities. Most were of two types: chairpersons of departments of pathology or directors of laboratories of immunology in research institutes. Two specific positions, however, were very different.

An attractive offer came from London, where the only existing chair in immunology was vacant at St. Mary's. It had been occupied until recently by Rodney Porter who shared the Nobel Prize with Gerry Edelman for their contributions to the structure of immunoglobulins. Porter had recently decided to move to Cambridge. St. Mary's was also famous because it was the school where Fleming had discovered penicillin. Annette and I flew to England to consider the position. I visited the school and was very graciously received by the dean and by Rod Porter. But I was apprehensive that it would be very difficult for me, considering my lack of familiarity with the British system, to build the type of research team I needed to bring my exciting research program on the genetics of the immune response to a successful conclusion.

Moreover, although I have always enjoyed visiting London and had many English friends, I did not think that I could adapt easily to the British style of conducting business. I like speaking my mind in the most direct manner and I do not suffer fools gladly. I am aware that this attitude has earned me a reputation for some ruthlessness. Whereas, since Queen Victoria at least, the British are masters in the art of understatement and avoid mentioning unpleasant truths, no matter how evident they may be. In English scientific circles, everyone speaks so carefully that one must pay particular attention to the hidden meanings of what is being said or not said.

Another position I considered briefly required that we return to Paris. A chair at the University of Paris and a laboratory were offered to me by Jacques Monod, in a new university complex to be built at the Halles au Vin. I did not consider this opportunity seriously since, by then, I had decided that it would be foolish for me to leave the United States. My reasons for leaving a secure place at NYU were the need for better resources to carry out my research program effectively and to support my young associates at a critical stage in the development of our work. It would have been unrealistic for me to go to Europe, where I would have to start everything anew, without Bill Paul and Ira Green. I was therefore limited to consider positions available in the United States.

The job which attracted me most was the chairmanship of the Department of Pathology at Cornell Medical School and New York Hospital which had just become available. That position had all the resources I required and would permit my team to remain in New York where Annette and I enjoyed our life and our apartment. Moreover, Beryl had been accepted at Barnard College and had to remain in New York for at least four years. I was interviewed by the search committee and I very much hoped that I had made a good impression. I was still too naive to realize that I had very little, if any, chance to be offered the Cornell position. Unlike NYU, where the chairmen of the Department of Pathology had been experimental pathologists, since the appointment of Lewis Thomas, the chairmanship at Cornell had been, and would remain, the exclusive reserve of traditional morphological pathologists.*

The other position which attracted me was the chairmanship of the Department of Pathology at Yale Medical School. There I felt I had a real chance. Dean Redlich explained to me that Yale was eager to build a strong experimental Department of Pathology and was very interested in my candidacy. I went to New Haven for an interview with the search committee and I brought along my friend and colleague Robert McCluskey who was an alumnus of Yale University. I found the position attractive and challenging but I felt that, since I would have the responsibility for service pathology at the hospital, I had to have the support of McCluskey, a classically trained pathologist whom I could trust implicitly and who was also a scientist. At the end of our visit, Dean Redlich offered me the chair but added that he was sorry that they could only make one professorial appointment to their Department of Pathology and not two as I required. I therefore declined the position.

I purposely began this story with the jobs that were not offered or with those that were offered but I wisely did not take. I can concentrate now on the two excellent positions which I considered seriously and between which it was difficult to chose: the chairmanship of the Department of Pathology at Tufts Medical School in Boston and the directorship of the Laboratory of Immunology of

*Pathology is the study of the mechanism of disease. However, the earliest pathologists were traditionally concerned with anatomical changes associated with disease, as detected at autopsy or from the study of diseased tissues. These studies were particularly effective when carried out with the microscope on tissue section to establish definitive diagnosis. Physicians with such skills and interests are known as morphological pathologists.

the Institute of Allergy and Infectious Diseases (NIAID) at NIH. I should add that, at that critical time, Lewis Thomas informed me that the chairmanship of pathology at Harvard would soon be vacant and that he was sure Dean Ebert, to whom he had strongly recommended me, would call me any day. Thomas was right after all, except for the timing. I did receive Ebert's call, but two years later, when I was Chief of the Laboratory of Immunology at NIAID. I did not yet appreciate how slowly the wheels turn in the hallowed halls of Harvard.

The main advantage of the Tufts job was that it was in Boston in an academic environment. But from the scientific point of view the position at NIH was exactly what I needed to fulfill my research ambitions. There were no responsibilities other than to mount a high-quality research program in immunology, in any direction I deemed appropriate. The physical and personnel resources were excellent. Moreover, among the assets of the laboratory was the unlimited access to the two strains of inbred guinea pigs, 2 and 13, which were essential for our genetic studies. Dr. John Seal, the scientific director of the intramural program at NIAID who recruited me, was a bright, generous, efficient, and wise administrator; the best of his kind I ever met. His primary concern was not power for himself, but rather the quality of the scientists he could attract and of the programs he could support. He offered me carte blanche in the manner that I would run the Laboratory of Immunology and promised he would help me in the personnel moves I would need to make to reorganize the research program. He offered appointments to Bill Paul and Ira Green at the level I thought appropriate.

I had a long discussion with Annette before making my final decision. Generously, she told me to decide solely on the basis of my research and career opportunities. I knew, however, how much she was attached to New York, her home, her daughter, and her friends, and how much the thought of living in Washington, which she disliked at first sight, as a town without personality and humanity, repelled her, but I did not suspect how depressed she would become when we moved there.

I decided to accept John Seal's offer and to start as Chief of the Laboratory of Immunology in September 1968. Both Ira Green and Bill Paul received concomitant appointments. They were to make their whole careers in that laboratory, which Paul was to head when I left in 1970. He still heads it to this day.

The National Institutes of Health are, in my opinion, one of the most successful achievements of Congress and, particularly, of a few legislators endowed with great vision, steadfastness, and generosity such as Congressman John Fogarthy and Senator Lister Hill, who fought for the NIH budgets year after year. The critical role of the NIH programs in the support of biomedical research throughout the nation is well known.

The NIH has been justly credited with the remarkable discoveries that have introduced scientific medicine and improved the health of the American people and that have ushered in the modern era of biotechnology. But what is much less known and publicized is the outstanding quality of the intramural program at NIH, which equals and outshines that of many prestigious universities. The intramural research programs of the different institutes, which had been initiated and supported by James A. Shannon, the brilliant director of NIH in the 1950s and 1960s, provided scientific leadership of outstanding quality for the nation and exceptional laboratories where many of our best biomedical scientists have been trained. It was to head one of those laboratories in the intramural program of the NIAID that I had been appointed. Moreover, traditionally the NIAID had been the institute primarily responsible for immunological research and its support throughout the nation.

The laboratory I was to head was expected to provide exemplary leadership in this field. The Laboratory of Immunology of the

NIAID had a history of excellence under the able leadership of Jules Freund, who, you may remember, had advised me in 1947 to train with Elvin Kabat. But the laboratory had sometime ago lost its effectiveness and productivity after Freund died. I found that several of the key scientists in that laboratory were, at best, marginally competent with the notable exceptions of Rose Mage, Rose Lieberman, and Ralph Reisfeld who were excellent scientists. My first task was therefore to get rid of unwanted personnel to make space and provide resources for new recruits better adapted to modern research. This goal was rendered particularly difficult by the government's civil-service regulations that provide job security at all levels, almost without regard for quality of performance. It is a credit to the professionalism of many superb scientists and technicians at NIH who perform at the highest level of quality that they must rely only on their conscience and high standards to motivate them. It is not surprising, therefore, that in addition to these outstanding professionals, there was also another group of barely competent individuals, equally protected by the government's system.

I reasoned that, since I lacked effective power over the fate of incompetent personnel, I would use psychology instead. I had noticed that, in order to satisfy the egos and professional standing of members of the laboratory, impressive titles of heads of units or programs had been granted to many individuals, regardless of their accomplishments. I decided to abolish all titles, except my own, as Head of the Laboratory, from one day to the next. As I expected, I soon began receiving letters of resignation from those who could not accept the injury to their self-esteem or their standing brought on by their demotion to the ranks.

Another interesting insight into the working of a government administration was given to me by my efficient and dedicated secretary, Mrs. Doris Day, a lovely Virginia lady with an excellent sense of humor and great wisdom. She said: "Dr. Benacerraf, there is a regulation that I must forward a copy of all your correspondence to Dr. Seal. Please let me know when there is a letter or document that you consider sensitive and I will direct the copy to the wastepaper basket." I answered that I could not imagine that anyone had enough time or curiosity to read my mail, that the copies were probably destined to the permanent files of the institute, and I instructed her to abide by the regulations without exception. Mrs. Day laughed when several months later I received a serious memorandum from John Seal stating: "In a letter that you wrote on such a date, to such a person, you stated that there are no positions available in the Laboratory of Immunology. You cannot make such a statement." I had been naive and Mrs. Day had been right. Big Brother was reading my mail!

The Laboratory of Immunology occupied two wings at one end of the eleventh floor of the Clinical Center building. The rest of the floor was assigned to the Laboratory of Clinical Investigation of NIAID. The director of that laboratory was Sheldon Wolff, a dynamic and skilled clinical researcher who was also an outstanding physician. Undoubtedly, the most significant benefit I have derived from my period at the NIH is my warm and intimate friendship with Sheldon Wolff. Sheldon took me under his wing and showed me the way through the complex structure of NIH and government regulations. We also had many scientific interests in common. His own work had focused on the mechanism of fever, research that would lead to his important discovery that interleukin 1 (IL 1) was the molecule responsible for fever and for other critical inflammatory defense mechanisms. Sheldon and his wife, Lila, were also warm and generous hosts to Annette and me in Bethesda during this difficult period of adjustment.

When I organized our family's move to Washington, D.C., we decided to keep our New York apartment, where Beryl would live while at Barnard, and to return to New York at least every other weekend. I hoped that the knowledge that her home remained undisturbed and that she could return to it regularly would make life in the Washington suburbs less painful for Annette.

The National Institutes of Health are located on a beautiful campus in Bethesda off Wisconsin Avenue, at least forty-five minutes by car from the center of Washington, a provincial city without the glamour and culture of New York, Paris, or London. The improvements which have been made since then to enhance Washington's cultural life—e.g., the Kennedy Center and other projects—were nonexistent in 1968. Life in the Washington area was pretty much a suburban existence, a far cry from the exciting experiences to which Annette had grown accustomed in New York. We bought some new furniture and rented a small apartment in a giant housing project in Chevy Chase. I reasoned that I could drive to work in Bethesda against the flow of traffic and that we would be closer to Washington and particularly Georgetown, but we seldom went to the city during that period except to Washington National Airport to catch a plane to New York.

My life during the next two years would be a strange mixture of exciting professional experiences in the laboratory and of sadness in the evenings at home, with the welcome break of our weekends in New York. I was not prepared for the depression that leaving New York, her home, and Beryl provoked in Annette. She felt an overwhelming sadness which she could not control.

Annette is usually a happy, buoyant, optimistic, and highly sociable person. I relied on her generally upbeat mood to lift my own spirits which, since childhood, have tended to often sag without any apparent reason. However, when Annette is hurt or depressed she clams up in a shell and finds it impossible to communicate with me or to break out of her self-imposed isolation. I have learned from experience that only time, or the correction of the offending situation which provoked her feelings of despair, will improve her condition and restore her normally gay mood. In spite of having agreed that my move to Washington and the NIH was the only logical decision to make, she could not cope with life as she perceived it in Washington.

My attachment to Annette and the intimacy of our lives made it difficult for me to enjoy and take full advantage of the golden opportunity that I was experiencing in the laboratory.

In contrast with our home life, work in the laboratory was going very well. I had dealt with all the technical issues that motivated our move. I had unlimited resources and time to work on an exciting and important problem that I was sure I could solve now. Bill Paul and Ira Green had secure positions and independent laboratories and were still collaborating with me on joint experiments. And last but not least, at NIH we had our choice of brilliant young physicians interested in a scientific career and desirous to work as postdoctoral fellows in our laboratories. Among these were David Katz, Joe Davie, Ethan Shevach, and Alan Rosenthal who, together with Bill Paul and Ira Green, were to make some of the important contributions that would clarify the role of transplantation molecules* in immune recognition.

In the two years I spent at the head of the laboratory I accomplished several of my goals. I reoriented the program of the laboratory toward immunogenetics and cellular immunology, which would be the most exciting fields for the next two decades. I staffed the laboratory with highly competent young scientists, and I initiated the experiments that would eventually solve the puzzle of antigen processing and presentation and the function of transplantation molecules as presenters of processed antigen to T lymphocytes, which I discussed earlier.

---

*Transplantation molecules are proteins expressed on the surface of cells that are endowed with great polymorphism, which means that they differ from individual to individual. Such molecules can, to some extent, be considered as the identity card of the individual bearing them. The immune system is programmed to recognize and identify such molecules as foreign when they belong to another individual which explains why we reject tissue transplant from others than identical twins. These transplantation molecules on our own cells have the additional property of binding foreign antigen peptide fragments for presentation to the immune system to initiate a specific immune response against such foreign antigens.

Looking back, I feel that I made the right decision—not only for myself, but for the field, and for my associates—by coming to NIH and rebuilding the Laboratory of Immunology. If I had only been moved by strictly scientific considerations, I would have stayed many years as head of that laboratory, which I consider a magnificent instrument in an ideal environment for pure research, without the need to worry about grant support, fund raising, curricular reforms, or academic politics, the inescapable concerns of those of us who have chosen to return to academic institutions.

14

---·─►•◄─·---

Move to Harvard Medical School

In the spring of 1969, when I no longer expected it, I received the call from Harvard Medical School (HMS) regarding the position which had been announced long ago by Lewis Thomas. Don Fawcett, chairman of the Department of Anatomy and of the search committee charged with the selection of the next chairperson of the Department of Pathology, called and informed me that I was high on their list of candidates for the position. He urged me to meet with the search committee in Boston.

I discussed it with Annette and agreed to go. I thought that I was not running much of a risk since I did not expect to be offered the position. I went to Boston alone and met with the committee on a Saturday morning in a conference room of the Countway Library. Dean Robert Ebert and Associate Dean Henry Meadow of the Medical School were present with Don Fawcett, as well as several other faculty members. I was asked how I visualized the future of pathology, and how I would organize the department at Harvard.

The special structure of the Department of Pathology at Harvard made the task of chairman challenging but manageable for me. Harvard Medical School is a multi-institutional center with the Medical School proper at the hub and in the periphery are the Harvard-affiliated hospitals, such as the Massachusetts General, the Brigham and Women's, the Beth Israel, Children's, and the Dana-Farber Cancer Institute, each with its own assets, managed by its own board of trustees. The essential feature of this system is the fact that Harvard does not own or manage the clinical facilities it uses for teaching, but controls the faculty appointments, which are jointly made by Harvard and the affiliated hospitals.

The Department of Pathology was comprised of: (1) a large departmental unit in the Medical School proper, concerned with research in experimental pathology and the organization of the teaching program, and (2) several clinical professorial units in the affiliated hospitals. The role of the chairman was primarily the staffing and management of the central department and the selection of the heads of each of the hospital units. It was clear to me that once the chiefs of each of the hospital units had been selected and appointed, the clinical operation of the hospitals was no longer the concern of the chairman. The job was manageable although complex and required the exercise of strong scientific and professional leadership.

I told the search committee that my first priority would be the building of strong professorial research divisions in the central department in the fields where I felt important advances would be made in our understanding of disease mechanisms in the next two decades. These areas were, in my opinion, immunology, vascular diseases such as atherosclerosis, and the mechanism of malignant transformation, i.e., cancer. I felt also that the heads of the hospital departments should belong to a new class of pathologists who could be both clinical morphologists and serious scientists in any of the areas of interest of the department. I had my friend Robert McCluskey in mind, who was then chairman of the department of pathology at State University of New York at Buffalo.

I was stunned when, after a short wait following my presentation, Dr. Ebert came back to me and said: "The search committee has recommended you for the job. Please tell me and Dean Meadow what your requirements would be to accept the position. I suggest that you return to Boston within a month with your wife to finalize the details."

Now I faced a serious problem: I had a critical decision to make which would affect the rest of our lives. When I called Annette in New York, she said: "I never doubted for a minute that you would be offered the chair. Come back quick and let's celebrate."

It was with a very heavy heart that I considered leaving, within a year, the experimental paradise I had created for myself at the NIH and where I had hoped to work for a long time. But I knew that we would all be happier in Boston where Beryl could join us some day to continue her studies after she graduated from Barnard. I knew that Annette would adapt very well to Boston, which was a university town where we could reconstruct a life different from but just as pleasant as our New York experience.

Professionally, I would have new challenges to face and more serious responsibilities to discharge than I had ever envisioned. I was not sure that I was up to the task at the age of fifty. I had always expected that, when I reached fifty years of age, I would decrease my activities rather than take on larger ones. I was fully aware of the magnitude of the task of building a modern Department of Pathology at Harvard as I have outlined it. I knew that I would have to rebuild my research program, to recruit and train new personnel since the closest associates I had trained, Bill Paul and Ira Green, would remain at NIH where they were very happy. But I guess I must be one of those who, after an initial reaction of fear and hesitation, always rises to face a new and exciting challenge. I carefully calculated what resources would be needed to build new laboratories and recruit scientists for the new divisions of the department to be built and prepared a proposal for Dr. Ebert and Mr. Meadow.

⚜ ⚜ ⚜

When I returned with Annette, I visited the various divisions of the department in the affiliated hospitals, and met Morris Karnovsky, who was acting head of the department. Karnovsky was a brilliant experimental pathologist and cell biologist with outstanding contributions to these fields. He was precisely the type of researcher I would plan to recruit to head a division of the department. I assured him that I would support his program wholeheartedly and enlisted his valuable help to rebuild the department.

Two named chairs were available in the central department, the Shattuck Professorship of Pathological Anatomy, which would go to Morris Karnovsky, and the Fabyan Chair of Comparative Pathology, which had been briefly occupied by René Dubos, to which I chose to be appointed. The central department was assigned to occupy the five floors of Building D2, with 22,000 square feet of space, on the impressive Harvard Medical School campus referred to as "the quadrangle." These buildings, which had been erected in the earlier part of this century, were impressive-looking but obsolete and antiquated. Some of the buildings had been renovated but not D Building, which was next in the plan for reconstruction.

In the meantime, I would be given unsatisfactory temporary laboratories. The D Building had two wings, D1 and D2, connected by a link and an amphitheater. The Department of Microbiology was assigned to D1 and pathology to D2. D1 Building was scheduled to be completely gutted and rebuilt. Henry Meadow gave me the option of doing the same thing for D2, at the cost of waiting two years or more for the work to be completed or of simply renovating the D2 laboratories without restructuring the building itself or its support facilities. According to this alternate plan, the laboratories would be ready in 1971 and expected to be functional for ten years only. I was in a hurry to resume my research, and I thought that ten years would be such a long time that I would surely be gone from the scene before 1980. I made the wrong choice. I would still be here in the 1980s and the building would be in a sad state of disrepair. D2 was eventually gutted in the 1990s, for the benefit of the next chairman of pathology and of his programs.

John Seal at NIH was very disappointed when I told him that I would leave in a year for Harvard. I recommended strongly that he consider Bill Paul as chief of the Laboratory of Immunology. I told Seal to feel reassured that all the necessary improvements had been introduced to make the laboratory the outstanding research instrument which I was leaving only reluctantly and for personal reasons. I committed myself to return every three months to NIH, during the first two years after I left, to help Bill Paul with our ongoing research projects and to ensure the growth and development of the laboratory. I am very proud of his performance of the last twenty-five years as head of the laboratory, which he has effectively built into the leader in immunological research I expected.

Though I had decided once again to move, this time it was with Annette's effective help and enthusiasm. We were very fortunate to find an apartment for rent on the top (thirtieth) floor of a residential tower in the Jamaica Plain section of Boston, within five minutes of the medical school. It was a magnificent apartment with a superb view of a lovely pond on one side and of the downtown skyline on the other. In fact, we still live in that very same apartment, which we were able to purchase when the building became a cooperative fifteen years ago. We kept our New York apartment for one more year only, since after Beryl's graduation from college, there was no longer any need for it and we no longer spent our weekends in New York. In 1971, I invested the proceeds from the sale of the apartment and our Shelter Island country house in the purchase of a magnificent waterfront property in Woods Hole on Cap Cod, into which we moved our New York furniture. We fell in love with this handsome estate at first sight. It had a magnificent view of Martha's Vineyard and three hundred feet of private sandy beach, in front of beautiful grounds with tall trees and a comfortable Cape Cod–style home.

I would like to reflect for a few minutes on the reasons that motivated my various moves. The move to New York occurred when I was thirty-six and was clearly determined by my ambition to initiate a serious scientific career. My move to NIH and Washington, at forty-eight years of age, was motivated again by the professional considerations of securing the resources necessary to pursue my immunogenetic studies and to establish my younger associates. My move to Harvard at fifty had much more complex reasons. In a way, it was a retreat from my ambition to build the best research instrument which had brought me to NIH. Instead, it attempted to reconcile and harmonize divergent goals. I cannot deny that I was flattered to be asked to chair a prestigious department in a world-famous university, and that I was tempted and challenged by the magnitude of the task ahead. I was also intrigued by the complex politics of academia in which I would become experienced. But a major consideration was my determination to restore some harmony in our lives. I felt certain that we could resume in Boston the harmonious and happy existence we had in New York.

The major price I would have to pay would be the necessity to rebuild my research operation entirely, and possibly even in different directions. The consequence of having gifted and successful students with whom one has worked on original problems is that one produces effective competitors. This is not only unavoidable but in my opinion beneficial for the field and also for the students and the teacher.

I have always felt that I must never compete with my own students and that they should have the opportunity to develop further, by themselves and for their benefit, the problems we have initiated together. This policy has required that I initiate new areas of investigation or more original approaches to old problems, and therefore that I always keep on my toes intellectually.

15

───►○◄───

I Am a Harvard Professor

Early in the summer of 1970, shortly after I arrived at Harvard Medical School, I attended a faculty meeting chaired by President Nathan Pusey in the Faculty Room of Building A, the administration building. The Faculty Room was an impressive place with high ceilings, antique furniture, and the portraits of previous deans decorating the walls and looking down on the new upstart who had just been appointed to this august faculty. In the official program of my first faculty meeting, the award of an Honorary Master of Arts degree to Dr. Benacerraf was scheduled. Harvard, to maintain the tradition that a Harvard degree is required for an appointment to its professorial faculty, has adopted the policy to award an Honorary M.A. to every new professor who does not hold a Harvard degree. I was to receive what I considered my naturalization papers from the gracious hands of President Pusey. It was a very hot afternoon, and the Faculty Room was neither air-conditioned nor adequately ventilated. I was extremely warm and I sweated profusely in my light summer suit. I was all the more impressed by President Pusey who appeared as cool as a cucumber in his formal dark suit, without a drop of sweat on his brow. I reflected on the many generations of New England up-bringing that would be needed to achieve such an appearance of impassivity and disregard for the discomfort of one's environment.

My first tasks at Harvard were the drafting of applications to the NIH to support my research program and the recruitment of personnel for my laboratory and for the Division of Immunology.

Rather than searching for and appointing seasoned scientists with established records of accomplishments, I always preferred, both in the Department of Pathology and later in my career, to make junior appointments and give a chance to young, recently estab-lished researchers who, one hoped, would grow in their jobs. This policy has several advantages. The initial financial commitments are smaller per individual and more appointments can be made. More-over, I strongly believe in the Darwinian principle of the survival of the fittest, particularly in research. I feel, accordingly, that the tenure principle, which has been appropriately created to ensure the intellectual independence of the faculty, should not be extended to a vested right to scarce university laboratory resources, which should be assigned based on a realistic assessment of the ability to make use of them. Those institutions or departments unmindful of this principle and who focus their recruitment on senior faculty are in serious danger of compromising their own chances to compete in the struggle for survival. It is also essential to provide one's junior faculty with all the support they need in equipment and personnel to give them an adequate chance to compete and move ahead.

It is equally important to be prepared to support junior faculty wholeheartedly with the university administration and to give the best of them a reasonable chance to achieve tenure.

I soon learned that this recipe, which I consider essential to the building of a strong and united department and of a dynamic institute, was in conflict with the university policy at Harvard which required that: (1) Junior faculty must make tenure in eleven years from the time of first appointment or leave the school. (2) All tenure appointments at Harvard must be the result of effective worldwide searches for the best candidate. (3) The result of those searches, which may take years, must be documented formally by comparison letters from experts in the field where the "candidates" considered, whether they are interested or not in the position, are ranked comparatively on the basis of arbitrary criteria. The complex selection process dictates, in addition, that the report of the search committees be scrutinized by special ad hoc committees appointed to insure that the best candidates have indeed been chosen. Lastly, the reports of these two committees must be reviewed and approved by a permanent subcommittee of professors, appointed by the dean, and, finally, approved by the president before a tenure appointment is made.

This system, meant to ensure that the department chairpersons do not attempt to unjustifiably promote inside candidates, does not take many factors into account: (1) Harvard no longer is such a uniquely prestigious institution that everyone asked will abandon their present positions to join our faculty. (2) Recruitment of valuable scientists requires negotiations conducted promptly and decisively if one is not going to be outbid. (3) Lastly, in my opinion, the best results are obtained when a department chairperson with vision and credibility, as was the case of Lewis Thomas at NYU fifteen years earlier, is delegated the responsibility to recruit and build a coherent group of junior researchers with growth potential, the best of whom will reach tenure.

Fortunately for our school, departmental chairpersons at Harvard have learned to define narrowly the job descriptions used in the charge to search committees, in order that they fit closely the attributes of inside candidates they sponsor, to give them a better chance to be selected.

Moreover, the cumbersome and transparent Harvard system is sufficiently known and understood throughout the scientific community that many referees refuse to cooperate in the hypocritical approach of comparing real candidates with imaginary ones. My old friend Salva Luria, a famous Nobel laureate and professor at MIT, confided to me that once he answered the request from a Harvard search committee that he compare two candidates' qualifications that one was taller and thinner than the other.

The only result of these fastidious rules has been a slowing down of the selection process and added work for everyone, since I have seen no evidence that our elaborate system has selected a better faculty than MIT, Stanford, Johns Hopkins, or Rockefeller universities, to mention a few of the leading institutions.

In the last few years, finally, a more realistic approach is beginning to be introduced, albeit reluctantly. In some selected cases, when requested by the sponsoring affiliated institution, the inside candidate can be evaluated honestly by an ad hoc committee and his or her accomplishments assessed in comparison with the field, without the need to invoke nonexistent, unrealistic candidates.

It has been a real education for me to build a department and to staff a research institute which, all agree, have unmistakably the imprint of my long-term plans, with the help—or I should say, the hindrance—of that system.

With the support of Harvard's prestige and the large combined resources of the Harvard-affiliated hospitals, we were fortunate to build a department of pathology ranked among the best in the United States and to recruit and promote, largely from our junior faculty, a competent professorial staff at the Dana-Farber Cancer Institute thereby placing it at the top of its field in immunology, genetics and cell and molecular biology. This could only have been accomplished, however, by exercising judgment and forceful leadership at the management level. In other words, the same principles apply for success in academia as in other more mundane enterprises. The responsibility for initiating choices and planning cannot be abdicated by management to a large committee, and even less, to a combination of committees with varying membership.

This plea for more candor, for more confidence by the university

in the leadership of departmental chairpersons, and for more opportunities for our junior faculty to achieve tenure does not mean that I
wish to abolish or bypass the essential ad hoc committee system of
evaluation of scientific and academic credentials, but that those
committees should exercise their control of academic standards in a
more candid manner. When a position is open to a worldwide search
and there are no inside candidates, it should be so stated and a true
search undertaken. However, if the intent and expectation of the rec-
ommending department is the promotion of an inside candidate to
tenure, the committee should simply consider whether he or she
merits promotion to tenure rank based on the candidate's qualifications and ability to meet the university standards.

These seem to be merely parochial issues that I alone faced in
my administrative position at Harvard, but I feel they give a flavor
of the life and politics in a major university and provide a background for what will follow.

When I started staffing the pathology department in 1970, I
chose to recruit Emil Unanue first, to help me run the Division of
Immunology. I offered him an assistant professorship and provided
him with an ample and well-equipped laboratory, the same size as
my own. I assured him that I would recommend him for promotion
to professor within a few years. Emil was a Cuban physician and
fellow Hispanic, who had fled his native land following Castro's
revolution. I had followed his career with considerable interest. He
had trained as a pathologist. He then worked as postdoctoral fellow
at Mill Hill near London, where he demonstrated the importance
of macrophages in presenting antigen to initiate the immune responses. As an immunologist, Emil Unanue's interest in antigen
processing and renal immunopathology and his general philosophy
of medicine meshed admirably with my own. In addition, we could
converse in Spanish. His training in morphological anatomy would
be most useful to our teaching program. Emil was a bright, ambitious, hands-on scientist, with very demanding standards and a
critical mind. He has been my most valued colleague and a close

friend at Harvard. As I expected, Unanue has had a brilliant career. Within a few years he would be promoted to the distinguished Mallinkrodt Professor of Pathology. Eventually, he was recruited from us to become chairman of the department of Pathology at Washington University in Saint Louis. Soon after, he was elected to the National Academy of Sciences.* The molecular analysis of antigen processing by macrophages and the documentation of the specific interaction between transplantation molecules and processed antigen stand out among his numerous contributions for which he received the Lasker Award† in 1996.

Emil helped me with the organization of the teaching, research, and graduate programs in immunology at Harvard Medical School. He and I shared all these activities equally. As early as 1970 I organized a graduate program in immunology, but I did not want it to be restricted to our department since there were competent immunologists in other departments at the medical school, particularly in clinical departments. I convinced the faculty to approve the first graduate program run by a faculty committee rather than by a department. For this purpose the Committee of Immunology was created under my chairmanship with representation by immunologists from several departments. It has been a very popular program, one that has stood as a model on which other highly successful committee-sponsored graduate programs have been designed in cellular biology and virology.

When I assumed the responsibility for the department in 1970,

---

*The National Academy of Sciences is a private organization established by Congress in 1983 for the furtherance of science. Members are elected yearly in recognition of their scientific contributions. The academy acts as an official advisor to the federal government on matters of science and technology. Membership in the academy is the highest distinction for an American scientist.

†The Lasker Award is a famous prize awarded yearly, in memory of Mary Lasker who established this prize, for the most important recent contribution to medical research. Many Lasker awardees were subsequently recipients of the Nobel Prize.

several of the well-known professors who headed the hospital departments of pathology were close to retirement. They were all classical academic pathologists with a strong background in morbid anatomy. They had made important contributions and built excellent clinical departments.

Sidney Farber was the most outstanding and nationally respected of the group. Besides being an excellent classical pathologist, he had carried out pioneering work in cancer research and had reported the first remission in childhood leukemia following chemotherapy. His interest in cancer therapy and his strong belief that this lethal disease would be cured, particularly in children, motivated him to raise the resources to undertake a major research effort in that direction. Fifty years ago he founded the Children's Cancer Research Foundation and built their cancer research laboratories, supported by the Jimmy Fund, named in memory of the first child who experienced a remission of his leukemia. These laboratories would eventually develop into the Dana-Farber Cancer Institute. Dr. Farber was a very impressive man for whom I had great respect and admiration. I was ill at ease when, very sensitive to protocol, he would address me, his chairman, as "sir" and offer to visit me in my office. I hurriedly paid a formal call on him and offered my help with his program.

The major task I faced my first years as chairman was the recruitment of appropriate replacements for the heads of the various hospital units. Dean Robert Ebert of the Medical School put me in charge of the search committees entrusted with these critical choices for the department. My basic plan was to staff the hospital units with pathologists who were also accomplished scientists with splendid records in the laboratory. I knew that a new generation of basic science-oriented pathologists not only existed but would control the discipline in the future. We were fortunate to be extremely successful in our searches. First, we selected my friend and close associate Robert McCluskey to replace Sidney Farber at Children's Hospital. When the chair of the Massachusetts General

Hospital (MGH) pathology department became vacant I convinced Bob McCluskey to move from Children's to take charge of the MGH department. Soon after that I was able to recruit Ramzi Cotran, a brilliant experimental pathologist who had trained with Morris Karnovsky, to chair the Peter Bent Brigham Hospital pathology department. I was able also to identify an excellent young immunopathologist from the MGH, Harold Dvorack, to head the department at the Beth Israel Hospital. Within a few years, a complete changing of the guard had taken place and a department that had been previously focused primarily on morphology had been completely changed—both on the medical-school campus and in the hospitals—into an experimental department with strong expertise in immunology, immunopathology, inflammation, cell biology, and vascular and renal pathophysiology.

I could now concentrate my efforts on restoring my research program and on my teaching responsibilities. I have always enjoyed teaching, because it provides an opportunity of contact with young, eager minds. I found the interaction with young people enormously refreshing and rejuvenating. I have had the opportunity to reflect on this experience from the perspectives of both a student and a teacher in a similar context. My memories of youth are still very vivid in my mind. I find that the child and adolescent I was are still very much alive in the older man I have become. Both Annette and I welcomed, also, the opportunity for social contacts with the students outside the classroom. For many years I have invited members of the first-year class to my home, in groups, for informal evening discussions over beer, wine, and cake. I was surprised to find that I was one of the rare faculty members to invite students to their homes.

Very little had changed in the style and atmosphere of medical-school teaching from my student days. Medical school is still a four-year experience, with two of those years spent largely in the classroom to give students the scientific basis on which to build their clinical expertise and skills. The second two years are spent in contact with patients in the hospital.

These requirements impose certain rigid limitations of time and material to cover, which make any meaningful change in the curriculum very illusory, in spite of the fact that such curricular changes are introduced all the time, depending upon the passing fad. As an illustration, I shall discuss at some length the recent curricular change at Harvard Medical School (HMS) known as the "New Pathway" about which I am not particularly enthusiastic.

The student body at HMS is divided into three distinct groups with very different personalities and interests. The HMS medical students constitute the largest group, with about 135 students per entering class. There is, in addition, a second separate group of thirty medical students known as HST (Health, Science, and Technology) program students, who are taught according to a separate curriculum by the combined efforts of both HMS and MIT faculties, for the first two years of the curriculum. Lastly, there is an important group of graduate students who belong to a division of the Faculty of Arts and Sciences at HMS called the Division of Medical Sciences. Since these various groups have different interests, different courses are offered in each of these programs. It is a testimony to the large and dedicated HMS faculty that these three efforts can be mounted in parallel, almost without pain.

My personal involvement, once I had made sure that the responsibility for the departmental courses of general pathology and organ pathology had been properly assigned, was the teaching of the courses of immunology, which I shared with Emil Unanue. There were two separate courses with different emphasis, one more general course for the large HMS class of medical students and the other a more scientifically oriented one for both the HST group and the graduate students. Initially, and for several years, I chose to teach the latter course because the HST and graduate students were a more homogeneous group, more oriented toward science than the large HMS class. They were more fun to teach and one could address the issues from a broad historical as well as deeply scientific point of view without fear of losing their interest. The larger HMS class, to which it was later my responsibility to teach immunology for many years, was a much more difficult group to manage. It was too large for intimate contacts, except with a selected number of very interested students. But the greatest difficulty was that the class was very heterogeneous in terms of the student backgrounds and interests. About 10 to 20 percent of the class had a strong basic science interest and might have ambition for academic careers, but the large majority did not care about science and only wanted to hear and learn the essentials which might be of use to them as physicians later. They no longer understood what my New York University students had clearly perceived, i.e., that medicine is not an accumulation of facts or recipes that need to be learned, it is rather the ability to develop mature judgment in the handling of scientific information to permit a judicious decision about a patient. Moreover, since science is always advancing, medical education must strive to teach physicians to keep informed of the latest scientific technologies applicable to their patients. This requires a deep interest in science on their part, as well as a capacity to understand the scientific basis of medicine.

In addition to teaching and administration, my major task at Harvard was to conduct research in immunogenetics and cellular immunology. I needed to rebuild not only a research laboratory from scratch and fund it, but I also had to train a new research team of young immunologists.

A measure of the success and impact of a scientist's laboratory is not only the number and quality of his publications but also the number and the successful careers of the students who have trained with him. The list would be too long if I were to name every student who worked and published with me during these exciting years. However, I am very proud that three of my trainees, William Paul, Lloyd Old, and Stuart Schlossman, were elected to the National Academy of Sciences, and six were made tenured professors at Harvard Medical School.

16

⎯⎯➤•◀⎯⎯

I Am an Immunologist

Immunology was born with Edward Jenner (1749–1823) and Louis Pasteur (1822–1895), who discovered that previous contact with infectious organisms is associated with lasting immunity, which can also be induced by specific immunization. Emil Adolf von Behring (1854–1917) later discovered that immunization caused the production of serum antibodies capable of neutralizing bacterial toxins such as diphtheria or tetanus. Jules Bordet (1870–1961), a Belgium immunologist, then found that serum contained heat labile* molecules, called complement, required for antibodies to be able to kill and coat bacteria to prepare them for phagocytosis.† Antibodies and complement factors are generally referred to

---

*Heat labile biological products are sensitive to heat, usually 56 degrees centigrade.

†Phagocytosis is the uptake of particulate matter by a cell as a defense mechanism. Certain cells, such as macrophages and polymorphonuclear leukocytes, are particularly specialized in phagocytosis.

as the humoral arm of the immune system* and bind to antigens in body fluids. Antibodies are now known to be synthesized by specialized white blood cells, called B lymphocytes and plasma cells.

There is, however, another major component to the immune system, responsible for the reaction with antigens on the surface of living cells, which is referred to as the cellular arm of the immune system. Cellular immunity is mediated by specific T lymphocytes and is responsible for the rejection of foreign-tissue grafts, the killing of cells infected by viruses, the destruction of tumor cells, and the regulation of both the humoral and cellular arms of the immune system. A major component of cellular immunity, the helper T cell, is the target of infection by the HIV virus in AIDS.

The role of the immune system is to identify foreign invaders or cells they have infected and to mark them for destruction by inflammatory white blood cells, killer T cells, macrophages, and the polymorphonuclear leukocytes, while leaving our own healthy cells unharmed. It is a tall order indeed because this specific recognition must be achieved for organisms and molecules with which our own immune system has never had previous contact, and which sometimes differ from our own proteins by very discrete structural (amino acid) changes. It is obvious that the primary role of the immune system requires an enormous capacity for discrimination and specificity.

Major issues for immunologists have therefore been: what is the specificity of antibodies and how is this brought about; also, what is the specificity of T lymphocytes responsible for cellular immunity? In other words, what is recognized by antibodies and by immune T cells as harmful and targeted as an enemy cell and how is it recognized?

---

*Serum antibodies are the humoral arm of the immune system and bind directly with their target antigens on bacteria or viruses, thereby initiating their destruction. In contrast, immune T cells are the cellular arm of the immune system and recognize antigen when presented on the surface of cells in combination with transplantation molecules.

Another major problem has been: what mechanisms can generate antibodies and T cells with such enormous diversity as to encompass the possible recognition of so many different foreign substances? It is to the credit of Niels Jerne and Sir Macfarlane Burnet (1899–1985) to have provided immunologists with the correct theoretical approach, permitting the resolution of this puzzle. Before their groundbreaking contributions, the prevalent hypothesis was that the antigen acted as a template on which the antibody was folded within the cells that made antibodies, a notion incompatible with our knowledge of protein synthesis. Jerne proposed that a large population of antibodies of all the different specificities are synthesized before antigen is injected and that antigen simply selects the antibody molecule to which it binds from the large population available to initiate the immune response. Burnet went one biological step farther with his clonal selection theory. He proposed in 1959 that different clones of lymphocytes are generated (by a genetic mechanism that has been resolved much later by Susumu Tonegawa) and each clone is capable of synthesizing a unique antibody with a distinct specificity. In the course of immunization, the antigen binds specifically to the antibody, which functions as a receptor on the surface of a clonal lymphocyte, stimulates the expansion of that specific clone, and thereby ensures the synthesis of large amounts of that unique antibody. Jerne (1984), Burnet (1960), and later Tonegawa (1987) were all awarded Nobel Prizes in medicine for their respective valuable contributions to solving this important problem.

The major issues as I saw them in 1960, when I became involved with basic immunological research, were: (1) What is the specificity of antibodies and of cellular immunity? Are they the same or different? (2) If they are different (as they were proven to be), how are antigens recognized by immune T lymphocytes? (3) Can the

Burnet clonal theory be proven correct? (4) What are the genetic mechanisms responsible for the recognition of a molecule as a foreign antigen?

The answers to these questions, which have occupied most of my life as a scientist, have depended very much upon accidental observations.

Contrary to the myth promoted by government-granting agencies that science is a predictable activity and that detailed grant applications can be written to support work that will result in foreseeable discoveries, the truth is that most important advances are made accidentally. Science is an unpredictable activity. Successful scientists owe most of their discoveries to circumstances that placed them and their laboratories at a critical point in the development of technical advances, and often to chance observations made in the course of experiments directed toward achieving entirely different goals. I do not mean to belittle the importance of a prepared mind and of an imaginative approach; but in my experience, success has often been the result of chance observations providing leads that I was fortunate to follow. Nature is extremely unpredictable in the manner in which she has provided elegant mechanisms for infinitely complex biological systems.

In the late 1950s Philip Gell, a distinguished English immunologist, joined our department at New York University as a visiting professor. I was delighted to find that we were both interested in a study of the specificity of cellular immunity, as exemplified by tuberculin and contact sensitivity (a form of immunity mediated by T lymphocytes), and in the manner in which the specificity of these reactions might differ from the specificity of serum antibodies. Gell had a vivid imagination, an artist's intuitive temperament, but a systematic mind. Our personalities and even our own idiosyncrasies complemented each other admirably. A collaboration of several years evolved between us.

Antibodies against foreign proteins were known to react specifically with the antigens in their native state. The structures they recognize on antigens are shaped by the folding of their amino acid chains and may be contributed by distant amino acids brought into close proximity by the shape of the antigens.*

We were very surprised, therefore, to discover that the specificity of cellular immune reactions differed markedly from the specificity of the antibodies elicited by the same antigens. Thus, cellular immunity to a foreign protein such as ovalbumin in immune guinea pigs, could be elicited equally well by the denatured, i.e., unfolded, molecule, as by the native protein, whereas antibodies to ovalbumin made by the same animals, did not bind the denatured protein. We concluded that antigen must be chemically processed to generate the determinants recognized by cellular immunity and that this type of immunity is specific for unfolded protein chains in contrast to antibodies, which react with the native unprocessed antigen. This was a most important observation, the first step indeed in a long journey of more than twenty years, which led eventually to our understanding of antigen processing to generate the immunogenic peptide capable of binding specifically to the transplantation molecule to be presented to the specific T cells.

Lacking inbred strains of animals to work with, we were unable, at the time, to appreciate the important contribution of transplantation antigens to the specificity of cellular immunity, which would be recognized in the 1970s by several groups of investigators following the discovery of immune response genes. However, it was only in 1985, twenty-six years after our initial report, that the precise mechanism to generate the specific deter-

---

*A native protein is made of a chain of amino acids, also referred to as a polypeptide chain. This chain is folded permanently to give a distinct and recognizable shape to the molecule. This permanent folding is maintained by chemical interactions between appropriate atoms of the protein such as S-S bonds. When the polypeptide chain of a protein is unfolded, the protein loses its shape and is denatured. T cells are programmed to recognize selected peptide sequences in the unfolded protein presented in combination with transplantation molecules.

minants recognized by T lymphocytes in association with the transplantation molecules had been finally elucidated in our department at Harvard Medical School by my colleague and friend Emil Unanue.

I do not remember precisely what initiated my collaboration with Gerald Edelman in 1961. Edelman is a highly unconventional, ambitious, and brilliant immunologist with a strong background in biochemistry. When I met him he had just been assigned his own laboratory at the Rockefeller University following his discovery of the two-chain structure of antibodies. Antibodies are indeed comprised of two heavy (H) and two light (L) polypeptide chains. This was not known previous to the demonstration by Gerald Edelman and Poulik that simple reduction and alkylation of antibody molecules (a technique which unfolds the molecules and separates them into their component amino acid chains) yielded both types of chains, which could be separated by gel electrophoresis, or column fractionation.

Antibodies produced against any antigens are a broadly heterogeneous population of molecules, with slightly different specificity, that, as predicted by Burnet, are the products of distinct clones. In contrast, myeloma proteins, the product of malignant clones of plasma cells, and more recently monoclonal antibodies, widely available commercially, are homogeneous populations of molecules produced by the progeny of clones of antibody-producing cells. The dissociation of the component chains of serum antibodies, therefore, yields heterogeneous population of H and L chains as analyzed by gel electrophoresis, whereas myeloma proteins, or nowadays monoclonal antibodies, yield homogeneous H and L chains.

To investigate the structural and molecular heterogeneity of serum antibodies, Edelman and I agreed to compare the migration

patterns, in acid urea starch gels, of the dissociated chains of purified antibodies isolated from the sera of individual guinea pigs
immunized with various antigens, in the hope that antibodies of
different specificities would yield distinctive patterns despite their
known heterogeneity. When these experiments were undertaken,
chemists such as Linus Pauling, who had proposed the template
theory of antibody specificity, were already fighting a losing battle
against the proponents of the clonal selection theory. Our experiments demonstrated that guinea pig antibodies of selected specificities yielded distinct, reproducible L-chain patterns in urea
starch gel, and were therefore among the first to indicate that the
biologists were right. Edelman would go on to elucidate the
detailed structure of immunoglobulins for which he was awarded
the Nobel Prize in medicine in 1971.

In addition to his wit, intelligence, and talent as a raconteur—
which made working with him stimulating—Edelman was an accomplished musician and a gifted violinist. To add a social note to
this story, Annette organized one of her musical parties in our
apartment of Manhattan House where the featured piece in the
program was J. S. Bach's concerto for two violins played by Gerry
Edelman and Lloyd Old, with Annette at the harpsichord. Among
our guests that evening were Annette's uncle, Jacques Monod, and
his Pasteur Institute colleague, François Jacob, who had been
Annette's teenage friend before the war.

It has been known for some time that immunity to an antigen
improves considerably with time after immunization. The late-
appearing antibodies display considerably stronger affinity for the
immunizing antigen than the antibodies produced earlier, as if the
immune system could learn how to produce antibodies with greater
binding affinity for the antigen with time. I elucidated the mechanism of this interesting phenomenon with Gregory Siskind, a gifted
postdoctoral fellow, who is today professor of medicine at Cornell
Medical School. We demonstrated that, as the injected immunizing
antigen is metabolized and destroyed progressively, the clones of

B lymphocytes with antibody receptors of highest affinity have a selective advantage in capturing the diminishing pool of antigen and are therefore selectively stimulated to expand and produce antibody. The result is a gradual increase in the average affinity of the antibodies produced and more effective immunity.

In 1965, I was appointed to an "immunology" study section that reviewed and evaluated the merits of grant applications to the National Institutes of Health (NIH) in this field. This study section had twelve members. On the basis of the study section's evaluations and peer reviews, the councils of the various institutes decided whether to fund the individual grants. In the 1980s I also served on the council of the Institute of Allergy and Infectious Diseases. I was, therefore, able to witness and contribute, firsthand, to the operation of the excellent system that makes scientific decisions regarding what work is supported in the United States. With the help of that system some of the best biomedical science has been supported in this country for decades. The important features of the system are: (1) The members of study sections were young midcareer scientists, themselves actively involved in the laboratory and therefore quite knowledgeable of the feasibility and opportunities. In other countries the decision-making process is often controlled by committees of senior scientists, heads of institutes or departments, who are often motivated by political considerations and their need to control younger colleagues. (2) Everybody on a study section worked very hard. We had to review an average of eighty grant applications for each of three meetings a year. I calculated that the equivalent of at least one full month a year was totally dedicated to this effort, since I always made a point of reading every application whether I was assigned to report on it or not.

✤ ✤ ✤

Historically, the genetics of biological phenomena has always proven to be a most productive and definitive approach, since, in the last analysis, every molecular interaction is encoded in the genetic information of all living organisms. This statement has proven to be eminently correct for immunology, the most complex of all biological sciences. In the last two decades, the identification of the genes that encode the critical immunological molecules concerned with specificity and with discrimination between self and foreign antigens, has resolved many puzzling problems that confronted immunologists for decades. This approach provided, also, an insight into the evolutionary process by which nature fostered the development of this most complex and aesthetically satisfying monument, our immune system. In an interview, quoted by *Time* magazine, I compared its beauty, complexity, and majesty to a cathedral.

I was fortunate that chance had given me a clue to the discovery of some of the key genes of the immune system and pointed to a tiny thread which, when followed, would lead to one of the major breakthroughs of this research.

As I related earlier, Edelman and I undertook experiments in 1961 designed to explore the molecular heterogeneity of purified antibodies against defined antigenic determinants. I reasoned at the time that we would stand a better chance to produce homogeneous antibodies if the antigen we used had itself limited structural heterogeneity. Luckily, thanks to the work of Ephraim Katzir at the Weizmann Institute in Israel, synthetic amino acid homopolymers and copolymers were available. Such molecules, if recognized as antigens, would present to the immune system a limited range of determinants to be recognized. By chance, Bernard Levine, a postdoctoral fellow in my laboratory, with a strong interest in penicillin hypersensitivity, had been using conjugates of penicillin and the homopolymer of the amino acid lysine, poly-

L-lysine (PLL).* I decided to immunize random-bred guinea pigs with the conjugate of the dinitrophenyl determinant with PLL (DNP-PLL), in the expectation of stimulating the production of antibodies with markedly restricted heterogeneity. This hope was not realized, but Fred Kantor, Levine, and I observed that only 40 percent of the animals responded to DNP-PLL.

We immediately thought that there might be a genetic basis for this intriguing difference in responsiveness to a relatively simple antigen. Our genetic analysis would have been much easier to perform if inbred strains of guinea pigs (genetically identical animals derived by generations of brother and sister matings) had been available to us at the time. The two inbred strains in existence at the NIH would have been very useful indeed, since strain 2 proved eventually to be a responder and strain 13 a nonresponder to DNP-PLL. We had no choice but to carry out extensive breeding experiments with our responder and nonresponder random-bred guinea pigs. We discovered that the recognition of DNP-PLL as an antigen is controlled by a single dominant autosomal gene in this species.

Parenthetically, as a price for this intriguing result and others that would follow, Bernie Levine and I became extremely allergic to both guinea pig hair and serum.

We extended our finding with DNP-PLL to other synthetic antigens with restricted structural heterogeneity, the L-amino acid copolymers of glutamic acid and either lysine, alanine, or tyrosine, and later to conventional protein antigens, injected at limiting doses to restrict recognition to their most immunogenic determinants. The immune response of guinea pigs to all these synthetic antigens and to limited doses of foreign proteins were

---

*Homopolymers are large molecules constituted by multiple units of the same compound. Thus poly-L-Lysine homopolymer is a polyaminoacid made solely of L-Lysines conjugated to each other by peptide bonds. Whereas copolymers are compounds made of two amino acids randomly conjugated. Thus, compared to proteins made of large numbers of different amino acids, poly-L-Lysine is a very much simpler compound to be recognized by the

under the identical control of a class of genes we called immune response (Ir) genes.

Since it had been established that nonmetabolizable polymers of D-amino acids were not antigenic, we needed to investigate, as a first priority, whether nonresponder animals were unable to metabolize the antigens, which would have made our discovery trivial. Fortunately, cells from responder and nonresponder animals were equally able to metabolize and digest PLL to its component amino acids. Ir genes were, therefore, concerned with an important recognition phenomenon in immunity, but which one?

Fred Kantor, having finished his fellowship, accepted a position at Yale Medical School where he would eventually rise to the rank of professor of medicine. At that time, as I mentioned earlier, two very bright and hard-working postdoctoral fellows, William Paul and Ira Green, joined my laboratory. They would be associated with our developing studies of Ir genes until their successful conclusion. The first experiments which shed some light on the function of these genes were our demonstration that the Ir genes were not concerned with the ability of the animals to produce antibodies. Nonresponder animals could be stimulated to produce antibodies specific for DNP-PLL, but not cellular immunity, if the molecule was presented to the immune system in association with an immunogenic antigen. The Ir gene defect concerned therefore the recognition of foreign molecules as antigens by T lymphocytes and not the capacity to make antibodies. Our guinea pig studies on Ir genes, published initially in 1963, were confirmed in 1965 by McDevitt and Sela in mice with another set of synthetic polypeptide antigens.

I alluded earlier to the discovery by Snell and Gorer of transplantation (histocompatibility) antigens, responsible for the rejection of allografts. The singular property of transplantation antigens is their capacity to exist in many forms (polymorphism); this accounts for our difficulty of finding another individual, at random, from whom we can accept tissue grafts without rejection. The study of transplantation antigens in mice, therefore, required the development by Snell of numerous inbred mouse strains that differ at the H-2 locus, the major genetic locus encoding for the histocompatibility molecules in this species. The transplantation of tissue, such as skin grafts, from a mouse of one of these inbred strains to a mouse of another strain is promptly rejected. The cause of the rejection is the very strong cellular immune response elicited by the transplantation antigens. HLA is the corresponding locus in human encoding for the major transplantation antigens in our species; identity at HLA is necessary to prevent the rejection of allografts.

In an attempt to map the Ir genes in mice, Hugh McDevitt and Chinitz demonstrated the linkage between Ir genes and the H-2 locus in this species. They discovered that tissue typing of an inbred strain of mice for their transplantation molecule allowed them to predict accurately the pattern of immune responsiveness of that strain to a panel of antigens under Ir gene control. We were soon able to confirm the linkage of Ir genes with the genes encoding transplantation molecules in guinea pigs, rats, and monkeys, illustrating the broad applicability of McDevitt's original observation.

For several years, until the final understanding of this complex problem, Hugh McDevitt and I worked in close association, although his laboratory was located at Stanford University and mine at NYU, NIH, and Harvard, successively. Our work was made far easier and more exciting by our policy of communicating our results immediately and discussing the experiments we planned to carry out. For several years Hugh and I worked in near isolation on this complex problem, which did not attract other immunologists until much later. The opportunity to work on an exciting problem without the pressure of many other competing laboratories is a rare privilege in modern biology. These privileged conditions did not last many years, and are an indication that one is either mistaken or far ahead of the pack. I was pleased to share this unique distinction with my friend Hugh. I was, therefore, sad and disappointed when he was not selected by the Nobel Committee to share the prize with me in 1980, for the work to which we had both contributed so closely.

The Ir genes we discovered were eventually shown by us and others to be identical with the transplantation molecules of the major histocompatibility complex.* The individual differences in responsiveness are due to the enormous polymorphism of these genes and the molecules they encode.

I shall deal later with the evolutionary value of this polymorphism for the species and the inevitable consequence of tissue rejection, which is the price we have to pay for this advantage. But let's consider first the process by which transplantation antigens control immune recognition. Studies carried out in the early 1970s by William Paul, Alan Rosenthal, and Ethan Shevach in the laboratory of immunology at NIH with the guinea pig systems I developed, showed that specific T cells recognized foreign antigen only when presented in association with autologous transplantation antigens. Similarly, Rolf Zinkernagel and Peter Doherty made the critical observation that immune cytolytic T cells† capable of killing virally infected cells were restricted to kill virally infected target cells bearing identical transplantation antigens. Zinkernagel and Doherty were awarded the Nobel Prize in medicine in 1995 for this contribution.

It is appropriate now to recall some of the work I carried out with Philip Gell as well as later experiments of Emil Unanue which led to the conclusion that protein antigens need to be denatured, unfolded, and sometimes digested by proteolytic enzymes of macrophages to initiate cellular immune responses. Putting these two observations

---

*Histocompatibility complex is a complex of genes coding for histocompatibility molecules (transplantation antigens) such as HLA in humans and H-2 in mice.

  †Cytolytic T cells are specific T cells capable of recognizing and interacting with target cells bearing surface antigens for which they are specific. Following this interaction the cytolytic T cell lyses and kills the target cell with which it interacts. This is one of the most efficient defense mechanisms of the immune system responsible for the rejection of grafts and the killing of virally infected cells against which the cytolytic T cells are specific.

together, i.e., (1) the need to process antigen to produce the immunogenic denatured fragment and (2) the role of transplantation molecules, in association with antigen, for the immune T lymphocytes to
recognize foreign antigens, I formulated a hypothesis in 1978 which
stated that: Transplantation molecules expressed on the surface of
cells are capable of specific interaction with processed peptide fragments of the processed antigen and serve therefore as specific peptide presenters to the T lymphocytes of the immune system. The
transplantation molecule of a responder is able to interact specifically with and present the processed antigen, whereas the transplantation molecule of a nonresponder is not. In other words, the transplantation molecule through its specific interaction with the
processed antigenic peptide acts as a selective mechanism for immunity. T lymphocytes with receptors capable of recognizing foreign
antigens complexed with autologous transplantation molecules are
selected in the thymus during differentiation of the immune system.
This system is the basis whereby we are capable of distinguishing
self from any foreign molecules. Those cells with receptors specific
for self-peptides presented in the context of autologous histocompatibility molecules are deleted during differentiation in the thymus.

     With the help of my Macintosh, I present a graphic represen-
tation of that 1978 hypothesis.

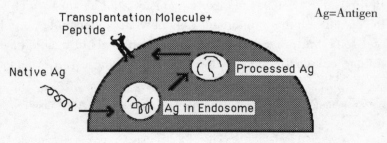

Section of a macrophage in the process of taking up a foreign antigen, then
breaking it down, enzymatically, into peptide fragments in order for these peptides to bind to transplantation molecules on the surface of the macrophage for
presentation to specific T lymphocyte, to initiate the immune response.

With my younger associate Kenneth Rock we obtained biological evidence in favor of this hypothesis in 1983. And it was Emil Unanue, who, as I stated earlier, provided the final proof in 1985, demonstrating that transplantation molecules from responder animals bind specifically processed peptides whereas those from nonresponder animals do not. Just about that time, two colleagues at Harvard, Jack Strominger, whose laboratory was primarily concerned with the structure of transplantation antigens, and Don Wiley, a brilliant crystallographer,* obtained an X-ray crystallographic picture of a human transplantation antigen which clearly demonstrated a groove for peptide interaction. Moreover, in one of the preparations, a peptide could be seen bound in the groove. I was very excited by that picture which illustrated a process that I had worked twenty-five years to elucidate.

What is the biological significance of the phenomenon I have been discussing and spent over two decades in studying? Why has Nature evolved such a complicated mechanism to initiate recognition by the immune system? The response to this question resides in the enormous polymorphism of transplantation molecules, the most variable of our body components.

The requirement for antigen to be specifically bound to these polymorphic molecules to initiate immune responses has as a consequence: that different individuals vary in their capacity to mount immune responses to a given foreign antigen, depending upon what transplantation molecules they express on their cells. Moreover, there will always be individuals in the species capable of mounting immune responses to foreign viral antigens, irrespective of the ability of such organisms to mutate their antigens. Therefore, there will always be some individuals capable of assuring the survival of the species.

---

*Crystallography is the technique which permits the visualization of the structure of complex molecules such as proteins once they are crystallized by X-ray analysis.

The unfortunate consequences of this enormous evolutionary advantage are: the uniqueness of each of us, immunologically, which prevents transplantation of tissues and assures the rejection of allografts, and the fact that some individuals will be at greater risk than others of immunological disease based on their HLA type, the major human histocompatibility complex.

From our initial experiments of 1959 and 1963, more than twenty years were to elapse before the picture I have drawn of the genetic, cellular, and molecular events that initiated the specific immune response could emerge. During those years, which encompass much of my scientific life, I very much enjoyed my involvement in the step-by-step resolution of this central problem of immunological science, which occurred as my career evolved through three laboratories, NYU, NIH, and finally Harvard. This central theme was also the source of many of the valuable personal relationships I built with students and colleagues.

17

Move to Dana-Farber
Cancer Institute

Late in 1979, I received a call from Lewis Thomas, who had been president of the Memorial Sloan Kettering Institute for several years. Lewis told me of his intention to step down as president, and said that he had recommended to the board of trustees that I be recruited to replace him. He graciously added that he felt that I was the most qualified for the job and that he would feel secure if he could leave the fate of the institution in my hands.

I was not prepared or inclined to consider moving from Harvard to another position. A few years earlier I had declined the request of Benno Schmidt that I consider the directorship of the National Cancer Institute at NIH. However, my long friendship and the debt of gratitude I felt toward Lewis Thomas, who gave me my first chance for a career in research and academic medicine, required that I carefully weigh his request. I thanked him for this new expression of confidence, on top of the many he had given me in the past, and told him that I would give the matter the serious consideration it deserved.

Within a few days I received a formal offer from Laurence Rockefeller and Benno Schmidt to come to New York to discuss with them how I would manage the most prestigious and richly endowed institution specializing in cancer research and treatment in the United States. I answered that I was honored to be considered. I further added that I was not sure that I was interested, but that I would be delighted to come and speak with members of the board of trustees about my plans for the Memorial Sloan Kettering, if I were to manage it. We agreed on a date for my visit, and Laurence Rockefeller insisted on sending his private plane, which he felt would be more convenient than the shuttle, which I always use to fly to New York. I suspect that he also wanted to impress me with the seriousness with which my candidacy was being considered. It was my first and last experience with the luxury of private jet travel. The jet, with two young pilots in civilian clothes, took Annette and me to the Marine Air Terminal, where Laurence Rockefeller's limousine was waiting to take us to my meeting at the Memorial Sloan Kettering.

I was enormously impressed with the seriousness and dedication of Laurence Rockefeller, Benno Schmidt, and their associates to their institution and to solving the cancer problem. I was easily convinced of their commitment and of their ability to provide the necessary resources for the job. If these were the only requirements for success, there is no doubt that the major scientific and technological advances needed to cure this dreaded disease would have soon been made, and indeed made in their magnificent institution. I had been familiar with the Sloan Kettering Laboratories for a long time, since I had worked with my friend and student, Lloyd Old, many years ago in their Rye laboratories and closely followed his remarkable career at Memorial Sloan Kettering.

I told the trustees that the cure for cancer, as is the case also for other diseases, would depend on: the continued generation of new scientific information in genetics, cell biology, and immunology related to the malignant process, and in the technological application of this scientific information to the development of new therapeutic approaches. I was, and still am convinced, that the present forms of therapy, such as surgery, radiotherapy, and combined chemotherapy, which have provided cures for many cancer patients and prolonged the lives of others, have reached their maximum effectiveness in eradicating cancer cells. Progress with these methods is reaching its limits, which cannot be technologically improved upon, unless a totally new approach is attempted. The strength of the Memorial Hospital resided in its superb cadre of surgeons who, because of their competence, had an enormous influence in determining hospital policy and priorities, a matter of concern to me, if I took responsibility for the institution.

After our meeting I was offered the presidency of the Memorial Sloan Kettering Institute, a very generous salary, and the use of any suitable apartment in Manhattan that I would find appropriate for our needs. The ball was in my court. I had to reexamine once more my career goals and family commitments in relation to this new opportunity and challenge presented to me.

The main attraction of this offer was that it came at a stage of my life when my creativity in the laboratory, while still considerable, was unlikely to generate new avenues of research of the quality and excitement of our previous contributions on antigen processing, Ir genes, and the role of transplantation molecules in immunity. Moreover, I noticed also that the willingness to involve oneself in new approaches, at the moving edge of emerging technologies, which is essential for imaginative research, becomes an increasing problem with age. To compensate, I had become more interested in the application of scientific knowledge to the development of new therapeutic approaches to disease. I have become increasingly aware that the explosive increase in knowledge and understanding of basic immunological phenomena, with the development of monoclonal antibodies, the discoveries and characterization of numerous lymphokines, have opened new windows of opportunity for technology transfer. This is the critical process, whereby the fruits of basic research are brought more rapidly to the patient's bedside and often commercialized in the process. I was convinced that cancer was one of the major remaining unresolved medical problems the solutions to which immunological science could make a tangible contribution. As president of a cancer institute, I reasoned that I would be better equipped to effectively conduct such programs, or to facilitate the emergence of new technological applications.

I had to face several issues: (1) Was the Memorial Sloan Kettering the right instrument to achieve my purposes? (2) If it was the appropriate institution, was the price I would have to pay in energy and time to manage such a large and complex institute, which included a major hospital, not only too high, but also of such magnitude as to be self-defeating, by not leaving me free enough to think creatively? (3) Did I want to cut myself off suddenly from basic immunological research to which I had dedicated most of my professional life? (4) Would Annette and I have the courage and the desire to move from Boston and resettle again in New York?

New York had changed very much since we left, and we ourselves had aged. Annette is fond of saying that New York is a wonderful town for the young because of the excitement and opportunity it offers. Maybe we were too old for New York?

For several weeks I weighed these issues. I decided first that my laboratory and scientific activity were too important for me and had to be preserved at all cost. Moreover, I also enjoyed and depended very much upon the academic atmosphere of a prestigious university such as Harvard because of the interactions with gifted colleagues and highly motivated students it provided. I would miss this essential aspect of my life at the Memorial Sloan Kettering, unless I could also have a faculty appointment at Rockefeller University. I inquired about such a possibility and was told by Joshua Lederberg, the president of Rockefeller University, that I could not be guaranteed an appointment. Such a statement, together with my realization that the hospital administrative responsibilities of the Memorial Sloan Kettering position would be heavy and complex, cooled my enthusiasm considerably.

I was very touched also by the efforts which had been made by my friends and the administration at Harvard to keep me. In the remarkably short span of a couple of weeks, this university, which is characterized, as I have experienced before, by moving slowly and deliberately, created a new position to satisfy my needs, and offered it to me. In January 1980, at the suggestion of President Derek Bok, Richard Smith and Morton Zuckerman, on behalf of the trustees of the Sidney Farber Cancer Institute, offered me the presidency of their institution, a position which would permit me to remain simultaneously chairman of the Department of Pathology and to continue to direct my laboratory in D2 Building. I accepted gratefully their offer and declined Laurence Rockefeller's.

It is rare in one's life that the opportunity presents itself to achieve what amounts to conflicting aims, with the minimal amount of sacrifice. The offer at Harvard satisfied my ambition for an opportunity to become more involved in technology transfer of science and medicine where I was eager to make a contribution. I would achieve this goal without disturbing my life and that of my family. Furthermore, I entertained, then, the illusion that I could undertake this new effort without slowing down my laboratory.

Time would prove that I was incorrect on this last point. Although I was careful to organize my schedule from the start to preserve a full half-day undisturbed for my laboratory, and to manage the institute's affairs in the afternoon hours only, I neglected to consider that the weight of responsibilities would by itself cause an appreciable slowing down of my scientific productivity. An analysis of my publication record, which I made years later, reflects a sharp drop that coincides with my assumption of the responsibility for the institute. I do not mention this to express regrets, which I do not harbor, but rather to acknowledge that nothing worthwhile is achieved without paying a price. The remarkable success of the institute, to which I contributed, was well worth this sacrifice.

A few months later, that same fateful year 1980, when I reached my sixtieth birthday, I would be awarded the Nobel Prize. I have never asked myself seriously what would have been my decision if the order of the events had been reversed.

The Sidney Farber Cancer Institute was the offspring of the Children's Cancer Research Foundation which had been created by Sidney Farber fifty years ago to carry out cancer research and treat children with cancer, with the support of the Jimmy Fund, a fund-raising instrument of the foundation named after the first child successfully treated for leukemia with chemotherapy by Sidney Farber. Later on, the goals of the foundation were enlarged to support the treatment of adult patients also. With the generous help of benefactor Charles Dana and a construction grant from the National Cancer Institute, a major building was erected to provide both laboratory facilities as well as clinics and beds to mount a major clinical research effort in cancer, and an agreement of affiliation with Harvard University was negotiated and signed by the board of trustees. Sidney Farber recruited Emil Frei as Professor of Medicine and Physician-in-Chief, a very able clinical researcher, to head the adult oncology program. When Sidney Farber died, the foundation was renamed the Sidney Farber Cancer Institute to perpetuate the memory of its founder, and Emil Frei was appointed director and entrusted with the administration of the institute. During my tenure as president, to honor Charles Dana and the Dana Foundation, which, in addition to their earlier gift, had contributed an additional ten million dollars in a matching grant to the institute endowment, the name was changed again to Dana-Farber Cancer Institute (DFCI).

The major problems I encountered at the DFCI were organizational, administrative, and financial. In addition, there were serious issues of recruitment and expansion to consider. Moreover, I had to deal with all the common problems every hospital experienced then, i.e., (1) The shortage of nurses; (2) the efficiency of operations; (3) the chronic deficits in the patient-care divisions and the difficulties in third-party reimbursement, particularly for patients treated on research protocols; (4) the concern to maintain an adequate census of occupied beds, and a sufficiently low average hospital length of stay. These problems were rendered more manageable by the small size of the DFCI's patient population, much smaller than that of Memorial Hospital.

I found that, before my appointment as president, the chairman of the board and other trustees had been heavily involved in the direct administration of the DFCI through a variety of trustee committees. I felt that this arrangement was highly unsatisfactory on several grounds. You cannot mix fiduciary responsibilities with direct administrative control. Moreover, in the absence of a strong administrative direction at the helm, the staff was generally not competent and the records grossly incomplete. I made it clear from the start that I had the responsibility for management and that I intended to exercise it personally. I would report regularly, on a monthly basis, to an executive committee of selected trustees on the basis of an agenda that I would prepare and control.

In addition to the administrative problems I had to correct, the weak financial condition in which I found the DFCI was a major concern for the banker in me. The annual operations, even after fund raising, had been running a deficit for several successive years. In addition, although our debt was negligible compared to our fixed assets, the endowment of DFCI, at the level of 1.5 million dollars, was practically nonexistent, considering the size of our operation and our contingent liabilities. These deficiencies were in desperate need of attention if the institution was to grow in effectiveness and importance. As far as the yearly deficit was concerned, I felt that prudent management and an increase in annual fund raising would rapidly correct this persistent problem.

Within two years we were running annual surpluses. The problem of the endowment required that I convince the board of trustees to have the courage to initiate a major fund-raising campaign, the first ever attempted by this young institution. The size of this undertaking was a matter of serious debate. I proposed, initially, a campaign to raise thirty-eight million dollars in five years. I felt that this figure was high but attainable. I had a hard time convincing the trustees that this goal was well within our reach. I told them that we had no choice, because the institute needed the endowment funds urgently, and these were always the most difficult funds to raise. I pledged the gift of my Nobel Prize to initiate the campaign. The project was approved subject to the results of a feasibility study on the ability of DFCI to successfully raise the large sums I recommended, in the short span of five years. A consultant was contracted to make such a study. The consultants came from New York and interviewed members of our staff and our faculty as well as a large number of our trustees. Then they asked my advice on how to draft their final report which, of course, was highly optimistic of our fund-raising capabilities.

As it turned out, we managed to raise in excess of sixty million dollars. This gratifying result very much depended on the considerable help we received, at the start of the campaign, from a most generous matching grant of ten million dollars from our dear friend and faithful supporter, the Dana Foundation. I am deeply grateful to David Mahoney, the chairman of the board, and Bob Kreidler, the president of the Dana Foundation, for their dedicated support at a critical time. After this successful campaign, the DFCI was at last, and has remained, in sound financial condition.

The recruitment of gifted scientists and clinicians, a high priority in my general plan for the DFCI, was very successful. We identified and attracted a large group of extremely competent young immunologists, cell and molecular biologists, pharmacologists, and virologists. As a consequence of this welcomed expansion, several new divisions were created: one focused on human retroviruses, concerned with the study of the infectious agent of AIDS, HIV, and also of related cancer viruses, headed initially by William Haseltine, a well-known investigator in the field; and a division of cellular and molecular biology, staffed with six capable young scientists, concerned with the mechanisms of growth and differentiation of normal and malignant cells.

Our immunology programs were also greatly expanded, making the institute a world leader in this field. Within a short time after these excellent appointments, our space was at a premium. Since there were no indications that substantial new space would be vacated through the retirement of scientists, because of the relative young age of our staff, the construction of new laboratories was necessary to relieve the crowding and to provide room for the natural expansion of existing programs. The project of erecting a new structure with 120,000 square feet of space, at a cost of about thirty million dollars, was approved by our board of trustees, whose members agreed to raise one-third of the sum and to borrow the rest through the sale of tax-free obligations.

Annette brought to my attention an excellent autobiography by Irene Mayer Selznick, in which the author wrote about her father, Louis B. Mayer. It was a most interesting book, very well-written, which gave an exciting picture of one of the giants of that fascinating Hollywood film era. Irene Selznick, as the daughter and wife of highly successful Hollywood producers, had been a privileged spectator to much of what had happened there. Her sensitivity, talent, and sense of humor captivated me as I read her book. Annette pointed out that Louis B. Mayer had been severely ill with leukemia, in California, and had insisted on consulting Sidney Farber, who came to see him in Hollywood. Apparently, Sidney Farber had helped Louis B. Mayer cope with the dreadful disease which eventually killed him. Both Mayer and his daughter Irene were deeply grateful to Farber, as she wrote in her book. Annette

thought that Mrs. Selznick might want to honor the memory of her
father by helping the institute, founded by Sidney Farber, eradi-
cate the disease which had killed her father. Mrs. Selznick, when
contacted, was most generous and through the Louis B. Mayer
Foundation offered to donate five million dollars to support the
construction of the Louis B. Mayer Laboratories of the DFCI, a
magnificent set of new facilities which have, at least temporarily,
solved the space problem at DFCI. A splendid photograph of Louis
B. Mayer graces the entrance of the laboratories.

One of my goals in accepting the added responsibility of the DFCI
was my interest in being involved in the transfer of scientific
information into new technologies to treat patients. I thought that
cancer presented an appropriate target to attempt to facilitate the
development of new therapeutic approaches based on sound scientific data. Moreover, I felt immunology presented an excellent
opportunity to carry out my plan. Two major projects, in which I
have had a favorable influence, illustrate this approach.

When I arrived at the DFCI, bone-marrow transplantation was
already an acceptable treatment for leukemias. The very high
doses of radiation or chemotherapy which have to be delivered to
destroy the malignant cells have a lethal effect on the patient's
highly susceptible bone marrow and particularly on the cells
responsible for the continuous generation of both our white and
red blood cells. In an attempt to treat this major complication
resulting from irradiation and chemotherapy, leukemic patients
are injected with histocompatible bone marrow from healthy
donors who share the same histocompatibility antigens at HLA,
the major locus, to restore their destroyed bone marrows. The
problem is that histocompatible donors are difficult to find and
often restricted to selected siblings. Moreover, even in cases of
matched histocompatible bone marrow, graft versus host reactions

occur whereby the healthy and mature adult lymphocytes in the donor's graft react against minor antigens of the host.

To obviate some of these problems, a team from the Division of Tumor Immunology at the DFCI, led by Lee Nadler, under the direction of Stuart Schlossman, has introduced the use of autologous bone-marrow transplantation in the treatment of malignant lymphoma, a tumor of B lymphocytes. According to their experimental protocol, bone marrow from selected patients with malignant lymphomas in remission is removed and stored frozen. The patients are then treated with a sufficient dose of chemotherapy or radiotherapy to destroy their malignant lymphocytes. Such a dose also destroys their own bone marrow. The patients are then injected with their own previously preserved bone marrow, after it is treated in the laboratory with a specific antibody (generated in the Division of Tumor Immunology of DFCI) and complement to kill all the malignant lymphoma cells and effectively clean the bone marrow of cancer cells. The patients are then able to reconstitute a normal lymphoid and hematological system from their own bone-marrow cells that were reinjected free of tumor cells. An impressive fraction of patients treated according to this protocol have remained disease-free after many years without the need of further therapy. I established a number of beds at the DFCI solely dedicated to this form of bone-marrow treatment, which is accepted and carried out in other institutions as well.

18

Partnership with Industry

The National Institutes of Health (NIH) and other government agencies that support basic biomedical research aimed at improving the health of all Americans and curing specific diseases, such as cancer or AIDS, have generously encouraged the grantee institutions to protect their discoveries by patents issued in the name of, and for the benefit of the institution where the discoveries have been made. The rationale behind this policy is to produce a strong incentive for the rapid evolution of basic scientific information into patentable discoveries beneficial to the population, and to provide the nonprofit academic institutions with important and legitimate sources of revenue that will facilitate their mission and diminish their eventual dependency on the federal government for research funds. The ownership of such patents permits, in turn, the licensing of corporations for the exploitation of the inventions.

To take the analysis of the situation one step further, successful academic institutions, whose scientists have accumulated much valuable basic research information over the years, can, with the support of public funds, present outside investors and technological innovators with golden opportunities for partnerships on specific research programs designed to accelerate the development of patentable discoveries in defined fields of common interest. This aim is achieved through the drafting of research agreements whereby the outside investors (or corporations) contract to support the research programs of selected laboratories and scientists in the institution, in defined fields, for the benefit of acquiring the licensing rights for the inventions made with their support.

The advantages for the institution are also readily apparent. Beyond finding additional support for its scientists and laboratories, the mission of the institution is also greatly benefited. For-profit corporations often can provide, in addition to research support, the valuable expertise of their technical staffs which, in contrast to the scientific staffs of academic institutions, are more apt to tackle and solve technological problems arising from the development of new therapeutic agents.

There is no question that these partnerships between academia and industry have become increasingly important and successful, as evidenced by the growing volume of such agreements (more than 15 percent of DFCI's research funds were generated by such agreements), and by the discoveries they generate, which would not have been forthcoming as rapidly otherwise.

The growth of these programs in a relatively short time have brought to light a series of problems that academic institutions have to consider seriously to permit the partnership between academia and industry to grow without compromising the traditional climate of openness and concern for the public good, which is the traditional heritage of nonprofit academic institutions. Academic institutions have had, therefore, to develop new departments of technology transfer, with both strong legal and technical representation. But, more important, they have had to redefine several times, the rules concerning conflict of interest of the faculty involved in the research covered by these research agreements.

Indeed, governed by the profit motive, the commercial partners of the universities and institutes have sought to stimulate the interest of academic scientists and attract them to their projects, with legitimate consulting agreements, and also, on a more questionable level, stock participations or stock options. It is a matter of record that, with the surge of interest and discoveries in biotechnology in the last two decades, numerous scientists have become wealthy through the ownership of stock in companies for whom they consulted or from whom their laboratories obtained support. As a former banker and businessman, well aware of the benefits of a market economy, I would be the last one to hold that it is wrong or inappropriate for a scientist or a physician to aspire to create an estate for his family, if the opportunity presents itself. But, I feel strongly that this unavoidable by-product of the necessary and beneficial partnership of academia and industry must not corrupt academia.

To prevent the degradation of academic tradition and standards, I believe that certain very strict rules must be respected. (1) Those in academe who have the decision-making power concerning these commercial agreements (which means those with administrative responsibility) must never be tainted by ownership of stock or stock options and can never function as consultants. (During my tenure as chairman of the Department of Pathology or president of the DFCI, I never had a consulting agreement or benefited from any stock ownership in corporations with which we were involved. (2) The involvement of faculty with industry must be closely monitored and the object of immediate thorough reports and annual reviews by specialized personnel responsible to the highest authority of the institution. (3) The interaction of faculty with industry must be the object of strict rules such as limited stock participation (not to exceed 3 or 5 percent), in a corporation that supports the laboratory, and no involvement as officers or directors. (4) Particularly, in the case of therapeutic agents, which are to undergo clinical trials, the principal investigator in charge of these clinical trials must never be a consultant or have stock involvement with the company providing the materials or supporting the trials, through direct ownership or option. I feel that these rules will ensure that the integrity of the academic institution will be preserved without compromising legitimate goals of the partnership with industry.

19

The Nobel Prize

I have never been guilty of overconfidence, but rather plagued with self-doubts most of my life. From the days of medical school throughout my research and academic career I have been astonished at my success. It took many decades to develop enough self-confidence to accept the reality of success. Annette, who had to boost my sagging morale on many occasions, would probably say that this systemic lack of self-confidence—one of the personality traits inherited by my successful daughter—has made me difficult to live with. But my chronic insecurity had a major advantage in that I never took anything for granted in the laboratory. I was the first to doubt and harshly criticize any discovery we would make, until it could be established by several independent methods and possibly verified through independent testing by different observers. I have also directed equally toward others this hypercritical attitude toward myself, which may have given me the reputation of being too demanding or motivated by impossibly high standards. On the whole, in spite of the emotional cost, I feel that this

220

attitude has been beneficial to me and also to my associates. They have argued that my ambition for them has helped them set higher standards for themselves.

By the time I was in my fifties I began to accumulate some of the tangible rewards of success. I was elected to the American Academy of Arts and Sciences (Cambridge, Massachusetts) in 1972, and to the National Academy of Sciences in 1973. I served as president of the American Association of Immunologists from 1973 to 1974, as president of the Federation of American Societies for Experimental Biology from 1974 to 1975, and as president of the International Union of Immunological Societies from 1980 to 1983. I was awarded the Nobel Prize in medicine in 1980, and the National Medal of Science by President George Bush at the White House in 1990.

The Nobel Prize, for historical reasons and because it is simultaneously awarded in several important disciplines, has taken on a prestigious importance that far outweighs the merits of the individual recipients. It is, indeed, unreasonable to expect that in such broad disciplines as physics or physiology and medicine only one or at most three scientists per year (since the prize cannot be shared by more than three recipients) are worthy of the distinguished honor. In addition to merit, therefore, chance plays a major role in determining who, in a particular year, is selected to receive these most coveted awards.

I do not mean to imply that Nobel laureates are not deserving of the award. On the contrary, much of the prestige surrounding the Nobel Prizes stems from the historically high quality of the laureates and the painstakingly careful choice of the Swedish selection committees. My contention is, rather, that since there exist other candidates equally deserving of receiving this unique yearly distinction (besides the ones chosen), there is a strong element of uncertainty in any year's selection. To give a few examples of this contention, I believe that René Dubos's contribution to the development of antibiotics should have been rewarded just as much as Waksman or Fleming, Chain and Florey, and that Avery deserved the prize for his discovery of the genetic transforming properties of nucleic acids.

In addition, because the awards in medicine rotate very much among areas and subspecialties, many years may elapse before an important discovery is recognized or rewarded. This situation favors those scientists endowed with longevity. Peyton Rous was eighty-seven years of age when he was awarded the prize, in 1966, for his discovery of tumor-inducing viruses—several decades earlier. Peter Gorer was not so fortunate. He discovered transplantation antigens with George Snell in 1948, but had died of lung cancer when George Snell received the Nobel Prize in 1980, jointly with me and Jean Dausset, when the important function of these polymorphic molecules in the immune response was finally recognized.

It is because I, and many other recipients of the award, whose lives have been transformed by it, are very much aware of these considerations and of the important part played by chance in being the chosen ones, that we are so uneasy about the enormous attention and honor that is forever attached to everyone who has been chosen by the Nobel Committee. Many of my colleagues, I have noted, have felt uncomfortable about talking or writing in their memoirs of circumstances related to the award. In my case, I have chosen to write about it for several reasons. First, since this is a story of my life, there is no question that the award of the prize was a most important event for me, well worth the time to set down my thoughts. Second, I promised to be candid when I began this story, and not writing about it would obviously be interpreted as deliberately evasive.

In spite of the very small statistical chance of being considered for, let alone being awarded, a Nobel Prize, every budding scientist has a secret yearning for this maximal award, just like West Point cadets fantasize about becoming a five-star general. Realistically, very few scientists have had the good fortune of having made contributions, which open new insights, or which have enough practical importance, for them to be seriously considered for the award. When I discovered immune response genes, and particularly when their relationship with transplantation molecules were brought to light, I had the hope that if I was industrious and fortunate to bring this important problem to its final conclusion, I had a chance to be at least considered. I knew that many friends had nominated me, but I had no real expectation of being selected.

To give the floor to an independent observer, I have relied on Annette for an accurate if not unbiased account of this exciting period. I shall transcribe verbatim what she wrote, at the time, of the manner we received the news of the award and of the subsequent events of that day. Annette's story was originally published by her in French in *L'Odyssée d'une Jeune Fille de Bonne Famille* (The Odyssey of a Well-Bred Young Lady), Editions Tirésias, Paris.

Annette's Story

October 10, 1980, is a day I shall always remember, a day of total madness and great happiness.

That morning, Baruj was completely unsuspecting. However, I had read in the press that the Nobel Prize in medicine was going to be announced that day and, as we had learned that Baruj had been proposed for the prize by several nominators, I thought he had a chance.

I had always heard that people who win the Nobel Prize usually learn the news early in the morning by a phone call from the press. So, putting this all together, I had trouble sleeping the night before and sat up in bed at 5 A.M. next to Baruj who, having wakened early, was calmly reading a book.

At 6:45 the phone rang. I jumped and picked up the phone. An unknown voice asked to speak to Professor Benacerraf. I handed the phone to Baruj and immediately realized what it was about. It was the United Press asking Baruj if he was aware that he had won the Nobel Prize. I have never seen Baruj so stunned. He could hardly believe it and kept repeating: "Are you sure? Are you sure?" As soon as he hung up, both phone lines started to ring nonstop and we were hardly dressed when our living room began to fill with reporters, photographers, and well-wishers.

We finally managed to leave the apartment and soon arrived at Harvard Medical School, followed by all the reporters and photographers. There, we found Baruj's office full of students, fellows, colleagues, and friends already assembled; a magnum of champagne was popped opened and everybody wanted to hug Baruj. The dean of the medical school arrived and we learned that this was the first Nobel Prize to be awarded to a member of the Harvard Medical School since 1954 when the prize was awarded to John F. Enders, Thomas H. Weller, and Frederick C. Robbins for their contribution to the growth of the poliomyelitis virus in tissue culture.

It was a mad scene and the phones were ringing off the hooks. One of the calls was from our friends from the Karolinska Institute. It was the first contact we had with Stockholm that day and I was happy to have the news confirmed. Indeed, shortly afterward, the official telegram arrived from the Nobel Committee and everybody wanted to see it and touch it. Another call came from the Richmond, Virginia, newspapers. They were very excited because Baruj was the first Medical College of Virginia graduate to receive such an honor.

Then, it was announced that a press conference had been organized in the big amphitheater of Harvard Medical School for the members of the press who were all clamoring to interview Baruj. So, we all trouped down there. The amphitheater was packed and Baruj was greeted with a standing ovation. He answered all the questions on his work, his feelings, his future plans, insisting that he was hoping that his new status will give him more power to help the young scientists obtain funds for their work.

After lunch, we all went to the Dana-Farber Cancer Institute, where a huge party had been organized in Baruj's honor. Hundreds and hundreds of people were there, all wanting to shake his hand. Champagne bottles were popping and there were speeches. It was all very touching.

Then, we went back to the medical school, where a faculty meeting had been scheduled. It was announced that the meeting had been changed to a party for Baruj. When we arrived, Baruj was again greeted with a standing ovation and toasted with champagne! We were all getting a little giddy with all the champagne!

When we got home, followed by several of Baruj's students, whom we had invited for dinner, we watched the news on television where Baruj appeared on all the channels. During dinner, the phones kept ringing and we all took turns answering. One call was from the president of Venezuela, who wanted to congratulate Baruj and tell him how proud the Venezuelan people were, since he was the first Venezuelan to receive the prize. Another call came from the local public television channel asking if Baruj would appear for an interview on the 10 P.M. news that evening. Everybody agreed that he should go, so we all piled into three cars.

While Baruj was being interviewed, we sat behind the glass partition with the show's producers. It was fascinating to watch how a news broadcast is monitored and directed.

Finally, we went home totally spent and exhausted, but still excited. We had a hard time going to sleep.

The next four weeks were intensely occupied in writing the paper I would deliver in Stockholm and in answering the hundreds of letters and telegrams I received. It is a remarkable experience how the award of the Nobel Prize brings back, in the span of a couple of weeks, warm messages from all the accumulated friends, family, and associates of a lifetime. I have carefully saved them in albums and files as a set of my most precious documents. I occasionally reread them, particularly when I feel somewhat discouraged by the unavoidable difficulties of my complex jobs.

The most touching aspect of my experience had to be the letters from friends and acquaintances I had not forgotten but had not heard from since childhood or adolescence. There was a sweet letter from a young lady whom I had met and was romantically involved with, when I was fifteen, in one of the summer resorts where I was with my parents. Then there were letters from others I was associated with during my life as a banker at the Colonial Trust Company. There were, in addition to official messages from presidents Jimmy Carter and Valery Giscard D'Estaing, Senator Edward M. Kennedy, and other officials, letters that were particularly meaningful to me from Lewis Thomas, who gave me my first faculty appointment at NYU, and Robert Ebert, who recruited me to Harvard's Medical School. Other precious letters, which I will always treasure, came from colleagues and students I worked with over the years.

To prepare for the Stockholm week of ceremonies which culminate with the official award of the prize in the Concert Hall from the gracious hands of the king of Sweden, Annette was busy purchasing evening dresses, and I rented the first set of tails I would wear since my wedding day.

Beryl and her husband, Peter, accompanied Annette and me to Stockholm. But there was also another most important person on this trip, my grandson, Oliver, Beryl's unborn child. He is very proud today to have been an unseeing participant at the ceremonies. We went by Paris to have an opportunity to visit with my eighty-three-year-old mother, who by then was very much incapacitated with osteoporosis and unable to travel.

I shall not describe in detail our week in Stockholm since the numerous accounts have been given of the elaborate pageantry with which the Swedes organize their major annual event. I would like to simply mention that we were for that week treated like royalty, with every wish attended to in extraordinary luxury at the beautiful Grand Hotel, where the other laureates and their families were housed. The only other time that I felt so extraordinarily pampered was several years ago when we were guests of President François Mitterand at the Elysée Palace in Paris. President Mitterand and Elie Wiesel organized a conference of Nobel laureates of all disciplines in Paris to discuss important world issues. It was an extraordinary feeling to be whisked through the streets of crowded Paris with motorcycle escorts. I must also admit that the ceremonial routine and the fare at the Elysée Palace far surpass those at the White House, where I was fortunate to have been invited by presidents Carter, Reagan, and Bush successively.

When we returned to Boston I was the same man as before, none the wiser. Yet, now, as far as the world was concerned, I belonged to an elite club of men and women who are expected to utter wise and authoritative statements on all subjects no matter how far removed from their individual expertise or past experience. I always felt awkward and uneasy to have gained that extraordinary level of public credibility which accompanies the award of a Nobel Prize. I promised myself never to use it except in speaking publicly about science and medicine, where my true expertise resides.

One aspect of the prize I have enjoyed very much is that it has finally given me some of the independence from authority, or at least the illusion of independence, that I have searched for all my life. Probably because I had very strong and stern parents, I have always been apprehensive of authority in all its forms; and, as I mentioned earlier, I sought to climb the academic administrative ladder far more in the illusory attempt to escape authority than to gather power or influence. I have enjoyed the mantel of protection which I feel the prize has given me.

The large number of Nobel Prizes in medicine that were awarded to American scientists in the past fifty-three years (seventy-two out of one hundred twenty, or 60 percent) reflects the success of American biomedical research supported by the National Institutes of Health (NIH). The impressive list of American laureates and the description of their discoveries, which spanned the fields of biochemistry, genetics, molecular biology, cell biology, microbiology, immunology, and neurobiology, can be found in Table 1.

I have also singled out below some of the contributions that have had considerable impact on our health and daily life. In 1952, Selman A. Waksman was recognized for his discovery of streptomycin, the first antibiotic active against the tubercule bacillus. In 1954, John F. Enders, Thomas H. Weller, and Frederick C. Robbins received the prize for their discovery of the technique to culture the poliomyelitis virus in the laboratory. This technique would soon permit the development of antipolio vaccines by Jonas Salk and by Albert Sabin and abolished the tragic poliomyelitis epidemics, one of which I was sad to witness in Richmond as a medical student. In 1956, André F. Cournand and Dickinson W. Richards Jr. were singled out for their introduction of the technique of cardiac catherization, which revolutionized the practice of cardiology. In 1962, James D. Watson was awarded the prize with Francis H. Crick and Maurice H. F. Wilkins for their discovery of the structure of nucleic acid, the genetic material. This finding opened the whole field of genetics to chemical analysis. Soon after, in 1968, Marshall W. Nirenberg, H. Gobind Khorana, and Robert W. Holley were recognized for their discovery of the genetic code. In 1979, the Nobel Prize was awarded to Allan M. Cormack for his discovery, with Geoffrey N. Hounsfield, of computer-assisted tomography, which is routinely used in our hospitals. More recently, in 1990, E. Donnall Thomas and Joseph E. Murray received their prize for discoveries that permit the transplantation of organs and cells.

TABLE I

American Nobel Laureates in
Medicine and Physiology, 1942–1992

Year	Name	Discoveries
1943	E. A. Doisy	The chemical nature of vitamin K
1944*	J. Erlanger H. S. Gasser	The highly differentiated functions of single nerve fibers
1946*	H. J. Muller	The production of mutations by way of X-ray irradiation
1947	C. F. Cori G. T. Cori	The course of the catalytic conversion of glycogen
1950	E. C. Kendall P. S. Hench	The structure and biological effects of the hormones of the adrenal cortex
1952*	S. A. Waksman	Streptomycin, the first antibiotic active against tuberculosis
1953	F. A. Lipmann	Co-enzyme A, its importance for intermediary metabolism
1954*	J. F. Enders T. H. Weller F. C. Robbins	The ability of poliomyelitis viruses to grow in culture
1956	A. F. Cournand D. F. Richards	The catherization and pathological changes in the circulatory system
1958*	G. W. Beadle E. L. Tatum	Genes regulating definite chemical events

*Years when the Nobel Prize was awarded solely to American scientists. In the other years the prize was shared with foreign scientists.

	J. Lederberg	Genetic recombination and the organization of the genetic material of bacteria
1959*	S. Ochoa A. Kornberg	The mechanism of biological synthesis of ribonucleic and dexoxiribonucleic acid
1961*	G. Von Bekesy	Physical mechanism of stimulation within the cochlea
1962	J. Watson	The molecular structure of nucleic acids and its significance in information transfer in living material
1964	K. Bloch	Mechanism of regulation of the cholesterol and fatty-acid metabolism
1966*	P. Rous	Tumor-inducing viruses
	C. B. Higgins	Hormonal treatment of prostatic cancer
1967	H. Hartline G. Wald	Primary physiological and chemical processes in the eye
1968*	R. W. Holley H. G. Khorana M. W. Nirenberg	The interpretation of the genetic code and its function in protein synthesis
1969*	M. Delbruck A. D. Hershey S. Luria	The replication mechanism and the genetic structure of viruses
1970	J. Axelrod	The humoral transmitters in the nerve terminals and their storage, release, and inactivation mechanisms
1971*	E. W. Sutherland Jr.	The mechanism of action of hormones

1972	G. M. Edelman	The chemical structure of antibodies
1974	C. De Duve G. Palade	The structural and functional organization of the cell
1975*	D. Baltimore R. Dulbecco H. M. Temin	The interaction between tumor viruses and the genetic material of the cell
1976*	B. Blumberg D. C. Gajdusek	New mechanisms for the origin and dissemination of infectious diseases
1977*	R. Guillemin A. V. Schally	Peptide hormone production in the brain
	R. Yalow	Radioimmunoassay of peptide hormones
1978	D. Nathans H. O. Smith	Restriction enzymes and their application to the problems of immunogenetics
1979	A. Cormack	Development of computer-assisted tomography
1980	B. Benacerraf G. D. Snell	Genetically determined structures on the cell surface that regulate immunological reactions
1981*	R. W. Sperry	Functional specialization of the cerebral hemispheres
	D. H. Hubel T. N. Wiesel	Information processing in the visual system
1983*	B. McClintock	Mobile genetic elements
1985*	M. S. Brown J. L. Goldstein	The regulation of cholesterol metabolism

1986	S. Cohen	Growth factors
1987*	S. Tonegawa	Genetic principle for generation of antibody diversity
1988	G. B. Elion G. W. Hitchings	Important principles for drug treatment
1989*	J. M. Bishop H. E. Varmus	Cellular origin of retroviral oncogenes
1990*	J. E. Murray D. E. Thomas	Organ and cell transplantation in the treatment of human disease
1992*	E. H. Fisher E. G. Krebs	Molecular pathways of signal transduction
1993	P. A. Sharp	Discovery of split genes
1994*	A. G. Gilman M. Rodbell	Discovery of G proteins and their role in signal transduction in cells
1995	L. B. Lewis E. F. Wieschaus	Discovery concerning the genetic control of early genetic development

The accomplishments of American biomedical science are illustrated by the fact that, in the span of fifty-three years reviewed in this table, American scientists received the prize in forty of these years, and in twenty-two of the forty years the prize was only awarded to American scientists. Moreover, in the last two decades, the prize was awarded to Americans 80 percent of the time.

All these advances, which have depended solely upon the benefits of basic and clinical research, can be surpassed by what the future will bring if we are wise to continue on the same enlightened program of government support of biomedical research that has produced so many discoveries at relatively low cost and has placed our country in a position of leadership in medical research and in biotechnology.

20

⟫•⟪

How to Be a Father

It is never easy to raise children since it is impossible to avoid the inevitable generational conflicts that are, in fact, essential to the maturation of the personality of the developing child. It seems that in addition to my own daughter, Beryl, I have successfully raised a whole crew of scientific offspring who have expressed toward me the complex feelings and reactions of children toward their fathers. But the natural experience, as a parent, is the education of one's own biological children.

Beryl was not an easy child to raise, and life was probably difficult for her also. Some children, particularly in our era when so many marriages are not harmonious or end in divorce, complain to their parents that their lives were rendered miserable by the conflicts they witnessed. In spite of all the attention we gave her, Beryl objected that Annette and I loved each other too much and that it was difficult for her to find a place for herself in our relationship. From an early age her supreme ambition had been to get between us in our bed in the morning. She suffered also from being an only child, with no siblings with whom she could plot revenge against her parents for her real or imaginary grievances. Moreover, she was brought up in two cultures, French and American, and was always bilingual. She valued her dual heritage and was never affected by the herd instinct, so powerful in American education, which pushes children to conform and belong to groups their own age. Another heavy cross to bear, I realized, was our successful example and the very high standards that I have always maintained and expected, almost unconsciously, of everyone around me. An instance of this behavior, for which she still reproaches me to this day as having marked her life, was my reaction when she came to me proudly with a grade of 99 on a major test at school. Instead of congratulating her, as she had the right to expect, I asked: "Why not a hundred?"

Beryl was a very pretty girl and is now a beautiful young woman. But she has a strange mixture of femininity and ruthlessness. She inherited personality traits from both of her grandmothers. From my mother's character I recognize the toughness and obstinacy with which she approaches any challenge, as well as a lack of innate tenderness. From Annette's mother, of whom Beryl was very fond, she has inherited a love for dramatics and a gift to survive emotional mäelstroms that would readily sink others. Another trait of Beryl's character which has been an enormous asset to her is her ability to focus her attention on the present to the exclusion of the past and preferably without much attention to the anxiety-provoking future. I have learned from watching her as a teenager that girls have an enormous resilience and a striking capacity to rebound from emotional despair, in no time, in comparison to boys of the same age. I often felt sorry for the numerous boys who were crushed when she would tire of them.

In spite of our age and sex difference and markedly divergent personalities, I am proud that, in addition to the mutual respect and deep affection which has always bound us together, I have achieved the essential in our relationship, which is a capacity and even a necessity for total communication. In an era when the greatest family tragedy is the inability of the generations to talk to each other and to make the effort to understand each other honestly, there has always been an absolute trust between Beryl and me, based on mutual respect for our dignity. She always felt comfortable talking to me freely about her thoughts or problems. The result of this ability to communicate is that Beryl would go through the 1968 student revolution at Columbia and four years of college, when many of her friends were on one drug or another, without the desire or the need to try any of these experiences. I convinced her when she was very young of the dangers of this path. She avoided the drug culture around her and was not affected by peer pressure.

In college at Barnard, where her mother had graduated, Beryl planned to satisfy the premedical requirements in case she decided to go to medical school, a career that I did not particularly encourage. Her main interest at Columbia was the radio broadcasting station WKCR. She was very gifted as a speaker and as producer of musical shows. Otherwise she found that the curriculum presented little challenge and breezed through it painlessly and brilliantly. She graduated cum laude in 1971.

Following graduation Beryl was not certain what long-term career plans to make. She had spent several summers in Italy, which she loved, and she spoke the language fluently. She decided to spend a year in Rome working as a technician in Rita Levi-Montalcini's Institute, until she felt clearer about her career plans. I was delighted with her decision to spend a year abroad by herself. She loved her year in Rome, where we visited her in the summer. She finally decided to apply to medical school at the last minute. With the help of my friend the Nobel laureate André Cournand, she had an interview at Columbia's College of Physicians and Surgeons, where she did better than her father, since she was admitted to start classes in September 1972.

In 1973 she transferred for her sophomore year to Harvard Medical School to be closer to us. Beryl graduated from Harvard

Medical School in 1976 and was elected to the Alpha Omega Alpha honorary fraternity, just like her father had been.

When Beryl was in her last year of medical school she met Peter Libby, a young medical resident at the Peter Bent Brigham Hospital. They soon became very much attracted to each other. Beryl introduced Peter to us and indicated their desire to get married. We both liked Peter and welcomed him into our family. They were married on November 22, 1975, in a small ceremony followed by a reception at the Harvard Club.

Beryl is tough, resilient, and ambitious. She is also extraordinarily skilled with her hands and has an unusual knowledge of anatomy. In her clinical years she had performed very well in her surgical rotations and wanted to become a surgeon. She applied to both Massachusetts General Hospital and the Peter Bent Brigham Hospital for a surgical internship. She preferred the MGH, where she had trained as a student and where she felt most comfortable. She was shattered by her interview with the Selection Committee. She had not been aware of, or rather had been blind to, the degree of sexual prejudice in surgery. Surgery is probably the last bastion of macho prejudice in medicine. The whole training program of surgeons, through five grueling years, with little sleep, constant stress, at the limit of physical endurance, is probably designed more to test the stamina of the men than to teach surgical approaches and techniques. By the time Beryl entered the operating room as a surgical intern, very few women had preceded her in that capacity at Harvard-affiliated hospitals. The great majority of females in the operating room were nurses. As an intern, Beryl had to change into surgical garb in the nurses' room, since the doctors' lounge was reserved for males only.

During her interview at the MGH, in addition to appropriate questions on surgery, Beryl was asked typically sexist questions such as: (1) Does your husband accept and approve of your career as a surgeon? (2) Will your marriage and marital duties interfere with your surgical training? (3) Do you plan to have children? (4)

Do you think you can have children and nevertheless be a successful surgeon? To break the reader's suspense, she was not selected by the MGH and complained to me bitterly of having been treated unfairly. In the meantime, she was accepted by Professor Francis Moore as one of the first female interns, and the first married one, at the Peter Bent Brigham Hospital.

I remember that I was furious at the manner in which my daughter had been treated at the MGH. I wrote an official letter of protest to Charles Saunders, the MGH director, complaining of the clear case of sex discrimination experienced by Beryl at the hands of the Surgical Selection Committee. I did not ask that her case be reopened but rather that an investigation be conducted on the manner in which she had been interviewed. After several weeks, I received a reply from Saunders admitting that the sexist questions had been asked, but as if this was a mitigating circumstance, only at the end of the interview and that Beryl's answers had been judged excellent! The last episode of this story is a report I received later that the procedures of the Surgical Selection Committees had been completely revised following my protest.

Beryl greatly enjoyed her year of surgical internship at the Brigham. Like her maternal grandmother, Suzanne, she liked drama. Being also impatient in nature, she was inclined toward the surgical approach to problems, which is drastic and immediate. During her internship year she truly tested the limits of her endurance. As she often would say: "After I survived a year of surgical internship, nothing appeared to me to be too taxing or impossible to tackle." After that stressful year, however, following my advice, she revised her career plans and switched to radiology, a specialty more compatible with her ambition to raise a family. With her great ability to visualize, Beryl was just as gifted in radiology as she was in surgery. After several uneventful years of training as a resident at the MGH (radiologists did not have sexist policies), she specialized in ultrasonography and today enjoys a thriving private practice in Boston and a successful academic career as a clinical professor of obstetrics and gynecology and a professor of radiology at Harvard Medical School and at the MGH.

For several years Harvard medical students have had the unusual distinction of being lectured by me, on immunology during their first year, and by Beryl, on the detection of fetal abnormalities by obstetrical ultrasound, in their second year.

My grandson, Oliver, who had traveled in utero to Stockholm, was born at the Brigham and Women's Hospital on April 24, 1981. Because of Beryl's and Peter's busy careers, and due to the fact that we lived in the same apartment house, Annette and I have looked after Oliver and then his sister, Brigitte, even more closely than we had after our own daughter. Brigitte was born on April 24, 1982, a year to the day after the birth of Oliver.

We have been very fortunate that both of our grandchildren are bright, intelligent, sensitive, considerate, and, on the whole, remarkably reasonable. Both, during Annette's and Beryl's pregnancies, I have been extremely anxious of the possibility of an abnormal child. There is, in my opinion, no greater sadness one can experience than to bring into the world a genetically impaired infant—a risk which, although small, is nevertheless appreciable, as I was able to verify regularly when I discussed her obstetrical ultrasound practice with Beryl. Largely because of modern advances in ultrasound, coupled with amniocentesis, parents increasingly have the option of terminating pregnancies that would result in genetically abnormal newborns. I am very proud of Beryl who, in a remarkable study she made of the ultrasonic abnormalities associated with Down's syndrome, has critically contributed to the early diagnosis of this condition in utero.

In late December of 1981 an urgent call from Marcel, my mother's chauffeur, informed me that Mother had had an unfortunate fall in her apartment in Paris and had broken her fragile hip. She had been immediately hospitalized and was scheduled to be operated on the next morning, when a pin was to be inserted in her femur.

I informed my brother, Paul, at Princeton and made immediate arrangements to leave for Paris with Annette by the first available flight the next day. On December 24, an early morning phone call from Marcel told me that Mother had just died. She had suffered a massive embolism following her operation and never recovered. I would not be able to kiss her one last time. My only remaining task was to bury my mother.

We met Paul in Paris and arranged for the religious burial ceremony to be performed at the Pantin Cemetery, where Mother was buried next to my father. As I said earlier, I had not returned to this cemetery previously, so painful for me had been the loss of my father. I grieved and cried at my mother's grave as her coffin was brought, and the rabbi said Kaddish, the traditional Jewish prayer for the dead, on that sad, bleak, December day.

There is no question that no matter how old one is, the loss of a parent is perceived as an irremediable event, which turns so many pages and cuts so many valuable ties in one's life course. The next few days in Paris were painfully occupied with the disposal of Mother's possessions and of her apartment. Paul and I agreed that there was little that we wanted to preserve. Mother's furniture was given to friends and relatives who wanted it. I was pleased that some of her best jewels, which she treasured, went to Beryl, whom, I knew, she loved and who shared with my mother her taste for jewelry. We made arrangements to sell both her apartment and the house in Montmorency, which had been allowed to deteriorate badly. I refused to ever return to it. To this day, I try to avoid going by the Avenue Paul Doumer where she lived and where I visited her so often. I have never returned to the Pantin Cemetery.

21

━━━◦◦◦◦━━━

Training Medical Scientists

Many of the scientific advances in medicine of the last fifty years were made by physicians who were also trained scientists. The motivation for physicians to go into science, which existed both in my generation and in that of my daughter, is rapidly vanishing in our medical schools. We stand to lose the scientific personnel best qualified to pick up the flag of biomedical research and direct themselves to the newer and more important discoveries waiting to be made. There are now considerably fewer doctors who apply for research fellowships.

The reasons for this decrease in interest in a research career on the part of physicians are numerous. Some are strictly financial. By the time they obtain their degree many physicians are deeply in debt and the earning prospects of scientists are hard to reconcile with their financial obligations. Moreover, the government support of research is much less assured than it was ten or fifteen years ago. Far fewer than 20 percent of approved grants are funded by the NIH nowadays, based on current budgetary support. This situation is not expected to improve in the foreseeable future. But most important, the interest of medical students in science and research has decreased considerably compared to what it was two decades ago. I fear that part of the reason for this disaffection for science is the responsibility of the faculty of the medical schools, which have not stood up for the necessity of a solid scientific education as part of the preparation for medicine.

The technological complexity of modern biology and medicine requires that groups of scientists with varying degrees of experience and often with expertise in different disciplines work together as teams. This consideration, together with the fact that creative science is conducted predominantly in academic institutions, has had as a consequence that successful and creative scientists have an important concomitant role to fulfill as teachers and trainers of new generations of young researchers.

Of all my activities I think that I have most enjoyed my role as a teacher in the laboratory where I collaborated with younger eager minds who shared with me that obsessive curiosity which is the central motivation of science. In a period of nearly forty years, starting in 1956 at NYU, eighty-one postdoctoral fellows and graduate students have worked closely with me in the laboratory. Many continued to collaborate with me in junior faculty positions for several additional years after their training period.

It is of interest that thirty-six of the eighty-one, i.e., 44 percent, came from abroad; my laboratory was very much an international enterprise with many foreign workers. To illustrate this interesting point, I have presented an analysis of the seventeen countries of origin of my young associates in Table 2.

TABLE 2

Countries of Origin of Foreign Postdoctoral Fellows

Australia	1	Hong Kong	1
Argentina	1	Hungary	1
Brazil	2	Israel	2
Canada	3	Japan	2
Czechoslovakia	1	Spain	1
England	1	Switzerland	5
France	10	Taiwan	1
Germany	2	Venezuela	1
Holland	1	TOTAL	36

The largest group came of course from France and Switzerland.

Another most interesting statistic concerns the academic degrees of my trainees; fifty-one of the eighty-one, or 63 percent, had earned medical degrees. These observations illustrate the strong interest of young physicians in basic immunological research during this golden era. It is very sad that, as I have mentioned, fewer doctors are entering our laboratories nowadays as a consequence of economic conditions in science and medicine and of the reduced emphasis on science in medical education. The decreased interest of M.D.s in biomedical research careers is also very alarming because they are indeed the best qualified to continue to make the scientific contributions that have transformed the practice of medicine in the last few decades.

One last issue that should be addressed in a discussion about training is the recent highly publicized problem of scientific fraud. Since biomedical research has become increasingly a team effort, which demands a considerable degree of trust, the real possibility exists that some individual, with a flawed or dishonest character, may manipulate the data for a variety of personal motives. It is unreasonable to expect that the scientific establishment would be spared from its share of dishonest people.

Being well aware of this possibility and of the acute embarrassment, to say the least, that the publication of unreproducible data* would cause, I have always had a rule in my laboratory that all significant observations must be independently confirmed by a different team or selected individuals, before being considered for publication. Moreover, I am naturally distrustful of Nature and of its willingness to reveal its secrets, and even more cautious not to be led astray by any prejudiced ideas I might hold. Lastly, the rules of complete openness in our laboratory are an added guarantee against anyone being able to conceal, at least for very long, a tendency to fudge or even to overinterpret their data. We have been very fortunate that no unpleasant incident, involving the fabrication or manipulation of data, has occurred in our laboratories, over the many decades of operation. But I have been familiar with a sufficient number of such cases and I have attempted to assess the real damage that these highly publicized cases have brought.

Historically, there have been two types of cases of scientific fraud: The first type concerns the fabrication of data about critical experiments on important problems, the publication of which are certain to cause considerable attention and ephemeral notoriety. The very nature of science, as a self-verifying and correcting process, ensures that such experiments will be rapidly repeated and disproved. The short-lived notoriety achieved in these unfortunate cases will be inevitably followed by shame and contempt.

It seems evident that those individuals who perform such obviously detectable frauds must be seriously disturbed and in some cases may even harbor the secret wish for self-destruction. The actual damage that these types of misdeeds cause to science is

---

*Published observations that cannot be repeated in other laboratories.

negligible since the false information is rapidly corrected. If one were to assess the actual added cost to the scientific community in terms of the experiments that had to be carried out in other laboratories to correct the error, I would venture to consider it minimal, since all laboratories are constantly engaged in confirming each other's findings, as part and parcel of the process of carrying out their own research programs. This expenditure of time and money can be considered to be the cost of the insurance policy that science must pay to check its results. The real damage caused by this type of scientific fraud is to the image of science in the public eye.

As was the case for medicine or religion, science had an untarnished reputation for the public as a selfless activity performed for the highest motives by dedicated and scrupulously honest individuals. The press, which is frequently interested in sensationalism, has overblown the importance of these unfortunate incidents, which, in all the cases where I have had firsthand knowledge, were simply the result of a sick mind, poorly supervised, and should in no way be construed to be representative of the scientific process. In one particular case, the perpetrator would introduce himself at night into the laboratory to add chemicals to the test tubes of other workers, carrying out related experiments, in order to manipulate their data to make it fit his fraudulent results! In another famous case, a student, carrying out faked experiments on contact sensitivity in guinea pigs, would also come back at night to paint the skin of the animals with irritants designed to mimic the inflammation of real contact sensitivity.

I have asked myself, What could explain such aberrant behavior, which is bound to be discovered sooner than later? I have concluded that the motives may be complex: in some cases the student may be trying to manipulate data to provide his supervisor with a result which would confirm his mentor's hypothesis and, oblivious of the future, expect an immediate reward for it. In other cases, the data could have been manipulated to obtain a result which was once really observed but could not be reproduced.

To combat this dangerous temptation, it is very important to instill absolute respect for data in experimenters and particularly the notion that the experimenter is never entitled to select the data he likes and suppress the rest. An experimenter must be an unbiased observer expected to record the data for posterity impartially.

It is, indeed, very difficult to preserve oneself and one's laboratory against such aberrant behavior except by being very suspicious of any personality traits that might reveal potential risk. The damage caused by these incidents to the reputation of institutions and individuals is very serious and has motivated a renewed increase in vigilance and awareness in our laboratories.

The other type of malfeasance concerns the fabrication of unimportant data in order to generate added publications, to foster one's career, or to increase one's bibliography. Such falsifications are much more difficult to detect, because the data concerned are generally of such marginal interest, if any, that they seldom have much chance to be reproduced or challenged.

There have been several publicized cases of this type of fraud and many more which were handled without media involvement. These frauds were discovered when a close inspection of the data and of the record indicated discrepancies, which could not be explained. No matter how talented and diligent fakers are, they are never able to duplicate absolutely the natural events so as to withstand the critical inspection of an experienced observer.

The damage of this type of fraud to science is even more minimal than the former, since the fake information is of no significance in the first place. The best method to deal with these annoying nuisances is to diminish the incentive for such dishonest behavior by restricting to a minimum the publication of unimportant data by scientific journals and by giving less weight to the number of publications as compared to their quality when considering the qualification of an individual for faculty promotion or appointment. It is indeed impossible to detect and remove the dishonest ones and the misfits from the start, but we can make their fraud less profitable and more difficult to carry out, thereby preserving the image of science.

Before closing the discussion of this important issue, I want to repeat that in my opinion, the consequences of these highly publicized cases have been negligible for the operation of biomedical research, but regrettably very damaging for its reputation and for the climate of suspicion it has introduced in the laboratories.

Part of this damage, which has been caused by the considerable publicity the media have given to these isolated events, is probably our own fault. We scientists in the modern era of media communication and public relations have solicited the press to advertise our findings, in the hope of motivating the public to further support scientific research. It is appropriate to expect that, in return, the same glaring light will be focused on scandalous behavior, when detected in our laboratories, even if it is a rare and generally harmless event.

22

—➤◦◄—

Research-Based
New Cancer Therapies

My most important responsibility as president of an academically based comprehensive cancer center for twelve years was to foster the development of new therapeutic approaches to cure cancer, grounded in the discoveries in laboratory-based research. The major advances in combined chemotherapy and radiotherapy, which have been successful in saving the lives of numerous cancer patients, particularly in children over the last two decades, are reaching their maximal effectiveness and are unlikely to be improved substantially. Thanks to these treatments over 70 percent of childhood leukemias are cured today. But we are still very ineffective, in spite of available therapies, in the control of many adult cancers such as cancers of the lung, the pancreas, or the gastrointestinal tract.

Fortunately, major contributions have been made and are still generated in our understanding of (1) the mechanism of malignant transformation; (2) the intimate process of vascularization, which malignant tumors must control to ensure growth and metastasis; and (3) the immune system, to make possible newer and more specifically effective therapeutic agents with much lower toxicity and side effects than present accepted treatments. I fully expect that the progress to be made in the next twenty years will be even more dramatic than those we witnessed in the last twenty years, with both the definitive cure of many lethal cancers and the eventual prevention of cancers through specific vaccination of genetically susceptible patients.

Until the last decade, the information was not available on the complex mechanisms of malignant transformation responsible for cancer. Fortunately, great advances in the laboratory have identified several specific mechanisms of malignant transformation, at the molecular and cellular level.

The stage is now ready for basic science to generate new drugs to specifically correct or control the damage in the individual cancer cells. Effective collaborative partnerships have been established between research institutions and pharmaceutical companies experienced in drug design and development to accomplish these goals in the foreseeable future. A significant fraction of our research program at the DFCI is supported by industries with common objectives.

The most important advances are expected to occur in three major areas: reversing malignant transformation, controlling new vessel formation (angiogenesis), and the generation of immune vaccines in the treatment of cancer.

Reversing Malignant Transformation

Major targets for these new agents will be the products of the mutated cancer genes. These may be, for instance, the growth factors, or the growth-factor receptors on the surface of cancer cells, or the molecules responsible for carrying signals to the nucleus of a cancer cell. It is expected that molecular and structural biology and designer drug technology will make it possible to inhibit specific cancer genes or their products.

Technically, such inhibition could be achieved at the level of the gene products (the malignant proteins responsible for the uncontrolled growth) by designer drugs that fit, and bind to, the active site on the target proteins. Such drugs should be expected to restore the normal growth capacity of the cell, or to inhibit a cancer cell's ability to reproduce.

Controlling New Vessel Formation (Angiogenesis)

Studies of new vessel formation (angiogenesis), which is essential for the growth and metastasis of cancer, have also made major contributions to our understanding and to the potential for treating cancers. The study of tumor angiogenesis was initiated more than twenty years ago by Dr. J. Folkman at Children's Hospital in Boston.

Blood vessels are stable structures unless they are part of a healing wound. It soon became apparent that in order for solid tumors to grow, they need to be able to signal the cells of the blood vessels to generate new vessels, particularly new capillaries, to provide the growing tumors with the necessary blood supply to support their growth. The capacity to stimulate this new vessel formation is clearly associated with the aggressiveness of the cancer.

Recently, the research on tumor angiogenesis has progressed at the molecular level, identifying some of the molecules capable of stimulating angiogenesis, and other molecules able to suppress new vessel formation. The identification of these agents opened a new field of therapeutic research, first in experimental animals and soon to be applied to clinical research. Agents capable of suppressing angiogenesis are being investigated for their ability to suppress the growth of metastatic tumors. Moreover, the search for drugs capable of inhibiting angiogenesis has become an important goal of pharmacological research by drug companies, now that the technology to identify such agents is available.

Indeed, several promising antiangiogenesis agents have recently been introduced into clinical trials. Dr. Folkman has just been awarded the Mott Prize of the General Motors Foundation for his contribution to the study of angiogenesis in relation to cancer growth and metastasis.

Immune Vaccines in the Treatment of Cancer

In addition to providing specific defense against infection with bacteria and viruses, immune mechanisms exist that can very efficiently destroy foreign tissues that bear recognizable antigens. These defense mechanisms, which involve the stimulation of specific cytolitic T lymphocytes, are responsible for the rejection of transplanted organs from nonhistocompatible donors.

For many years, immunologists have speculated that if those immune mechanisms could be specifically directed against the cancer, they could cause the definitive destruction of the tumor and also prevent its recurrence. In order for this to happen, the tumor must produce one or more specific molecules which distinguish it from the normal, nonmalignant tissue. Moreover, the tumor-specific molecules must be perceived as a foreign antigen by the immune system.

Studies in the laboratory have revealed that the immunologist's dream to stimulate the immune system to respond to unique tumor antigens is not unreasonable. Indeed, the study of how malignancies occur has demonstrated that the cancer process involves mutations in critical genes. To the extent that the products of these genes are different from those expressed in the normal cells, they can be antigenic and they could stimulate an immune response.

These antigens referred to as tumor-specific associated antigens (TSTAs) have recently been identified in experimental animal tumors, and also in some human tumors, by Thierry Boone of the Ludwig Institute in Brussels. These antigens are unfortunately very weak; moreover, the dynamic growth of the tumors generally overwhelms the immune responses to the TSTAs.

In the last few years many of these difficulties have been resolved, however, and a window of opportunity exists for the development of effective T-cell-mediated immunotherapy for established metastasized tumors.

It has been recognized that immunity capable to effect tissue rejection must involve significant cytolitic T cells (CTL) responses. But, until recently, such responses could not be regularly elicited following immunization with soluble protein antigens, but required that the antigen be produced and metabolized in the target cell themselves for effective presentation by class I MHC molecules.

Fortunately, recent studies by my close associate Kenneth Rock have demonstrated that some macrophages have the capacity to process and present exogenous protein antigens with class I MHC antigens, provided these antigens are administered associated with a particle of appropriate size. In these antigen-presenting cells, particle-associated proteins are interiorized into phagolysosomes, gain access to the cytosol, and eventually share a final common pathway with endogenously synthesized proteins for class I MHC presentation.

This technique opens an effective approach for the generation of CTL-specific responses against antigens produced by the tumor cells, and can cause efficient destruction of the tumor.

In addition, several types of major cancers such as prostate, breast, and ovarian cancers present a unique advantage: they occur in tissues that are not essential for survival. The immunologists' target in these cancers, when developing effective antitumor therapy, need not be the weak TSTAs, although these are acceptable targets for building immunity. The CTL immune response against these tumors could conceivably be elicited against tissue-specific antigens for these cancers, particularly in patients with metastatic disease, since tissue-specific proteins are certainly more numerous and potentially more antigenic than discrete TSTAs.

The existence of autoimmune diseases specific for several tissues such as thyroid and pancreas, and the historical demonstration several decades ago that destructive autoimmunity could be initiated by classical immunization with tissue extracts in experimental animals indicate that tolerance is an unlikely problem, particularly if we attempt to immunize against a significant number of tissue-specific antigens rather than a single one.

Fortunately, recent advances in the analysis of the human genome in several laboratories whose purpose is to identify genes by the isolation of messenger RNAs and the subsequent hybridization made this approach feasible. The genes for human tissue antigens of the prostate or breast can be identified. The proteins they code for can be produced in quantity, and patients with metastatic tumors could be immunized with them. These treatments would be devoid of systemic toxicity.

23

———⇒»o«⇐———

Science and American Medicine

I have always considered myself a physician as much as a scientist. These dual identities have been far less difficult to reconcile than my professional activities with my performance as a business manager, since medicine has progressively increased its scientific basis in this century.

I agree with the clinicians that every patient is an individual who requires decisions and treatments adapted to his or her unique set of circumstances. Fortunately for the public, however, the amount and quality of scientific information which can be used to make these individual judgments has dramatically increased in the last half century, thanks to the spectacular contributions of biomedical research. Based on our increasing scientific understanding of many important diseases and of their pathogenic mechanisms, new therapeutic approaches have been introduced and their effectiveness has been statistically evaluated. Moreover, biomedical research has provided valuable information that is at last reaching the public to aid in our understanding of those factors in our food and our environment which are potentially harmful to us. The scientific education of the public in these topics is changing our diet and our lifestyles dramatically.

In addition, medical educators, since the Flexner revolution, have recognized and emphasized the need to train physicians with a strong background in the biomedical sciences to give them a greater opportunity to understand their patients' diseases and to make educated judgments on the course of treatment.

So great have been the changes in medical knowledge and practice in the span of just one generation that an illustration of some of the benefits we now enjoy (and often take for granted) from the contributions of biomedical research would serve a useful purpose.

Initially, I would like to mention the advances that have directly affected my own health and that of my immediate family. My father suffered from severe essential hypertension from the age of forty, and died of the consequences of this condition, which could not be effectively treated in his era, except for the prescription of a poorly effective salt-free diet. When I reached my forty-second birthday (thirty-four years ago), I was also diagnosed with hypertension. By then, effective treatments, initially with thiazide diuretics, later with beta blockers, and eventually angiotensin antagonists, were available. I have remained essentially normal through the last three decades under this form of treatment, whereas I would probably have had a stroke or a heart attack by now without the benefit of the modern scientific medical treatment.

As I mentioned earlier, I suffer from a genetic disease called Familial Mediterranean Fever (FMF), typical of Mediterranean peoples. It causes severe recurring, noninfectious peritonitis. I would have been totally incapacitated for the last twenty-five years were it not for colchicine, a drug shown by my friend and physician Sheldon Wolff, in a scientific double-blind study carried out at the NIH, to prevent FMF attacks.

I have already mentioned the enormous benefits derived from the discovery of antibiotics, which have saved innumerable lives.

If streptomycin had been available in 1945, as it is today, Annette would not have had to spend almost a year in bed, and neither the child I diagnosed with tubercular meningitis or the young lady I treated for miliary tuberculosis as an intern would have died. When I was a student, my first patient, who suffered from progressive glomerulonephritis and died of kidney failure, would have the chance today to be treated with hemodialysis and possibly a kidney transplant.

When Beryl was born we had no means to determine the sex of the fetus in utero, and much less opportunity to check for possible genetic abnormalities, in spite of my acute anxiety concerning the possibility of giving birth to an abnormal infant. With the availability of ultrasound imaging and amniocentesis, which are my daughter's medical specialties, the sex of the child is determined early on; but more important, mothers are given the option to decide whether to give birth to abnormal infants or to terminate the pregnancies. Other feats of modern obstetrical ultrasound technology performed regularly by Beryl are the possibility of giving blood transfusions to fetuses in utero and thereby saving numerous fetuses who suffer from Rh disease.

Equally spectacular advances have been made in the treatment of cancer, particularly in children. Combined chemotherapy, which was pioneered by my predecessor Emile Frei at the Dana-Farber Cancer Institute, has increased the cure rate of leukemia in children to over 70 percent.

All these advances, which have depended very much upon the benefits of laboratory research, can be surpassed by what the future can bring if we are able to continue on the same undisturbed path that has brought so many advances at relatively low cost. As my friend and mentor Lewis Thomas appropriately said to me: "When biomedical science is sufficiently advanced to allow definitive technologies to be generated to treat selected diseases, the treatments are absolutely effective and the cost of treatment easily affordable." The best examples of definitive technologies are the antibiotics, the antihypertensive drugs, and the polio vaccines. Such discoveries prevent or cure definitively at very low cost. The costly treatments are those which involve effective, or marginally effective, but as yet imperfect technologies. These modes of treatment, such as autologous bone-marrow transplant, which I discussed earlier, or coronary bypass surgery are extremely expensive. Until definitive technologies are generated these treatments are sufficiently effective to warrant offering them to patients in spite of their high cost. The high cost of certain treatments, and the scarcity of materials needed (for instance, histocompatible donors for organ transplants) create serious ethical and sociological problems regarding access to optimal care for everyone, which will have to be faced in the future and which can only be definitively solved by further research directed to the development of less expensive but better technologies. Research is therefore the only effective and economical method to decrease the cost of expensive care. It is the only way to generate curative approaches to replace useful but imperfect therapeutic ones.

One of the major problems in delivering medical care these days is its increased cost, which has escalated much faster than the rate of inflation and which is considered by some to have reached the maximum affordable share of our gross domestic product. As chief executive officer of a small hospital specializing in treating very sick and sometimes terminally ill patients, I have had to address this issue.

Some of the cost increases have been inevitable. We practice a technologically more advanced medicine than twenty or even ten years ago, with the advent of such expensive diagnostic imaging instruments as computerized tomography or, more recently, nuclear magnetic resonance. Similarly, the availability of ultrasound imaging for obstetrics has increased the cost of prenatal care, but with considerable benefits in return. When considering the added costs of these and many other technological advances, one always neglects to compute the considerable social and economic benefits for society in terms of patients returned to effective lives, because such advantages are difficult to quantify precisely on a balance sheet.

Other increases in medical costs relate to the defensive medicine which must be practiced with a constant concern for the potential liability to the physicians or the institution that may arise from possible errors in judgment and technical mistakes or oversights. This costly state of affairs has been compounded by: the litigious tendency of the American people, the very large numbers of lawyers willing to take on malpractice cases on a contingency basis, and the growing feelings of jurors that plaintiffs who have suffered a poor medical result should be compensated for their misfortune, sometimes without much concern for the degree of responsibility of the physician or the hospital. This attitude appears to stem from the jurors' desire to overlook the fact that most medical interventions carry a certain percentage of risk, independent of the skill or judgment of the physician. Because of the contributions of all these factors, the latest estimates indicate that less than forty cents of each settlement dollar goes to the plaintiffs in malpractice cases, a most inefficient system of compensation. This is a major problem, obviously, which can only be dealt with by appropriate legislation.

Furthermore, the same legal considerations have also changed the essential patient/physician relationship into one that may deteriorate into an adversarial attitude. The concern for potential liabilities can also motivate the physician to be not only candid with patients about their conditions and the potential hazards they may experience—which is commendable—but quite possibly brutal to the point of insensitivity for the patients' feelings and expected anxieties.

Other unnecessary medical costs concern the efficiency of administrative operations, which vary from institution to institution. Unavoidable wastage and inefficiency creep into any system when the organization paying for the services has no direct relationship with the individuals who are the recipients of those services. These conditions can also stimulate fraud and overbilling. Dedicated administrators, who are proud to couple efficiency with cost saving, can sometimes correct such deficiencies in selected institutions, but this cannot be realistically offered as a national solution for this serious problem.

Eventually the rising cost of medical care stimulated a revolution in the financing of medical care. Progressively, health maintenance organizations (HMOs) have become responsible for an increasingly higher percentage of the care of patients, thereby displacing the traditional individual physician. This has further compromised the patient/physician relationship and made it very difficult for patients to chose their personal physicians. These market financial pressures will lead to worse conditions still, as the power of the insurance companies will lead, with the increased desire for profit, to further changes in managed care.

Other major benefits which the American people have derived from their support of biomedical science have been the progressive improvements in their dietary habits and in their lifestyles. The scientific advances, which are the basis for these changes, took a relatively long time to reach the awareness of the public and to motivate them to act decisively. The evidence that cigarette smoking is a major cause of lung cancer, and contributes seriously to cardiovascular diseases was available for decades before cigarette smoking was banned in airplanes and in theaters and recently at both the DFCI and Harvard Medical School. In the 1950s we could not have a dinner party without providing cigarettes, and we were surrounded with tobacco smoke before the evening progressed. It is to the credit of physicians and scientists that in the late 1960s smoking had started to decrease considerably. I stopped smoking cigarettes, cigars, and even the pipe to which I was very much addicted. By the 1970s, rare were the physicians and the biomedical scientists who smoked, and neither cigarettes nor ashtrays could be found in our home.

The evidence for the harmful effects of animal fats, saturated fatty acids, and cholesterol in causing atherosclerosis has been accumulating for the last two decades. Those of us who were keenly aware of the data changed our eating habits at the time. For the last thirty years Annette and I, who were brought up on such delicacies as *foie gras,* creamy desserts, and cheese soufflés, and who enjoyed thick steaks, had to totally change our eating habits. We stopped eating cheeseburgers and french fries. Eggs and cream are no longer in our kitchen; butter is not used in cooking nor served at our table; only low-fat milk and milk products are used. We seldom eat beef and the fat of all meats is carefully trimmed off before cooking. Moreover, we have become very fond of fish and vegetables, long before such foods were shown to be healthy. Annette has been enormously gratified to see such eating habits progressively gain wide acceptance by an informed public.

When I discovered I had hypertension, and began taking diuretics, I became very conscious of the sodium content of foods, of which I had been totally oblivious before. I have tried to avoid such obviously salty foods as ham, or smoked beef, of which we were very fond. I discovered, however, that sodium in the form of monosodium glutamate (MSG) is added to a great many prepared foods (not just Chinese food). Practically all soup manufacturers add MSG to their canned soups. Eating a meal with MSG is always followed by considerable thirst and a temporary gain of nearly two pounds of water, which requires at least two days to be eliminated. I was so indignant at the apparent unconcern with which manufacturers added MSG to their products that, when I was president of the Federation of American Societies for Experimental Biology (which included the Society for Nutrition) in 1974, I wrote to several food manufacturers on official stationary (hoping that they would pay attention) protesting their indiscriminate use of MSG in their soups and other foods. I received letters explaining that they were catering to the public taste and not to the needs of people on special diets! Fortunately, the information on the harmful effects of too much sodium in foods has finally reached the public and enough demand has been generated that in the last few years, soups without MSG and with low salt are finally found on our supermarket shelves.

Another issue of concern to me has been the extensive use of a set of highly saturated and harmful oils, such as palm oil or coconut oil, and animal fat, solely because they are less expensive. They are, indeed, cheaper for the manufacturer but more dangerous for consumers, who, now that they are aware of the harmful effects of saturated oils and can read the labels themselves, have begun to demand foods without these artery-clogging oils.

In this respect the greater advantage of democracies, of which America is probably one of the most open, is the degree to which truth cannot be permanently suppressed. The data will, at some time, reach the public who, in its infinite wisdom, will eventually protect its own interests when properly informed. It is one of the important duties of science and biomedical researchers that the information they generate reach the public as rapidly as possible. Such dissemination of scientific information relevant to the public's welfare is the responsibility of the Surgeon General and also one of the missions of the NIH.

The conclusions I would like to draw from this discussion are the considerable beneficial consequences that the contributions of biomedical research have had for human health and welfare, not only in terms of more effective diagnosis, treatment, and prevention of diseases, but also in providing vital information to help us manage our daily lives in a healthier and more wholesome manner. I have also stressed the critical need to continue training America's physicians in biomedical science. The future of American medicine and the continued progress of science depend on it.

I alluded earlier to the present disaffection of medical students and recently graduated M.D.s, with careers in biomedical sciences. I also expressed the fear that recent curricular changes and the consequence of the 1968 student revolution are compromising the scientific basis of American medicine. I am deeply concerned that unless meaningful efforts are made to counteract these trends before they become irreversible, and unless the policies of funding of medical research and training by the federal government are maintained at an adequate level and even increased, the past era of spectacular achievements in biomedical science in America will be a matter of history and the banner of leadership will pass to another civilization.

24

————→•←————

Problems in American Education

I have been very fortunate to have spent much of my life in an academic environment. When I was a college student at Columbia University I had been immensely attracted by the ambiance and the lifestyle of American universities. Our universities are our modern hallowed temples, the most treasured possessions of our civilization, entrusted with the most vital and precious resources of our society, our youth and the body of knowledge painfully acquired through centuries of scholarship. Our universities have grown and prospered because of their tradition of scholarship and research. Dogmas are rejected outright and all ideas must stand the test of challenge and scrutiny before being accepted.

Our students and professors are committed to the belief that all concepts and previously accepted laws are open to question and to the test of experimentation. So imperfect is our knowledge of our universe that it is constantly subject to revision and improvement. In fact, scientists understood long ago that the progress of science is discontinuous and that our understanding of Nature advances

262

only by challenging an obsolete perception of our physical environment and of its laws and by replacing it with a more accurate set of relationships. These are, in turn, destined to be revised and reassessed in the light of future observations made by better-prepared minds with more advanced technology.

Our universities are the exciting places where both our cultural heritage is preserved and this process of constant revision takes place in an open, unprejudiced environment. These essential activities of our universities, at the frontier of knowledge, together with their role in the training, instruction, and inspiration of our future generations, make them exhilarating places in which to work and live. The stimulation of eager and ambitious minds and the heady environment they create also add to the attraction of university life. The privilege we enjoy as students and scholars of working in this protected environment on such important issues for society and education has traditionally carried a significant price, generally accepted cheerfully, which is embodied in the academic ethics that govern the acquisition of knowledge in our universities: no effort is too great to undertake; both students and professors are committed to a life of scholarship and dedication to the highest standards of truth, openness, and accuracy; our cultural heritage must be historically preserved and respected, even in circumstances where the conclusions of the past need to be revised and corrected. Above all else, scholarship and intellectual achievement must be encouraged, rewarded, and respected. It must be understood by everyone and accepted by all that, as far as our cultural heritage is concerned, the original contributions of any one person enriches the lives of us all in the manner in which Einstein's discoveries have changed how we perceive our physical environment. Exceptional scholarship must, therefore, be encouraged and rewarded, not resented and envied.

To educate our students and to stimulate their desire to carry out the type of achievements that will enrich our culture, they must be convinced that nothing is accomplished without considerable effort, particularly in the intellectual sphere. They must be motivated to exert their energies without limits. Such an attitude should be associated with a respect for the accomplishments of classical scholarship and accompanied by a suspicious and even contemptuous attitude toward the media culture of make-believe, and of appearance versus reality, which has contaminated our way of life for the last decades.

I did not realize, at the time of the student revolution in 1968, because it appeared to me then to be motivated by a number of legitimate causes, such as the opposition to the Vietnam war, military training in universities, and government secrecy, that it had another most important agenda, which concerned the destruction of the ethical basis of academic pursuits as we knew them. To avoid confusion, I should define what I mean by "ethical" in this context. It is not simply the adherence to conventional honest behavior which dictates that one should not cheat, steal, or lie; these were not the issues at the time. I am addressing the deeper meaning of the word *ethic* which signifies a set of values on which to base behavior and to motivate one's existence and which are the scaffolding of any society. It is precisely these values which were under attack in 1968 when the confrontation with the rebellious students occurred in our universities, where the destruction of these ethical norms could do the most harm.

As part of their revolt against authority and their resentment against society, the students tore apart the structure and authority of academia. They successfully challenged the importance and significance of grades, curriculum, and standards that required centuries to generate, as well as the prestige and authority of the scholars who taught them. These attacks on "elitism," which were fueled by the understandable desire of students to promote equality in our universities, overlooked that there is a fundamental difference between equality of opportunity and uniformity of performance. As a consequence of this error, the students in revolt refused to recognize that there are unavoidable inequalities in accomplishment in academia, which not only should be recognized but encouraged for the good of any society. These fundamental differences which should be very much striven for are the very basis for the excellence on which our academic culture is built. One must recognize from the start that not everyone is endowed to become an Aristotle, a Copernicus, a Spinoza, an Einstein, or a Pasteur, but that everyone should be given a chance to develop their individual potential to the utmost. This requires that we subscribe to "elitist" goals of accomplishment, and accept such anathemas of the 1968 revolution as competitive grading, and the respect for the achievements of the past and of our elders.

It is unfortunate indeed that the success of the 1968 revolution, not only in the United States but also in other Western democracies, led to the deterioration of the scale of values in our universities which had promoted scholarship for its own sake. This revolution was also responsible for the curricular changes which would contribute to the production of a generation of inadequately trained and motivated teachers. I was also depressed to observe that, during this period, the trustees of our academic institutions, fearing this revolutionary movement, promptly surrendered the administrative direction of our most prestigious universities, traditionally headed by scholars with records of brilliant accomplishments, into the undistinguished hands of "professional managers" whose qualifications were based more on public relations or even politics rather than academic credentials. It is of interest that, parallel to the introduction of these managerial types at the administrative helm of our universities, the same brand of lawyers, accountants, and public-relations specialists also rose to the administrative management of our major industrial corporations, replacing in those positions the technically trained managers who had headed them in the past. I feel that it is not a coincidence that this nationwide process has been associated with a decrease in inventiveness and long-term planning by industry.

In the years following this revolution, my small microcosm saw the grading system at Harvard Medical School abolished as elitist, and the scientific content of the curriculum constantly eroded. Criticism of students had to be muted, but criticism of teachers by students was very much encouraged. One of the consequences of that attitude in our school was that the student demanded to be entertained rather than enlightened. The most popular teachers were those who would compare with Ronald Reagan in their ability to tell jokes and to be generally likable, but not those who would stimulate one's curiosity and intellect.

Fortunately, in the last ten years, I have noted a small trend back toward the realization that scholarship is worthwhile and that nothing useful is accomplished without effort. But it is still such a small sapling that I am not confident that it will grow, in time, into a fruitful tree.

Finally, the consequence of the 1968 revolution has also reached medical education in terms of curriculum reform. It has become fashionable and popular to state that: (1) The didactic lecture style of teaching is passé. (2) Students are exposed to too much material. (3) The student must be entertained as well as taught. (4) The teacher and the student must learn together through discussion of cases, as is done in business school. (5) It is acceptable for students to discuss a topic and to form an opinion before they have fully searched the literature for the facts. (6) Expertise and experience are not required for competence. (7) It is just as important to discuss the social and economic consequence of a disease as the biomedical aspects of the condition.

These considerations have contributed to the birth of a new curriculum at Harvard entitled the "New Pathway" where the formal lectures by experts in the field, who had often made the original contributions, have been drastically curtailed. The students instead meet, in smaller groups, with instructors, not necessarily expert in the field of study, to discuss in depth all the issues, scientific or otherwise, that arise from the study of the case of a particular patient. The hope is that enough science will be learned by this device to prepare the student to understand medicine. Of

course the student is encouraged to investigate and look up anything relevant to the case. But who can honestly believe that the
average student, under pressure, will have the time to exercise
judgment concerning what to find and where to look.

To give an example, the popular immunology course I used to
teach comprised twenty-two lectures precisely aimed at the student
level and I spent a long time preparing it. Now it is reduced to a set
of seven lectures integrated in a larger course called Identity and
Defense in the New Pathway. I cannot conceive how immunology
can be adequately taught in so few lectures with strong clinical
emphasis. Moreover, the use of general terms such as "identity"
and "defense" in the title of the course rather than the classical
scientific titles of immunology, microbiology, and pathology, which
are the topics that this course is meant to cover, is already evidence
of a surrender to the glamour of appearances versus substance,
which is the plague of our media-inspired century.

But except for its unfortunate long-term effect on biomedical science, which is my major concern, I am probably ill-advised to become very exercised about curriculum reform in medical education.
I have seen several such monsters in a lifetime. None have really
made any difference in the preparation of medical students. I found
that medical students are an extremely bright group quite capable of
identifying what is important to them through any curriculum.

Moreover, medical students really begin to learn medicine
when they leave medical school and become interns. The most
extreme example of the accuracy of this statement concerns my
own daughter. When Beryl went through medical school at Harvard, a course in obstetrics and gynecology was not part of the
compulsory curriculum. Contrary to my own experience, she graduated without having seen a baby delivered. Much later, after an
internship in surgery, residencies in radiology, and a fellowship in
ultrasound, she specialized in obstetrical ultrasound and is now
the foremost expert in New England in her specialty and a valued
resource for obstetricians and gynecologists.

A vastly more important issue which, in my opinion, also has its roots in the 1968 revolution is the deterioration of standards in our primary and secondary schools, and the fact that the newer generations we produce in this wealthiest of all democracies are not as well prepared as their fathers and mothers and grandparents were in fundamental knowledge of science, mathematics, and even plain English, not to mention their grossly inferior performance compared to the children of much poorer countries, particularly in Asia.

There are in my opinion several important reasons for the choking deterioration of our primary and secondary schools, which if understood could be remedied, if it is not too late. First, many of the teachers we produce in our universities are not adequately prepared to teach the fundamental subjects they are responsible for, because of the poor education they have received. Second, the same anti-elitist philosophy that has produced our inadequate teachers has also contaminated our lower schools. It has become inappropriate to demand intellectual effort on the part of the students, to insist on accomplishment, and to reward scholarship. Instead, it is fashionable to insist that students must have fun while learning. As a result, young students are not given sufficient homework to do. At a time when their minds are most active and eager to learn, they are left with too much free time which is wasted on television and playing games. A most important reason for this deterioration, also, is the overemphasis on social and public-relation issues over academic values in our schools. The teaching of the standards of behavior in society has become an extremely important concern of our schools, a task which was heretofore appropriately considered to be the responsibility of the parents and of the family. Last but not least, there has been a deterioration of the willingness of parents and teachers to exercise authority at all levels. This trend, originating with the disastrous influence of Jean Jacques Rousseau's philosophy of natural goodness, was perpetuated by generations of psychologists, and has had a perverse effect on the philosophy of education. My experience in successfully raising a daughter, contributing to the education and training of my grandchildren, and training a large number of scientists, many of whom have told me that they have evolved a parental relationship with me, has taught me that it is impossible to train human beings without exercising authority and leadership and without making sure that such authority is respected and unquestioned. In fact, it has been my experience that children who need to develop a Freudian super ego require our help to do so. We must be stern in defining what is right and wrong and what is expected of them as ideal behavior and what will never be tolerated as unbecoming behavior in order for our children to be able to build a similar ethical construction in themselves. This is particularly important when they are small. Children brought up without the stability of benevolent authority are uncomfortable and unbalanced. Later on, one must accept the natural evolution toward independence which demands that the developing adult revolts against authority. This revolt must be welcomed and anticipated; it indicates that the appropriate evolution of the personality has occurred, but must be handled with understanding and firmness.

25

—»⊙«—

Conclusions

I have had the good fortune to have been influenced by several distinct cultures and societies all of which have molded my personality but remained sufficiently separate in my consciousness to grant me the luxury of being both a participant and a spectator. I am indebted to my French upbringing and to the classic French cultural education I have received for my tendency to examine and analyze everything rationally, and for my compulsion to organize my thoughts and plan my work carefully. Other aspects of my French upbringing are my dislike of hypocrisy, my commitment to say what's on my mind, my passion for privacy, and my natural reserve. I have never felt comfortable with the American custom of being addressed by one's first name, even by perfect strangers. I do not use first names myself unless a substantial bond exists to justify it. When a medical student in one of my laboratories asked me how to pronounce my first name, I answered, without a moment's hesitation: "You don't." I am apparently known and feared for my willingness to be open and even blunt.

My Jewish ancestry and the necessity to flee Hitler and anti-Semitism, as well as the few times that I was confronted with discrimination, have fostered in me the feeling (one I had also inherited from my forefathers) that I belong to a vulnerable group. As a consequence, when, at last, I felt comfortable and secure, as is the case in modern American society, I never lost sight of the fact that these are abnormally privileged times in the history of the world. Past history has taught us that they may not last forever.

This brings me to the enormous influence that America and the Anglo-Saxon (or more appropriately, the WASP culture) has had on me. First and foremost, I am immensely grateful for the warm welcome I received as an immigrant and for the opportunity to study, work, and progress in America with as much support and encouragement as if I had been born here. I do not know of another land, culture, or people who has the innate generosity and sense of fairness of the American people. I have felt immediately at home in the United States because it is largely a country of immigrants and sons of immigrants, who have never forgotten their origins and are ready to offer the recently arrived ones the same helping hand that was given them or their forefathers.

Moreover, all of us, who were not brought up on the Anglo-Saxon Protestant ethic, which together with the ideas of the French Revolution have influenced the drafting of the American Constitution, owe an immense debt of gratitude to the ideals and values that motivated the enlightened and generous men who created this country and foresaw its future. I am a great admirer of the respect for the individual which is the central theme of the American civilization, and also of the tradition of free speech, free press, unimpeded flow of information which, in my opinion are the most valuable of all the contributions of the American Constitution. It is comforting to feel that in the free market of ideas, and with the increasing availability of information, reason will always prevail and anyone can be heard. The latest advances in media communication, together with the increased sophistication in the technology of advertising, as applied to the selling of ideas and of political candidates, by appealing to emotions rather than to reason, have put a damper on my enthusiasm, however, and darkened my optimism that reason will ultimately triumph.

I have been much less impressed by a regrettable custom of our American civilization inherited from the British: our innate inability to express unpleasant truths, even when everyone knows them. It is considered very bad manners to acknowledge the obvious, if it is in anyway damaging. No one will admit that the emperor has no clothes. As a consequence, most sayings and public statements are notably incorrect and are meant more to hide the truth than to reveal it. To mention two obvious examples, when a cabinet secretary is fired from the government, the fiction is presented that he offered his resignation. Similarly, when a defeated candidate concedes after having lost an election, he or she has only praise for the opponent who was denounced viciously only days before.

As I reach the end of this book, I am inclined to reflect on the reasons for my project, and on the conclusions I have reached. The summer of 1942, when I entered medical school in Richmond, I read an autobiography that moved and impressed me deeply. It had been written by Hans Zinsser, the famous bacteriologist, chairman of the Department of Bacteriology at Harvard Medical School (today we would say microbiology). Zinsser's book, published in 1940, was titled *As I Remember Him* and he had written it after he had learned that he would soon die of leukemia. Rather than describing himself, he pretended to be writing about a close friend, who had confided in him his most intimate thoughts and feelings.

Although our respective lives, personalities, and backgrounds were very different, there were nevertheless enough similarities to merit reflection. I went to the Countway Library of the Harvard Medical School, to borrow Zinsser's book and reread it with the same fascination and admiration that I experienced over forty years ago. Zinsser, in addition to being an excellent microbiologist and epidemiologist, was also a poet and a writer. He had a profound knowledge of both French and German in addition to English and American literature. Rereading his book, and comparing it with mine, I found that we addressed many of the same issues about medicine, education, the governance of academia, and the destiny of man. There were, nevertheless, marked differences. Zinsser was candid about his thoughts and feelings, but was very reticent to speak of his own immediate family, his wife and children, and of the important events of his life that were not directly related to his professional activity.

When I began this volume, I pledged myself to be candid and thorough and to leave nothing unsaid which might enlighten the reader about my character or motivation, and to express my views freely on the issues about which I care most: education, science, and cultural heritage. I have been candid about myself and my family. I feel that the significance of the message for the reader might be heightened by a keener understanding of the personality and motivation of the writer.

My main purpose when I began writing this book was to preserve an experience for others to read about. I have never been a religious person. None of the existing faiths have ever tempted my imagination or my sensitivity, as I am highly suspicious of revelations and hostile to any form of dogmatism. This attitude has not prevented me from speculating about the meaning of life, the significance of existence, or the nature of reality, however. The only valid conclusion I have been able to come to after a lifetime dedicated to science concerns the miracle of communication. I find it extraordinary not only that we can communicate meaningfully, but that the message in the form of relationships can be translated into so many different media and still remain understandable to our senses and our brains. For instance, J. S. Bach's conception of the Goldberg variations* can be played, heard, and enjoyed, but it can be written and preserved in sheet music; encoded on magnetic tape, CD records, computer language; or transmitted through hertzian waves by radio. The permanent sets of relationships of sounds and rhythms which were born in Bach's brain originally, and which have been preserved for our culture through these various forms, owe their significance to the miracle that other human beings can understand them and transcribe them.

I cannot help fantasizing that, in addition, these relationships have a reality and permanency of their own, as a message, independent of the genius who formulated them, or of the humans who enjoy them. The real puzzle, therefore, resides in the organization of our brain, the miraculous machine that is capable of communicating not only with other brains, but also to analyze and appreciate the reality of relationships as they exist in Nature. I am pessimistic that we shall ever be able to elucidate how and why we understand, which is the ultimate puzzle.

In the meantime I could not miss this opportunity of transcribing my message in a more permanent form before the relationships as they exist in my perishable brain vanish forever.

---

*Clavier masterwork of J. S. Bach.

Index